Natural Materials

Natural Materials

Sources, Properties, and Uses

Jean Frances DeMouthe

California Academy of Sciences
San Francisco, California

AMSTERDAM • BOSTON • HEIDELBERG • LONDON • OXFORD • NEW YORK
PARIS • SAN DIEGO • SAN FRANCISCO • SINGAPORE • SYDNEY • TOKYO

Architectural Press is an imprint of Elsevier

Architectural Press
An imprint of Elsevier
Linacre House, Jordan Hill, Oxford OX2 8 DP
30 Corporate Road, Burlington, MA 01803

First Edition 2006

British Library Cataloguing in Publication Data
DeMouthe, Jean Frances
Natural materials: sources, properties, and uses
1. Natural products – Conservation and restoration 2. Museum
conservation methods
I. Title
069.5'3

Library of Congress Cataloguing in Publication Data
2005932979

ISBN 0 7506 6528 9

For information on all Architectural Press publications
visit our website at www.architecturalpress.com

Typeset by Charon Tec Pvt. Ltd, Chennai, India
www.charontec.com
Printed and bound in Great Britain

Contents

Preface   xi

Acknowledgements   xv

Illustration Acknowledgements   xvii

1   Introduction to Materials   **1**
Properties of matter   4
   Physical properties   4
   Optical properties   9

2   Geological Materials   **15**
Minerals   15
Metals and alloys   26
Gemstones   30
Rocks   40
Meteorites and related materials   49
In collections   51

3   Introduction to Organics and Organisms   **57**
Some organic compounds   57
Classification of organisms   59
Type specimens   61

4   Plants   **63**
Introduction   63
   Plant classification   63
   Plant structure   64
   Fossil plant materials   66

Products 68
  Wood 69
  Bark 71
  Paper 72
  Fabric and cordage 73
  Woven and dried plant materials 77
  Plant fluids 85
  Oil, resin and wax 87
  Perfume and other scented things 90
  Tar and asphalt 91
  Dyes 91
Plant materials in collections 93
  Botanical specimens 93
  Created objects 94

5 Invertebrate Animals 97
Introduction to animals and classification 97
  Porifera 98
  Cnidaria or Coelenterates 99
  Mollusca 100
  Arthropods 101
Products 104
  Silk 104
  Shellac, dye and wax 105
  Shell 107
  Pearls 111
  In collections 112

6 Vertebrate Animals 115
Introduction to animals and their classification 115
Body parts 119
  Skin 120
  Hair and fur 122
  Feathers 128
  Bone and antler 134
  Teeth 136
  Muscles and other tissues 140
  Eggs 141
  Keratin materials 142
Products 147
  Tools and weapons 148

Fat, oil, and wax   148
Leather   151
Teeth and ivory   155
Blood, milk, and excrement   157
Animals in collections   158

Appendix A: References and Further Reading   163

Appendix B: Glossary   167

Appendix C: Measurements   173

Index   175

This book is dedicated to my family:
my sister Peggy, my brother Scott, and my mother.
Few things would be possible without their love and support

Preface

There are natural materials in museums and private collections throughout the world, from traditional collections of plants and animals to components in artwork, historical objects, and anthropological specimens. These materials come from animals, plants, and from the Earth. Some of them have been used in their original state, while others have been processed and may not now resemble the original material.

This book is intended as a guide to natural materials in all their various forms, both natural and as they are likely to be found in collections. Chapters are devoted to the major types of natural materials, their properties and the products derived from them. It is intended to be a resource for anyone working with natural materials in any type of collection, including students, private collectors, and museum professionals.

Natural history collections contain preserved specimens of organisms and inorganic materials such as rocks, meteorites, and minerals. There are standards for the care, storage, and use of each type of specimen, which are usually well known to the curators and managers of each particular collection. Most natural history museums do not employ registrars or conservators, but rather rely on the professionals in each department to maintain their collections to professional standards. Museums and galleries devoted to art and historical artifacts are organized differently, and may have both registrars and conservators on staff.

In order for anyone to make decisions regarding the storage, care, and use of collections, they must be aware of the materials present. In natural history collections, this is usually simple. A butterfly is a butterfly, and a worm is a worm. But art and historical collections are devoted to "made" objects; things fashioned for a purpose. Specimens may be made of a single material, sometimes natural, sometimes synthetic. These collections also contain composite objects; things made of a combination of materials, many of which have been altered from their original state.

Jean Frances DeMouthe
San Francisco, California

Natural materials can be found in many forms in museum collections. The items in this photograph include wool, cotton, wood, leather, dried plant materials, paints, and metal alloys. Rug/carpet: kurdish mid-twentieth century wool on cotton, natural pigments/dye. Basket: Hopi piki-bread tray, wicker, early twentieth century. Kachina: c. 1970 cottonwood root with water-based (poster) paint, fabric, wool, feathers, yarn, fur ruff, unsigned (cloth "cape" is also painted). Books: calfskin, marbled paper, gold. Baseball: leather, linen cord, pen ink. Glove: leather, metal (grommets). Gun: wood, metal (brass, steel).

Composite objects like this Hopi Kachina may contain many different materials. This doll is made of cotton-wood root, decorated with paint, fabric, feathers, metal, plastic, and hair. Pahlik-mana (butterfly maiden) kachina c. 1980. Cottonwood root, acrylic paint, wool garments, feathers, yarn, plastic (artificial plant in right hand), metal (sequins, necklace), artificial pearl, down feathers.

Acknowledgements

The author would like to acknowledge and thank the people who have helped and supported her during the production of this work. These include Roberta Brett and Gary Williams, who gave their time and expertise on insects and invertebrates. And Gary lent some of his photographs to the project. Helen Von Ammon assisted with the text relating to animal fibers. Michael E. Gray and Patricia Gray contributed their expertise to the mineral and gemstone sections. Anne Malley, the Academy's head librarian, was generous with her time and advice, and assisted with acquiring animal photographs.

The California Academy of Sciences provided access to computers and other equipment, and to specimens in their collections. The Academy's library was the source of some of the photographs presented herein, and the library staff was very helpful. The Department of Invertebrate Zoology and Geology provided moral and practical support as well as technical assistance.

Illustration Acknowledgements

The author and publishers would like to thank those who have kindly permitted the use of images in the illustration of this book.

Figure	Page	Photographer	Copyright	Ownership
Preface	xii	P. DeMouthe	P. DeMouthe	P. DeMouthe
Preface	xiii	P. DeMouthe	P. DeMouthe	P. DeMouthe
2.1	25	Author	California Academy of Sciences	California Academy of Sciences
2.2	25	Author	California Academy of Sciences	California Academy of Sciences
2.4	38	Author	California Academy of Sciences	California Academy of Sciences
2.6	48	P. DeMouthe	P. DeMouthe	P. DeMouthe
4.4	73	P. DeMouthe	P. DeMouthe	P. DeMouthe
4.5	77	Author	Author	J.A. DeMouthe
4.7	78	Author	Author	P. DeMouthe
4.10	81	P. DeMouthe	P. DeMouthe	P. DeMouthe
4.12	83	P. DeMouthe	P. DeMouthe	P. DeMouthe
4.13	86	P. DeMouthe	P. DeMouthe	P. DeMouthe
5.1	99	G. Williams	G. Williams	
5.2	100	Author	Author	California Academy of Sciences
5.4	104	C. Fiorito	California Academy of Sciences	
5.5	107	Author	Author	California Academy of Sciences
5.6	109	Author	Author	California Academy of Sciences
5.7	110	Author	Author	California Academy of Sciences
6.6	127	G. & B. Corsi	California Academy of Sciences	
6.7	129	G. & B. Corsi	California Academy of Sciences	
6.10	133	G. & B. Corsi	California Academy of Sciences	
6.11	134	J.H. Tashjian	California Academy of Sciences	
6.12	135	G. & B. Corsi	California Academy of Sciences	
6.14	137	Author	Author	J.A. DeMouthe and S. DeMouthe

(Continued)

Figure	Page	Photographer	Copyright	Ownership
6.16	139	G. & B. Corsi	California Academy of Sciences	
6.17	142	C. Kopp	California Academy of Sciences	
6.18	143	Author	Author	J.A. DeMouthe and author
6.19	144	G. Williams	G. Williams	
6.20	145	P. DeMouthe	P. DeMouthe	
6.21	145	Author	Author	J.A. DeMouthe
6.23	146	L. Elrod	California Academy of Sciences	
6.24	151	G. & B. Corsi	California Academy of Sciences	
6.25	152	P. DeMouthe	P. DeMouthe	P. DeMouthe and D. Carnahan
6.26	153	P. DeMouthe	P. DeMouthe	P. DeMouthe
6.27	155	H.V. Davis	California Academy of Sciences	
6.28	156	Author	Author	California Academy of Sciences
6.29	157	Author	Author	J.A. DeMouthe and S. DeMouthe

All other photographs were taken by the author, who holds the copyrights. All drawings are by the author.

Introduction to Materials

The building blocks of all matter are atoms, which are in turn composed of much smaller subatomic particles. Although atoms contain over 100 different types of these smaller particles, only three are of general interest: protons, electrons, and neutrons. The dense central nucleus of an atom contains particles called protons, which have a positive electrical charge, and neutrons, which have no charge. Electrons are particles with a negative charge that orbit the nucleus. Electron orbits or "shells" close to the nucleus are small and may contain only a few particles. Larger atoms that have more of these moving particles also must have more orbits for them to occupy. Each successive orbit can accommodate more electrons than the one before it.

Traditional diagrams of an atom show a round nucleus with rings of orbiting electrons. This model has been replaced by a more accurate one that depicts clouds of electrons moving very fast around the nucleus in pod-shaped, three-dimensional orbits.

The number of positively charged protons must equal the number of negatively charged electrons for an atom to be stable and neutral. An atom that is out of balance, having more positive or negative particles, is itself a charged particle, called an ion.

The atomic number of an element is the number of protons in the nucleus of the atom. The atomic mass is basically the sum of the number of protons and neutrons in the nucleus, since the electrons contribute little to this calculation.

Elements are defined by the structure of their atoms, determined by the number of each type of subatomic particle present. Each element has been given a name, which is shown in Figure 1.1 as a two-letter abbreviation. These are the abbreviations that are used to write out chemical formulae.

The simplest elements contain only a few subatomic particles. Hydrogen and helium have one and two electrons, respectively. These electrons orbit the nucleus in the first orbital shell, which is only big enough to accommodate two electrons at most. The third element in the sequence is lithium, with

Key:

element name
atomic number
Symbol
atomic weight (mean relative mass)

1	2		3	4	5	6	7	8	9	10	11	12	13	14	15	16	17	18
hydrogen 1 **H** 1.0079																		helium 2 **He** 4.0026
lithium 3 **Li** 6.941	beryllium 4 **Be** 9.0122												boron 5 **B** 10.811	carbon 6 **C** 12.011	nitrogen 7 **N** 14.007	oxygen 8 **O** 15.999	fluorine 9 **F** 18.998	neon 10 **Ne** 20.180
sodium 11 **Na** 22.990	magnesium 12 **Mg** 24.305												aluminum 13 **Al** 26.982	silicon 14 **Si** 28.086	phosphorus 15 **P** 30.974	sulfur 16 **S** 32.065	chlorine 17 **Cl** 35.453	argon 18 **Ar** 39.948
potassium 19 **K** 39.098	calcium 20 **Ca** 40.078	scandium 21 **Sc** 44.956	titanium 22 **Ti** 47.867	vanadium 23 **V** 50.942	chromium 24 **Cr** 51.996	manganese 25 **Mn** 54.938	iron 26 **Fe** 55.845	cobalt 27 **Co** 58.933	nickel 28 **Ni** 58.693	copper 29 **Cu** 63.546	zinc 30 **Zn** 65.39	gallium 31 **Ga** 69.723	germanium 32 **Ge** 72.61	arsenic 33 **As** 74.922	selenium 34 **Se** 78.96	bromine 35 **Br** 79.904	krypton 36 **Kr** 83.80
rubidium 37 **Rb** 85.468	strontium 38 **Sr** 87.62	yttrium 39 **Y** 88.906	zirconium 40 **Zr** 91.224	niobium 41 **Nb** 92.906	molybdenum 42 **Mo** 95.94	technetium 43 **Tc** [98]	ruthenium 44 **Ru** 101.07	rhodium 45 **Rh** 102.91	palladium 46 **Pd** 106.42	silver 47 **Ag** 107.86	cadmium 48 **Cd** 112.41	Indium 49 **In** 114.82	tin 50 **Sn** 118.71	antimony 51 **Sb** 121.76	tellurium 52 **Te** 127.60	Iodine 53 **I** 126.90	xenon 54 **Xe** 131.29
caesium 55 **Cs** 132.91	barium 56 **Ba** 137.33	57–70 *	lutetium 71 **Lu** 174.97	tantalum 73 **Ta** 180.95	tungsten 74 **W** 183.84	rhenium 75 **Re** 186.21	osmium 76 **Os** 190.23	iridium 77 **Ir** 192.22	platinum 78 **Pt** 195.08	gold 79 **Au** 196.97	mercury 80 **Hg** 200.59	thallium 81 **Tl** 204.38	lead 82 **Pb** 207.2	bismuth 83 **Bi** 208.98	polonium 84 **Po** [209]	astatine 85 **At** [210]	radon 86 **Rn** [222]
francium 87 **Fr** [223]	radium 88 **Ra** [226]	89–102 **	lawrencium 103 **Lr** [262]	rutherfordium 104 **Rf** [261]	dubnium 105 **Db** [262]	seaborgium 106 **Sg** [266]	bohrium 107 **Bh** [264]	hassium 108 **Hs** [269]	mertnerium 109 **Mt** [268]	ununnilium 110 **Uun** [271]	unununium 111 **Uuu** [272]	ununbium 112 **Uub** [277]		urunquadium 114 **Uuq** [289]				

Note: hafnium 72 **Hf** 178.49 appears between lutetium and tantalum in period 6.

***lanthanoids**

lanthanum 57 **La** 138.91	cerium 58 **Ce** 140.12	praseodymium 59 **Pr** 140.91	neodymium 60 **Nd** 144.24	promethium 61 **Pm** [145]	samarium 62 **Sm** 150.36	europium 63 **Eu** 151.96	gadolinium 64 **Gd** 157.25	terbium 65 **Tb** 158.93	dysprosium 66 **Dy** 162.50	holmium 67 **Ho** 164.93	erbium 68 **Er** 167.26	thulium 69 **Tm** 168.93	ytterbium 70 **Yb** 173.04

****actinoids**

actinium 89 **Ac** [227]	thorium 90 **Th** 232.04	protactinium 91 **Pa** 231.04	uranium 92 **U** 238.03	neptunium 93 **Np** [237]	plutonium 94 **Pu** [244]	americium 95 **Am** [243]	curium 96 **Cm** [247]	berkelium 97 **Bk** [247]	californium 98 **Cf** [251]	einsteinium 99 **Es** [252]	fermium 100 **Fm** [257]	mendelevium 101 **Md** [258]	nobelium 102 **No** [259]

Figure 1.1   Periodic table of the elements.

three electrons. As the first orbital can only hold two electrons, lithium and the next elements in the series must have more and larger orbits to hold their electrons. The second shell holds up to eight electrons. So the element having an atomic number of ten (neon), will have two full orbitals, two electrons in the first and eight in the second. The third row of elements all have three electron shells, and so on. As the elements become larger and larger, having more and more electron shells, some of the electrons are in orbits far from the nucleus.

Elements having similar electron orbital configurations tend to display similar properties. Because of the way the periodic table is organized, elements that tend to behave the same way can be found in the vertical columns. For instance, the halogen elements, near the right edge of the table, combine in the same ways with other elements. Thus, chlorine, bromine, and fluorine readily form compounds with sodium, calcium, and other similar elements.

Atoms of a single element may combine into one molecule, and atoms of different elements may combine to form compounds, which are also molecules. The latter usually happens when elements having incomplete electron shells interact. Atoms of different elements can attain full and stable electron shells by transferring or sharing electrons with each other. When this happens, these atoms are then held closely together by chemical bonds. Elements whose atoms have full electron shells, like helium and neon, tend to be the most stable and least likely to form compounds with other elements.

A molecular formula is a written expression that lists the identity and number of all atoms present in a molecule. The positive ions in a compound are always listed first, followed by the negative ions. Whole molecules that may be part of the compound, like water, are tacked on to the end as a unit. The number of atoms of each element present are shown as a subscript to the right of the abbreviation for that element. Thus the formula H_2O shows that this molecule contains two hydrogen atoms and one oxygen atom. Gypsum is a common mineral that contains water. Its formula reads: $CaSO_4 \cdot 2H_2O$. The sulfate molecule, SO_4, is a strongly-bonded group of atoms that acts as a unit, combining with other elements just as if it were a single negatively-charged ion. There are a number of such molecules or anionic radicals.

Organic molecules or hydrocarbons are those that contain some combination of the elements carbon and hydrogen. All other compounds or single-element molecules are referred to as inorganic.

Water is necessary for life on Earth, and it is an essential component in many natural materials. The water molecule may seem simple, having just three atoms, but it is unique in many ways. The two hydrogen atoms each share one electron with the larger oxygen atom. The result is a V-shaped molecule that is polar in nature, having different electrical charges at each end of it. The positively charged hydrogen atoms in each water molecule can be weakly attracted to the negative oxygen atoms in other water molecules. One water molecule can be attached to as many as four others. These hydrogen bonds do not last long, and within liquid water they are continually breaking and forming.

The cohesion within water that results from these transitory hydrogen bonds allows water to move upward in plants against the force of gravity. Where water and another, less dense, substance meet, the bonds between water molecules contribute to surface tension.

When water is between 0° and 100°C, the hydrogen bonds continually form and break. Below 0 degrees, there is less energy acting on the water molecules, the hydrogen bonds do not break, and a solid forms. Water is one of the only natural compounds that is less dense in solid form than it is in liquid form. This is why ice floats.

Properties of Matter

There are three natural states of matter: solid, liquid, and gas. Most collections are limited to solids, although the occasional liquid or gas may be included. There may still be bourbon in that Elvis-shaped decanter, mercury in that antique thermometer, or neon in that advertising sign.

A substance is defined by its chemical composition and internal structure, which in turn define its properties. Knowledge of physical and optical properties is essential for anyone who needs to identify, care for, or describe natural materials in any form.

The following are some of the basic properties of solid matter. The terms listed here are not applicable to all natural materials. Some are specific to either organic or inorganic materials, and some of them will be used only occasionally.

Many of these properties may be useful in the identification of natural materials. The tests for most physical properties are destructive and so should be used with care, and only when absolutely necessary. Optical properties are most easily tested and can often be done with minimal handling of an object. Optical properties should be tried first, before potentially harmful physical tests are performed.

Physical Properties

Crystal structure describes the orderly arrangement of atoms within a substance. This term is most often applied to crystalline solids such as minerals, but organic compounds may also be described in this way.

Crystal structure is described in terms of symmetry. In mineralogy, there are six crystal systems and within those, thirty-two crystal classes. All crystals of

Table 1.1 *Crystal systems and common forms.*

Crystal system	Internal symmetry	Common forms	Examples
Isometric (cubic)	Three equal axes, at right angles to each other	Cube, dodecahedron, octahedron	Halite (salt), pyrite, diamond, fluorite, garnet
Tetragonal	Two equal axes and one longer, all at right angles to each other	Prism, pyramid	Vesuvian, rutile, chalcopyrite
Orthorhombic	Three unequal axes, at right angles to each other	Prism, pyramid	Aragonite, marcasite, sulfur
Hexagonal	Four axes; three in a plane at 60 degrees to each other, and one through the intersection of those axes	Prism, pyramid, rhombohedron	Quartz, beryl, tourmaline, calcite
Monoclinic	Three unequal axes; one angle not 90 degrees, two at right angles	Prism	Gypsum, orthoclase, mica
Triclinic	Three unequal axes, no right angles	prism	Microcline, albite

one substance will always have the same internal crystal symmetry, regardless of crystal size or how it formed. Substances that have no orderly internal arrangement of atoms are amorphous (i.e. glass). These rules of crystal symmetry apply to organic and inorganic solids.

The six crystal systems are described in Table 1.1. The hexagonal system is sometimes divided into two, the rhombohedral and hexagonal systems, making a total of seven.

Tenacity is the force of cohesion within a substance. These words describe how a material holds together under stress or pressure. Some of these, like ductility and malleability, refer only to metals. The words flexibility and elasticity are often used interchangeably and incorrectly; they really are two very different properties:

- *Ductility*: the ability of a substance to change shape under pressure.
- *Malleability*: the ability of a substance to be flattened into thin sheets without breaking.
- *Sectility*: the ability of a substance to be cut or shavings taken without breaking.
- *Flexibility*: the ability of a substance to bend and stay bent.
- *Elasticity*: the ability of a substance to bend or stretch and return to its original shape.
- *Brittleness*: the ability of a substance to separate into fragments under sudden pressure.

Fracture describes the pattern in which a substance breaks when stress is applied to it. In some materials, this is a very distinctive property. Unfortunately, it can only be observed on a broken surface. Sometimes, incipient cleavage or fracture planes may be visible in an undamaged object, but fracture is best observed on a freshly broken surface. This may not, of course, always be possible. "You want to break off a piece??!!":

- *Cleavage:* occurs when a crystalline substance breaks along planes that are parallel to crystal faces or structural planes (diamond, fluorite, calcite).
- *Parting:* occurs when a substance breaks along a plane of structural weakness, like the boundary between two crystals or two parts of a natural object. This is never the same in any two specimens, while cleavage directions are always the same within a given material.
- *Fracture:* the way a substance breaks when it neither cleaves nor parts. The three most common kinds of fracture are:
  - *Conchoidal:* produces curved smooth surfaces or concentric ridges (glass, quartz, garnets, obsidian)
  - *Fibrous or splintery:* produces splinters or fibers on surface (asbestos, ivory, bone, some fabrics)
  - *Uneven:* produces irregular, rough or jagged surface (clay, wood).

Hardness is a measure of the degree to which the surface of a substance resists scratching. Since testing for hardness is destructive, it can only be used on materials where scratches will not destroy or damage the scientific or historical value of the object.

A commonly used scale is "Moh's Hardness Scale". This is a scale of relative hardness, and is not quantitative. Something with a hardness of 6 is not twice as hard as a hardness of 3. All this scale says is that something with a hardness of 6 is harder than all those things having hardnesses of less than 6 (Table 1.2).

Quantitative tests of hardness involve indenting a material with a ball, cone, or wedge of hardened steel or other metal under a pre-determined pressure for a specific amount of time. The size and depth of the cavity left in the material being tested is then measured and a formula applied. The resulting value is the hardness, which, like Moh's hardness, has no units of measure.

Table 1.2 Moh's hardness scale.

1	Talc
2	Gypsum
3	Calcite
4	Fluorite
5	Apatite
6	Orthoclase (feldspar)
7	Quartz
8	Topaz
9	Corundum (sapphire, ruby)
10	Diamond

The hardness number is usually combined with the name of the method used, to indicate how the value was obtained. The commonly used tests are the Brinell, Rockwell, and Vickers hardness tests. The results of these tests are presented as the HB or Brinell hardness number, or the HV, and so on.

Conductivity is the ability of a substance to transmit energy in the form of heat or electricity. Most materials that are good conductors are either metals or alloys. This property may be measured in non-metallic materials, and is a common test to separate diamonds from imitations.

Magnetism is a measure of the effect of a magnet on a substance, or the action of a substance as a magnet. There are only a few natural materials that will attract a magnet, all of which contain significant amounts of iron. These include the minerals magnetite, pyrrhotite, native iron, and several types of iron-bearing meteorites. Processed metal alloys such as steel and cast iron will also react to a magnet.

Sensory effects will vary from person to person and may be affected by environmental conditions. They also may not be consistent for all specimens of a particular substance. These properties are most useful in describing a particular specimen at a particular time, as in condition reporting:

- *Taste*: subjective measure of the reaction of a person's taste buds.
- *Smell*: subjective measure of the reaction of a person's olfactory sense to a substance.
- *Feel*: description of the way a surface feels to the touch.

Toxicity is the relative effects of a substance on living organisms. This is not important as an identifying feature, but should always be considered for all materials in collections. There may be toxic substances in the objects in a collection and in the treatments those objects have received. Toxins are often the products of deterioration of natural materials. A person's reaction to toxic substances varies according to individual susceptibility, body weight, age, physical condition, and previous exposure.

Solubility is the ability of a substance to dissolve in a particular liquid, usually water or acid. This is obviously a destructive test and should not be used routinely. But this is an important property in many materials since it will determine how a substance reacts to moisture in any form, whether it be relative humidity or fire sprinklers.

Absorbency is the ability of a substance to absorb liquid, gas, or energy (i.e. heat). This is another property that is more important as a conservation consideration than as a tool for material identification.

Acidity and alkalinity are expressed in terms of the numerical pH scale on which 7 is the neutral middle (see Table 1.3). Compounds at either end of the scale are highly reactive. This scale actually reflects the concentration of hydrogen ions in a substance. Low pH corresponds to a high concentration of hydrogen ions. A compound that, when added to water, increases the

Table 1.3 *pH scale with examples.*

	pH value	Concentration of hydrogen atoms (compared to pure water)	Examples
Acids	0	10,000,000	Battery acid, hydrochloric, sulfuric, and other strong acids
	1	1,000,000	Stomach acid
	2	100,000	Citrus juices, vinegar, grapes
	3	10,000	Beer, soda
	4	1000	Tomato juice, apples
	5	100	Coffee, bananas, garlic
	6	10	Human urine and saliva, milk, onions
Neutral	7	1	Distilled (pure) water, human blood
	8	1/10	Sea water, eggs
	9	1/100	Baking soda
	10	1/1000	Milk of magnesia
	11	1/10,000	Ammonia
	12	1/100,000	Bleach
	13	1/1,000,000	Oven cleaner, lye
Bases	14	1/10,000,000	Drain cleaner

hydrogen ion concentration is called an acid. The reverse is also true; compounds that decrease the number of hydrogen ions when added to water are called bases, and have a high pH.

Acid rain can vary from pH 1 to 5, normal rain is in the pH 5 to 6.5 range, and normal surface water (streams, lakes, etc.) falls between pH 5 and 8. Most living cells have an internal pH of 7.

Flammability is the susceptibility of a substance to fire or burning. This is not a property commonly used for identification purposes, but there are a few materials where the "burn test" is traditional. Amber, plastics, and other substances that emit a distinctive smell when heated are commonly tested with a hot needle or candle flame. This is not recommended, as it is destructive to the object and may be hazardous to the person doing the testing (the smell can only be detected from very near the object).

Melting point is the temperature at which a substance goes from the solid to the liquid state. The next stage is at the boiling point, where a substance goes from a liquid to a gas. These properties are most often used with metals and liquids.

Radioactivity is the release of energy caused by the decay of unstable elements, in the form of charged particles (α and β) and/or γ radiation. It is a natural property of some minerals, and the rocks and fossils that contain them.

Radioactivity may also found in objects that have been treated with radiation, like some gemstones. Uranium salts have been used in pigments in paint and ceramic glazes, some of which retain measurable levels of radiation.

Density is the ratio of a substance's mass and its volume. It should not be confused with weight, which is related to the effects of gravity on a mass.

Density can be expressed in terms of weight per volume (e.g. pounds per cubic foot or grams per cubic centimeter). In geology, it is expressed in terms of specific gravity, which is a numerical expression of the ratio between the weight of a substance and the weight of an equal volume of water:

$$\text{Specific gravity} = \frac{\text{Weight in air}}{\text{Weight in air} - \text{Weight in water}}$$

The specific gravity or density of a substance is constant for all pure specimens of that material. Synthetics or natural mixtures, like rocks (granite, sandstone, etc.), are not consistent because the component substances within them vary in type and amount. Specific gravity is a simple test, but since it requires the object to be immersed in water, it should be used only on homogeneous materials known to be insoluble.

Optical Properties

Translucency or opacity is an expression of how much light can penetrate a substance. There are three levels of light transmission, the first two of which are often modified by words such as "slightly" or "moderately." Semi-transparent is a stage between transparent and translucent. This term is used most in describing gem materials.

Translucency can be used to describe individual objects only, since it is not consistent for any given material. Even some metals become translucent when in very thin sheets:

- *Transparent*: substance clear enough that objects can clearly be seen through it.
- *Semi-transparent*: substance transmits light but objects cannot be seen clearly through it.
- *Translucent*: substance transmits light but objects cannot be recognized through it.
- *Opaque*: substance does not transmit any light.

Luster describes the way a surface reflects light, independent of color. There are two basic types: metallic and non-metallic. Metallic luster is rarely described further, but there are a wide variety of non-metallic lusters.

The luster of a natural translucent or transparent material is dependent on its refractive index. Something with a very high refractive index may display

adamantine luster, an uncommon appearance that is hard to define. It sometimes looks waxy or slightly metallic. Materials that have been polished also have
a luster, but it is often not the same as the luster it had before it was worked.
Some common non-metallic lusters are:

- *Dull*: self-explanatory (like mud or worn linoleum)
- *Vitreous*: shiny, wet-looking (like window glass or freshly-broken obsidian)
- *Silky*: fibrous, with a directional sheen (like asbestos or silk fabric)
- *Waxy or greasy*: not highly shiny; it may appear to have a thin coating on the
  surface even though it does not (like wax candles or talc)
- *Pearly*: a soft sheen (like pearls, nacre, or moonstone)

Color describes the appearance of a substance in terms of which portions of
the visible spectrum of light are absorbed. The visible spectrum is only a small
part of the complete spectrum of light (see Figure 1.2). If none of the light
reflected or refracted by a substance is absorbed, it appears colorless. If all
light is absorbed, it appears black.

The structural and chemical causes of color in natural materials can be
very complex. But basically, visible colors are caused and affected by the amount
of a pigment or impurities present in a material, or the physical structure of
its surface. Color is consistent for some materials, and not for others. This
depends on the causes of the color.

Some colors fade or change over time. This may be due to the breakdown
or alteration of color-producing pigment compounds, which can be caused
by heat, ultra-violet radiation, dehydration, or other chemical changes.

Idiochromatic substances contain a specific coloring element, called a chromophore, which is part of their normal composition. The colors of idiochromatic materials tend to be constant and predictable. Examples of this are the
minerals malachite and azurite, both carbonates of copper. These minerals
are colored by the copper in their compositions, and are always green and
blue, respectively.

Allochromatic compounds are colored by trace elements or impurities
that are not part of their normal, basic chemical composition. In these cases,
color may vary widely among specimens of a single species or pieces of a certain material.

Figure 1.2

Wavelengths of light.

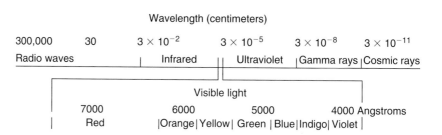

Structural colors may be caused by the diffraction or interference of light by tiny, regularly-spaced structures within a substance. Many insects and bird feathers display structural color. Structural defects in a material's crystal lattice can also affect its color. Excess or missing ions act as "color centers" and may affect the way the substance absorbs light.

The true color of a substance is the *streak*, which is the powdered material. This can be obtained by drawing the specimen across a piece of white, unglazed porcelain. This test is used most often in mineralogy, but it can be applied to other compounds as well.

Luminescence describes a substance that emits light when exposed to ultraviolet light or x-rays. Something that glows under these types of light is *fluorescent*. If luminescence continues after removal of the exciting light source, the substance is said to be *phosphorescent*. This can be used as a diagnostic characteristic for a variety of substances, including some adhesives. Some materials, like diamonds, are not consistently fluorescent, but this property may affect how some specimens appear in certain types of light that have a strong ultraviolet component.

Dispersion is the separation of light into the colors of the spectrum within a substance. It is expressed as the difference in the refractive index of red light and violet light inside the material in question.

The velocity of light varies as it passes from one medium to another. Light with long wavelengths travels the fastest and is refracted (bent) the least. Thus, red light changes direction less than violet light when they enter the same substance. Colorless or light-colored materials having a high dispersion (diamonds, zircon, cubic zirconia) may produce spectral colors in white light, giving them a fiery appearance.

Refraction describes the amount light is turned or bent inside a non-opaque material. Light falling on a non-opaque surface is partly reflected and partly refracted by the substance (see Figure 1.3). Light passing from air into a substance slows down and its direction changes. The index of refraction (IR) is a numerical expression of the relationship between the angles of incidence and refraction. The IR is constant for all pure specimens of the same substance.

There are two principal optical classes: *isotropic* and *anisotropic*. In an isotropic material, light travels at the same speed no matter which direction it goes. In anisotropic materials, the velocity of the light depends on which direction it is going relative to the crystal structure.

Isotropic substances are those having no internal structure (i.e. glass, liquids), and all compounds crystallizing in the isometric (cubic) crystal system. These all have a single refractive index because light moves through them at the same speed in all directions. All other crystalline substances are anisotropic. The velocity of light passing through these materials varies with the crystallographic direction. This results in a range of refractive indices, rather than a single value.

Figure 1.3

Refractive index measures the amount light is bent going from one substance into another, i = angle of incidence, r' = angle of reflection (= i), r = angle of refraction.

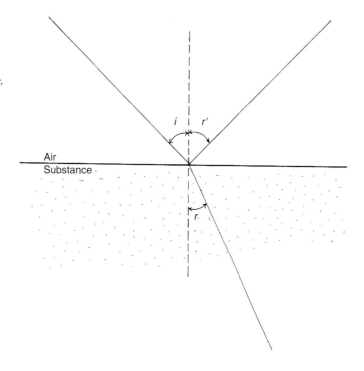

Refractive index (RI) of a solid can easily be measured using a refractometer, as long as an object can be placed in contact with the prism on the instrument. Liquid refractometers exist for the determination of RI of solutions. Both the RI and the birefringence (range between refractive indices) are diagnostic and constant for a pure substance.

Play of color is the term used to describe the internal spectral colors that appear inside some specimens of materials like opal and some synthetics. The colors seem to move when the specimen is turned or the light source is moved. Labradorescence is a broad play of colors common in labradorite and other minerals (mostly feldspars) having polysynthetic twinning.

Iridescence describes the display of spectral colors on or just below the surface of a specimen. This affect is often due to a coating, and may not be a diagnostic characteristic of a material.

Opalescence is a pearly or milky internal reflection, most common in white or light-colored minerals such as some opal or "moonstone" (albite or orthoclase feldspar). This is also known as adularescence. Like iridescence and play of color, these properties are not consistent within any natural material, and can only be used to describe individual specimens. Some synthetic materials have been created specifically to display these properties and so always show them.

Chatoyancy is the "cat's eye" effect. A band of light is revealed in a substance under a strong focused light. This is a common characteristic of fibrous materials or substances that contain fine parallel inclusions. Minerals that may display chatoyancy include chrysoberyl (the classic cat's eye), gypsum, and asbestiform species. The effect is also common in fibrous glass and some plastics.

Asterism describes the appearance of a "star" within some materials and gemstones cut from them. It is caused by the transmission of light within the crystal along crystallographic axes or aligned inclusions. The number of rays in the star is determined by the crystal structure of the substance. Those crystallizing in the Hexagonal crystal system may produce stars with rays in multiples of 3, like quartz or corundum (ruby and sapphire). Those in all other crystal systems can only produce rays in multiples of 2, like the mineral enstatite (often sold as the "black star of India"). Figure 1.4 shows a diagram of a sapphire crystal and how a cabochon would be cut to reveal a six-pointed star.

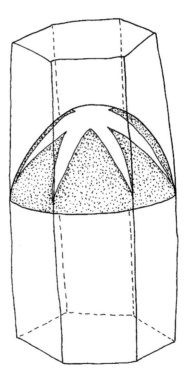

Figure 1.4   In order for a stone to exhibit asterism, it must be cut perpendicular to the long axis of a crystal to reveal a star.

2

Geological Materials

By weight, about 98% of the Earth's crust is composed of only eight elements: aluminum (Al), calcium (Ca), iron (Fe), potassium (K), magnesium (Mg), sodium (Na), oxygen (O), and silicon (Si). All other naturally occurring elements are rare by comparison.

The materials that make up the earth's crust are described at two levels. The smallest unit of classification is the mineral, which is defined as a natural, homogeneous inorganic solid having a definite chemical composition and a crystalline structure. The second, more complex classification unit is the rock, which is defined as any natural solid made up of one or more minerals.

Minerals

Every mineral has physical and optical properties that make it different from all others. Minerals are referred to as species, and each has a unique name. About 3600 mineral species have been identified and described, but only about 20 of the most common make up most of the Earth's crust.

Some chemical compounds occur in more than one form in nature. These are known as polymorphs ("many forms"). In minerals, two or more minerals may share the same chemical composition, but have different crystal structures. Two common examples of this are calcite and aragonite (calcium carbonate), and diamond and graphite (pure carbon).

Varieties have been named within some mineral species, usually based on appearance. For example, the mineral beryl has five color varieties: aquamarine (blue), emerald (green), heliodor (yellow), goshenite (colorless), and morganite (pink). Any specimen not falling within one of these colors is referred to simply as beryl. Varietal names have no legitimate mineralogical standing, since they do not differ from the parent mineral species in composition or crystal structure. Most varietal names are used in reference to gems or ornamental stones.

Minerals are usually organized according to their chemical compositions. This systematic arrangement of minerals, developed by Swedish chemist Jons Berzelius, was enlarged by James and Edward Dana in the late 1800s. Dana's system, expanded and updated, is the most widely used today.

Some collections, particularly those used for teaching, may be organized alphabetically or by some other simple criteria, such as mode of formation or by locality. Gem collections are usually organized by Dana's system or alphabetically.

In addition to the chemical groups of the Dana system, there are also structural groups of minerals. These describe two or more mineral species that have the same or similar crystalline structure, while differing chemically. Not all species are placed within structural groups. Well-known groups include garnets, tourmalines, feldspars, clays, and micas.

In the Dana system, the simplest minerals are placed at the beginning, followed by progressively more complex compounds. The silicates are last, and have been divided into six structural groups. Table 2.1 lists the chemical groups of minerals, with some examples of structural groups and species within each. This is by no means a complete list of species. The following paragraphs are descriptions of the major groups, with a brief discussion of those minerals in each group that are most often found in museum collections (other than traditional geological collections).

Native elements are minerals composed of a single element. This group also includes natural alloys, which are mixtures of two metals. Based on their physical properties, the native elements can be separated into three divisions: metals (such as Ag, Au, Cu, Fe, Hg, Pb, Pt, Sn), semi-metals (such as As, Bi, Sb, Te), and non-metals (C, S, Se).

The metallic elements and alloys will be discussed in a later section. Diamond and graphite are polymorphs of carbon. Diamond, the hardest natural substance, is also chemically inert. It is used in abrasives and cutting tools, as well as in jewelry. Graphite is an artist's material, a dry lubricant, and is combined with clay in the core of modern pencils.

Native iron is most common in iron meteorites. Native mercury is a liquid and extremely volatile. The low boiling point of this fluid can be reached in hot sunlight, so specimens containing free mercury are rare.

Although native arsenic, bismuth, iron, and other elements are known, they are not common. For commercial purposes, these elements are derived from more common, more complex, natural compounds.

Sulfides, Antimonides, Selenides, and Tellurides are minerals in which sulfur, antimony, selenium, or tellurium combine with one or more metals, or with one metal and one semi-metal. Some sulfide minerals are valuable sources of such elements as copper, silver, zinc, and mercury.

Pyrite and marcasite have been faceted and used in jewelry. Galena, cinnabar, and other sulfides have been ground up and used as pigment and in cosmetics and medicine. Cinnabar is the red sulfide of mercury. Chinese "cinnabar" tableware and jewelry is actually layered lacquer that was

Table 2.1 Examples of species in the Dana system of mineral classification.

Chemical group	Structural group	Species	Composition
Native element		Diamond	C
		Graphite	C
	Gold	Gold	Au
	Gold	Silver	Ag
		Sulfur	S
Sulfide	Pyrite	Pyrite	FeS_2
		Galena	PbS
		Cinnabar	HgS
Oxide		Chrysoberyl	$BeAl_2O_4$
	Hematite	Corundum	Al_2O_3
	Hematite	Hematite	Fe_2O_3
		Rutile	TiO_2
	Spinel	Spinel	$MgAl_2O_4$
Halide		Fluorite	CaF_2
		Halite	NaCl
Carbonate	Calcite	Calcite	$CaCO_3$
	Calcite	Magnesite	$MgCO_3$
	Calcite	Rhodochrosite	$MnCO_3$
	Aragonite	Aragonite	$CaCO_3$
		Azurite	$Cu_3(CO_3)_2(OH)_2$
		Malachite	$Cu_2CO_3(OH)_2$
Sulfate		Gypsum	$CaSO_4 \cdot 2H_2O$
		Barite	$BaSO_4$
Phosphate		Variscite	$Al(PO_4) \cdot 2H_2O$
		Turquoise	$CuAl_6(PO_4)_4(OH)_8 \cdot 4H_2O$
	Apatite	Fluorapatite	$Ca_5(PO_4)_3F$
Nesosilicate	Olivine	Forsterite	Mg_2SiO_4
	Garnet	Pyrope	$Mg_3Al_2(SiO_4)_3$
	Garnet	Almandine	$Fe_3Al_2(SiO_4)_3$
	Garnet	Spessartine	$Mn_2Al_2(SiO_4)_3$
	Garnet	Grossularite	$Ca_3Al_2(SiO_4)_3$
	Garnet	Andradite	$Ca_3Fe_2(SiO_4)_3$
	Garnet	Uvarovite	$Ca_3Cr_2(SiO_4)_3$
		Andalusite	Al_2SiO_5
		Kyanite	Al_2SiO_5
		Zircon	$ZrSiO_4$
		Topaz	$Al_2SiO_4(F,OH)_2$
Sorosilicate		Epidote	$Ca_2(Al,Fe)Al_2O(SiO_4)(Si_2O_7)(OH)$
		Zoisite	$Ca_2Al_3O(SiO_4)(Si_2O_7)(OH)$
		Vesuvian	$Ca_{10}(Mg,Fe)_2Al_4(SiO_4)_5(Si_2O_7)_2(OH)_4$
Cyclosilicate		Beryl	$Be_3Al_2(SiO_3)_6$
	Tourmaline	Elbaite	$Na(Li,Al)_3Al_6B_3Si_6O_{27}(OH,F)_4$

(Continued)

Table 2.1 *(Continued)*

Chemical group	Structural group	Species	Composition
Inosilicate	Pyroxene	Diopside	$CaMg(SiO_3)_2$
	Pyroxene	Jadeite	$NaAl(SiO_3)_2$
	Pyroxene	Spodumene	$LiAl(SiO_3)_2$
	Pyroxene	Enstatite	$MgSiO_3$
	Amphibole	Actinolite	$Ca_2(Mg,Fe)_5Si_8O_{22}(OH)_2$
		Rhodonite	$MnSiO_3$
Phyllosilicate		Antigorite	$Mg_3Si_2O_5(OH)_4$ and $Ca_2Mg_5Si_8O_{22}(OH)_2$
	Clay	Montmorillonite	$(Na,Ca)_{0.3}(Al,Mg)_2Si_4O_{10}(OH)_2 \cdot nH_2O$
	Mica	Muscovite	$KAl_2(Si_3Al)O_{10}(OH,F)_2$
		Talc	$Mg_3(Si_2O_5)_2(OH)_2$
		Chrysocolla	$Cu_4H_4(Si_2O_5)_2(OH)_8$
		Sepiolite	$Mg_4(OH)_2Si_6O_{15} \cdot 5H_2O$
Tectosilicate	Quartz	Quartz (crystalline and microcrystalline)	SiO_2
		Opal	$SiO_2 \cdot nH_2O$
	Feldspar	Orthoclase	$KAlSi_3O_8$
	Feldspar	Microcline	$KAlSi_3O_8$
	Feldspar	*plagioclases*: albite to anorthite	$NaAlSi_3O_8$ (*solid solution series*) $CaAl_2Si_2O_8$
		Sodalite	$Na_8(AlSiO_4)_6Cl_2$
		Lazurite	$(Na,Ca)_8(AlSiO_4)_6(SO_4,S,Cl)_2$
	Scapolite	Marialite	$Na_4(AlSi_3O_8)_3(Cl_2,CO_3,SO_4)$
	Scapolite	Meionite	$Ca_4(Al_2Si_2O_8)_3(Cl_2,CO_3,SO_4)$
	Zeolite	Natrolite	$Na_2Al_2Si_3O_{10} \cdot 2H_2O$

originally colored with cinnabar. Modern "cinnabar" ware contains no mercury.

Sulfosalts are compounds of one or more metals, a semi-metal and sulfur. Many sulfosalts are rare, but some of them are important ore minerals.

Oxides and hydroxides are combinations of one or more elements with oxygen. Some oxides contain water, which is itself a simple oxide. Oxides of silicon are not included in this group, but are classified as silicates, and are organized by their molecular structure.

A number of oxides are economically important ore minerals, such as hematite (iron), chromite (chrome), zincite (zinc), and cassiterite (tin). Some gemstone species are oxides, including corundum (ruby and sapphire), spinel, and chrysoberyl. Corundum is the second hardest natural substance and is used as an abrasive.

Some simple oxides are brightly or strongly colored, and have been used as pigments. This includes the common oxides of iron, hematite, which is red and black, and goethite (syn. limonite), which is yellow or brown. These compounds have also been called ocher, yellow ocher, or brown ocher. Minium and massicot are earthy, red/orange and yellow oxides of lead that are also used as pigments. Hematite is sometimes also found as carvings or faceted in jewelry.

There are only a few minerals that are attracted to a magnet, and only one that sometimes is itself a natural magnet. Those species that are attracted by a magnet include magnetite, pyrrhotite, and native iron. Magnetite occasionally occurs as naturally magnetic specimens, which have the common name "lodestone."

Halides are compounds that include one of the halogen elements: fluorine, chlorine, bromine, or iodine. The simplest halides are combinations of one element, such as sodium (Na), with a halogen element, such as chlorine (Cl). Complex halides combine two or more elements with a halogen, and some contain water. Some halides are economically important minerals, such as halite (common salt), fluorite (fluorine), and chlorargyrite (silver ore).

Salts are important in the processing of some natural materials and may be found as residues on or in objects. Fluorite, which is also called fluorospar, is commonly used for carvings, particularly in Asia. The translucent pastels of this material make it attractive, but its softness and perfect cleavage combine to make fluorite objects very fragile.

Carbonates contain the simple molecule CO_3. Some carbonate minerals also include the hydroxyl (OH) radical. They combine with other elements, such as calcium or iron, to form carbonate minerals.

Some carbonate minerals are sources of important elements like zinc (smithsonite) and magnesium (magnesite). Other members of this group are used for carving and ornaments because of their striking colors and patterns. These include calcite, rhodochrosite, azurite, and malachite.

The minerals calcite and aragonite are polymorphs of calcium carbonate. Calcite is the more stable of the two, and aragonite is most often seen in objects made of speleothems, the rocks formed in solution caverns. Aragonite is also an important constituent in many materials of organic origin, such as mollusk shells and the outer skeletons of sand dollars and coral. Calcite is the major component of the rocks limestone and marble, and as such is found in collections as sculpture, building stone, in mosaics, and in inlay or intarsia.

Borates contain some combination of boron and oxygen. Members of this group are sources of boron, which has many industrial uses.

Chromates are a small group of minerals that contain the simple CrO_4 molecule. Crocoite is the most common species in this group, a bright orange compound that is sometimes used as a pigment.

Sulfates contain SO_4, which combines with metals and other elements. Gypsum, the most common sulfate, is used to make plaster and wall board. It is often used as gesso or filler in paints, and its massive form (alabaster) has been used for carving. Other sulfates are ores of rare elements such as barium (barite) and strontium (celestine).

Chalcanthite is copper sulfate, often used as a poison, and sometimes as a pigment. Melanterite is a highly poisonous product of the decomposition of pyrite and marcasite. This white powdery material can often be found on deteriorating jewelry or other items made of iron sulfides. It is mentioned here because of its extreme toxicity.

Phosphates, arsenates, and vanadates contain a simple molecule of oxygen combined with phosphorous, arsenic, or vanadium. Compounds of PO_4 are most common. Although this is the largest group of non-silicate minerals, only a few of them are found in museums outside of mineral collections. The most notable exception is turquoise, a phosphate of copper. Variscite is a blue-green phosphate sometimes used as an imitation of turquoise. Callais is variscite from Spain and France that was used in the Early Neolithic as a pigment and to make trade beads.

Vanadium oxysalts are minerals that contain some combination of oxygen and vanadium. These differ from the generally simpler vanadates, which are included in the phosphate group.

Molybdates and Tungstates contain one of the simple molecules, MoO_4 or WO_4. Some members of this group are important ores, including wolframite and scheelite (tungsten), and wulfenite (molybdenum).

Silicates make up over 90% of the Earth's crust. The silicates are the largest chemical group in minerals, comprising about 25% of all known species. All species in this large group contain a molecule composed of silicon and oxygen. The simplest and most stable combination of these elements is SiO_4, in which four oxygen atoms are closely bonded to one silicon atom. This form is called a tetrahedron. These simple units or building blocks combine with each other to form a variety of silicate structures. The silicates are divided into six groups, each defined by a particular molecular structure.

Nesosilicates are the simplest silicates. They contain isolated or independent SiO_4 tetrahedra. This group has also been called the orthosilicates. A secondary classification, the nesosubsilicates has been designated by Strunz (1957), who was the originator of the silicate classification. This subclass included species having a second anion or anionic radical. The nesosilicates include the gem minerals zircon, topaz, and the garnet and olivine groups.

Sorosilicates are minerals in which two SiO_4 tetrahedra combine to produce Si_2O_7. Many members of this group are complex compounds that contain several elements, the (OH) molecule and water, as well as the silicate radical. Most species in this group are rare. The gem minerals tanzanite, a variety of zoisite, and vesuvian (idocrase) fall within this group.

Cyclosilicates are those compounds with three or more tetrahedra linked in closed, ring-like structures. The ratio between Si and O is 1:3. This group includes the important gem species beryl and the tourmaline group. The 11 members of the tourmaline group display an unusual property known as piezoelectricity. When pressure is applied to a crystal, an electrical charge builds up at either end of it. This makes these minerals useful in pressure gauges and other electrical equipment. Quartz and a few other, less common minerals, also display this property.

Inosilicates contain single or double chains of tetrahedra. In a single chain structure, the Si to O ratio is 1:3, and in a double chain, it is 4:11. This structural class contains many common rock-forming minerals, including the amphibole and pyroxene groups. Both jade minerals, jadeite, and nephrite, fall within this group.

Phyllosilicates are those minerals in which the SiO_4 tetrahedra combine in sheets, forming a layered structure. The Si to O ratio is 2:5. This class includes the clay, mica, and serpentine groups of minerals. Some clay minerals are economically important in the manufacture of everything from ceramics and cosmetics to cat litter. The common name for the clay mineral kaolinite is china clay, which refers to its use in making fine ceramics. Another clay mineral, sepiolite, is a white, soft material used for carving pipes and small household items. Its common name is meerschaum. Some clay minerals, like montmorillonite, are intensely hydroscopic and will absorb large amounts of water. These are sometimes used as desiccants and may be found as powder or tablets in older collections.

There are 30 species in the mica group, all of which have large, flat molecules that are weakly bonded to each other. These weak bonds make it possible to separate or cleave thin sheets of mica. The resulting sheets are flexible, resistant to thermal shock, and transparent or translucent. They may be quite large, up to several feet across, depending on the size of the original crystal. Muscovite, known as white mica or isinglass, is the most common mica used, although other species, such as phlogopite and lepidolite, may also yield transparent sheets. Mica has been used to make windows, particularly in situations where flexibility and heat resistance are important. Lamp shades were also made of light-weight sheets of mica. Soft enough to be cut with a knife, mica has also been used to make microscope slides and to support fragile plant or algae specimens. Delicate specimens may be pressed between two sheets of mica, which are held together either with glue or by binding around the edges.

Serpentine is a metamorphic rock made mostly of three similar phyllosilicate minerals, chrysotile, lizardite, and antigorite. A highly variable material, serpentine occasionally occurs in masses suitable for carving or for use as building or decorative stone. Chrysotile is one of the minerals known

Table 2.2   Asbestiform minerals.

Mineral species	Mineral group	Chemical composition
Ferrogedrite	Inosilicate	$(Fe,Mg)_5Al_2(Si_6Al_2)O_{22}(OH)_2$
Riebeckite (syn. Crocidolite)	Inosilicate	$Na_2(Fe,Mg)_3Fe_2Si_8O_{22}(OH)_2$
Tremolite	Inosilicate	$Ca_2(Mg,Fe)_5Si_8O_{22}(OH)_2$
Anthophyllite	Inosilicate	$(Mg,Fe)_7Si_8O_{22}(OH)_2$
Actinolite variety Byssolite	Inosilicate	$Ca_2(Mg,Fe)_5Si_8O_{22}(OH)_2$
Chrysotile	Phyllosilicate	$Mg_3Si_2O_5(OH)_4$
Grunerite (syn. Amosite)	Phyllosilicate	$(Fe,Mg)_7Si_8O_{22}(OH)_2$
Erionite	Tectosilicate	$(K_2,Ca,Na_2)_2Al_4Si_{14}O_{36} \cdot 15H_2O$

commonly as asbestos. There are a number of minerals that sometimes occur as long, flexible fibrous crystals. Although these minerals are not related, and are very different chemically, their mineral fibers share common properties that have made them useful (Table 2.2).

Mineral fibers are known commercially and collectively as asbestos, with little or no differentiation of mineral species. These materials are poor conductors of heat and other forms of energy, and they will not burn. Fabrics have been made by either weaving the fibers or, more commonly, by compressing them into felt-like mats. Asbestos fibers were often combined with other materials like cotton or wood pulp to give the product bulk. The primary use of asbestos is as an insulator against heat, and as such can be found in many forms, including brake shoes and engine gaskets. These fibrous minerals are also flexible and resistance to chemical attack, which increased their usefulness in industry.

Talc is a soft, large-molecule phyllosilicate mineral having a characteristic waxy luster. Ground to a floury texture, it used as bath powder and as a base for cosmetics. It is also used as a filler in food, as a dry lubricant, and in the manufacture of some kinds of paper.

Tectosilicates have a three-dimensional structure of linked SiO_4 tetrahedra. These minerals make up about 75% of the Earth's rocky crust. These are also called *framework* silicates. Every oxygen in each tetrahedron is shared with neighboring tetrahedra. This class includes the feldspars, a large group of important rock-forming minerals, and quartz, the most common mineral on Earth. This group also contains the zeolites, some of which are economically important, and the gemstone species lazurite (lapis lazuli) and opal.

There are 21 different feldspars, most of which are common rock-forming minerals. It is estimated that feldspars make up at least 50% of all the rocks in the Earth's crust. A few members of this group are sometimes used as gems or decorative stones. These include albite and microcline, light-colored specimens of which sometimes display adularescence ("moonstones"). Labradorite may display an internal play of color due to the presence of tiny parallel twin planes, giving specimens a blue internal sheen. This material is used as a decorative building stone, sometimes under the trade name larvikite.

The zeolites are a group of about 50 complex tectosilicates that have a number of industrial uses. These compounds tend to have an open, porous crystal structure and are chemically inert. This makes them useful in filters, water purification, and as fillers in animal feed and soil conditioners.

Quartz is the most common mineral in the Earth's crust. It occurs in a wide variety of forms, colors, and lusters, but other properties are generally consistent for all specimens. All quartz has the same basic chemical formula, silicon dioxide (SiO_2). It has a hardness of 7, and a distinctive conchoidal fracture. The color and translucency of quartz can be affected by a disruption of the molecular structure, as in smoky quartz, or by the inclusions of tiny amounts of other elements or minerals. In some classifications, quartz is listed with the oxides, but it is most often placed with the silicates.

There are two types of quartz: crystalline and cryptocrystalline or microcrystalline. Crystalline species often occur as terminated hexagonal prismatic crystals, while cryptocrystalline varieties never form crystals, but occur in homogeneous masses. All quartzes have the same crystalline structure at the molecular level.

Flint is a common name applied to any material, rock or mineral, that is composed mostly of massive cryptocrystalline quartz. This word is usually used to describe dark-colored chert nodules found in limestones. The term flint is often used by anthropologists to describe homogeneous siliceous materials that have been used to make tools or weapons, regardless of their actual composition.

Many of the names used to describe quartz varieties are obsolete, popular or common names. Tables 2.3 and 2.4 list the correct name for each variety, plus synonyms or archaic names for each.

Quartz is the most common mineral found as a pseudomorph, where it has chemically replaced another substance, retaining the form of the original material. These can be pseudomorphs after fossils, or other minerals. Quartz commonly forms pseudomorphs after wood, bone, calcite, barite, siderite, and fluorite. Those listed here are the forms most often used as gems or decorative stones (Table 2.5).

When quartz forms after or at the same time as another mineral, this can result in one mineral being inside, or included, in the other. Individual crystals of one mineral can be visible within another material, as with rutilated quartz, or one material may be evenly distributed throughout another, as

Table 2.3 *Cryptocrystalline quartz varieties.*

Variety	Synonyms	Description
Chalcedony		Any color, translucent to opaque, rarely transparent, several varieties may mix in any one specimen
	Moss agate, mocha stone	Clear to gray translucent white/black or green tree-like inclusions (dendrites); not a true agate, should be referred to as chalcedony with inclusions
Carnelian	Sard	Red-brown to red, translucent
Chrysoprase		Green to yellow-green, translucent
Jasper	Prase (green), Plasma (dark green)	Any color; opaque; most often red, green, brown and/or yellow, often multicolored
	Bloodstone, heliotrope	Dark green with red spots or streaks
Agate		Any color or combination of colors, forms concentric or curved layers, opaque or translucent
Onyx	Sardonyx (brown)	Any color or combination of colors, forms flat parallel layers or bands, opaque or translucent

Table 2.4 *Crystalline quartz varieties.*

Variety	Synonyms	Optical	Physical
Quartz	Rock crystal Rhinestone	Colorless, translucent to transparent	Usually as terminated hexagonal prisms; sometimes massive
Smoky quartz	Cairngorm Smoky topaz Morion (black)	Gray, brown, black, transparent to opaque	Terminated hexagonal prisms; rarely massive
Citrine	Madeira rio grande	Yellow to orange, translucent to transparent	Terminated hexagonal prisms; rarely massive, rare in nature, often achieved by heating amethyst
Amethyst/ Citrine	Ametrine	Bi-colored purple and yellow, transparent to translucent	Terminated hexagonal prisms; sometimes natural (mostly from Bolivia), but most is heat-treated
Amethyst	Oriental sapphire	Purple to violet, transparent to translucent	Terminated hexagonal prisms; rarely massive, color fades on exposure to heat or sunlight
Rose quartz	Bohemian ruby	Pink to rose-red, translucent to semi-transparent, rarely transparent	Usually cloudy with fractures, massive, rarely forms crystals, color fades on exposure to heat or sunlight
Veridine		Green, translucent to transparent	Vitreous masses, rare as crystals, may be produced by heat-treating amethyst
Milky quartz		Milky- to grayish-white, translucent to opaque	Common as vein-filling or irregular masses; rare as crystals

Figure 2.1

Moss agate. "Moss agate" is a term applied to chalcedony with black, green or brown branching inclusions. This term is inaccurate, since these are not agates, and the inclusions are not plants.

Figure 2.2

An agate is banded micro-crystalline quartz (chalcedony). The bands are curved, and can be any color, opaque or translucent.

Table 2.5   Some common quartz pseudomorphs.

Name	Common name	Description
Chalcedony after wood	Petrified wood Limb cast	Variable color, massive, translucent to opaque; often shows cell structure or some relic form of the wood
Chalcedony after bone	Petrified bone	Usually red or brown, opaque, often shows cell structure (usually dinosaur bone)
Chalcedony after Crocidolite	Tiger eye Red tiger eye	Yellow-brown; opaque; looks fibrous; red or dark brown is tiger eye that has been heat-treated
Chalcedony after Riebeckite	Hawk's eye	Blue-gray; opaque, looks fibrous

Table 2.6   Some common forms of quartz with inclusions.

Mineral inside quartz	Names and synonyms	Descriptions
Green mica	Aventurine	Green, massive, bright luster and color due to inclusions of small, shiny flakes of chrome-rich mica
Rutile (titanium oxide)	Rutilated quartz Needle stone Venus hair stone Sagenite	Colorless to smoky quartz, often as crystals, with needle-shaped yellow, red, or brown crystals of rutile randomly scattered or in radiating sprays
Tourmaline (usually black schorl)	Tourmalinated quartz Sagenite	Clear to smoky quartz, often crystals, with black or dark green needle- or thin lath-shaped crystals randomly scattered needle-shaped or prismatic black crystals of schorl (tourmaline)
Lepidochrocite (iron oxide)	Strawberry quartz	Clear to light smoky quartz with red platelets scattered or aligned along crystal axes

with aventurine. In Table 2.6 above the correct name for a type of included quartz is underlined.

Opal is silicon dioxide with a variable amount of free water. It is written $SiO_2 \cdot nH_2O$, the small n before the water indicating this variability in the amount present in any given specimen.

Opal is a common mineral in chemical sediments, as deposits around hot springs, replacing fossils such as wood, or as secondary vein-filling. Most opal is "common" opal, without the internal play of colors that makes some opal "precious." Common opal is usually light colored, and has a distinctive waxy luster.

Precious opal is usually defined by the background color, black, white, or fire (orange). There are terms used to describe the distribution of the internal colors, and which colors are dominant.

Metals and Alloys

The metals are those elements that combine as cations (positive ions), that are good conductors of energy, that have a metallic luster, and that can be

Table 2.7 Properties of some metallic elements.

Element	Iron*	Copper*	Zinc	Silver*	Tin	Platinum*	Gold*	Lead*
Chemical symbol	Fe	Cu	Zn	Ag	Sn	Pt	Au	Pb
Atomic number	26	29	30	47	50	78	79	82
Atomic weight	56	64	65	108	119	195	197	207
Specific gravity	7.87	8.93	7.14	10.50	7.30	21.45	19.30	11.34
Melting point	1535°C	1082°C	419°C	800°C	232°C	1755°C	900°C	300°C
Conductivity	Moderate	Very good	Moderate	Very good	Good	Poor	Good	Poor
Chemical reactivity	Reactive	Reactive	Reactive	Reactive	Reactive	Inert	Inert	Reactive
Malleability and ductility	Poor	Very good	Moderate	Good	Good	Good	Very good	Very good

*Those elements that occur in nature as native elements (minerals).

deformed without fracture. These elements can be found in the middle region of the periodic table (see Figure 1.1). "Noble metals" are those that are resistant to oxidation and corrosion under normal conditions, and "precious metals" are those that are considered rare or valuable.

At room temperature and normal atmospheric pressure, all metals are solids except mercury, which is a liquid. Over 60% of the known elements are classified as metals, but of those only about 40 are of any economic importance. From this group, only a small number have been selected for discussion here. These are the metallic elements found most often in museum collections as manufactured items. Their properties are summarized in Table 2.7.

Some metals occur in nature in an elemental state, and as such are minerals (native elements). Most metals, however, are stable only when in combination with at least one other element.

Gold possesses a unique combination of physical and optical properties. Its malleability, ductility and flexibility make it useful in industry as well as in ornamentation. As it is so soft, gold must be combined with other elements, usually silver, nickel, copper or palladium, before it can be used in coins or jewelry. Ancient gold objects may have a very high gold content because the metal was used just as it came out of the ground.

Gold is very stable chemically and seldom forms compounds. The most common and important ore of gold is the native element itself. Native gold often contains small amounts of silver, and sometimes copper or iron. Pure gold is not soluble in any single acid, nor does it tarnish.

Most native gold is actually a natural alloy of gold with a small amounts of silver (10–12%). Electrum is an natural alloy of gold that contains 20% or more silver, written Au, Ag.

The purity of gold is usually expressed in karats. Pure gold is "24 karat", while any lower number denotes the presence of some other metal(s). Twenty-two karat gold is 22 parts gold and 2 parts something else; 18 karat is

Table 2.8 Fool's gold minerals.

Mineral species	Composition	Color	Luster	Specific gravity	Hardness	Tenacity
Biotite (weathered)	Complex silicate (black mica)	Brown or gold-brown	Submetallic to dull	2.7–3.1	2.0–3.0	Perfect cleavage in one direction; may be flexible
Chalcopyrite	Copper iron sulfide	Brassy yellow	Metallic	4.1–4.3	3.5–4.0	Brittle, no cleavage
Marcasite	Iron sulfide	Pale bronze to gray	Metallic	4.85–4.9	6.0–6.5	Brittle, no cleavage
Pyrite	Iron sulfide	Brassy yellow	Metallic	4.95–5.1	6.0–6.5	Brittle; poor cleavage in two directions
Pyrrhotite	Iron sulfide	Bronze yellow	Metallic	4.58–4.64	3.5–4.5	Brittle; parting in one direction
Gold	*Gold*	*Golden yellow*	*Metallic*	*19.33*	*2.5–3.0*	*No cleavage; malleable, ductile, flexible*

18 parts gold and 6 parts not, and so on. The lower the number, the less gold there is present.

"Fool's gold" is any specimen that looks like gold, but does not contain any of that precious element. Not all specimens of any one mineral species could be called fool's gold, because there are none that could consistently, in all its forms and color variations, be mistaken for gold. The minerals most commonly found as fool's gold are pyrite, chalcopyrite, biotite, marcasite, and pyrrhotite.

The physical and optical properties of the "fool's gold" species are summarized and compared with those of gold in Table 2.8.

Silver is another native metal found in museum collections in a variety of forms. Chemically, silver differs greatly from gold in that it is highly reactive. Silver occurs in its native state, but is more stable in compounds with other elements. The black tarnish so common on silver items is silver sulfide. Silver objects that have been buried for any length of time may be completely altered, particularly if water is present. When the alteration that begins as tarnish is complete, and all native silver has been combined with other elements, a worked piece will usually lose its integrity and disintegrate. If silver is subjected to moisture in the presence of the element chlorine, as it would in seawater or brackish water, "horn silver" or silver chloride may develop.

Most modern silver mined has been used to make photographic film emulsions, in plating, and in alloys for tableware, jewelry, and electrical equipment. Sterling silver is an expression of purity, being at least 92.5% silver. This is expressed either with the word "sterling," "0.925" (the "." is often omitted), or the Lion Passant hallmark. Fine silver is 99.9% pure, but is too soft for most applications. This is the standard purity for silver bullion, as a commodity.

Lesser known standards are coin silver, which is 90% silver, 10% copper, and Mexican silver, which is 95% silver. Britannia silver also is more pure than sterling, with at least 95.84% silver and up to 4.16% copper. It may be marked with a lion's profile, the number 958, or the word Britannia. This is different from Britannia metal, which is mostly tin (90% Sn, 8% Sb, 2% Cu). This was also known as Vickers plate in the late 1700s.

Sheffield plate silver is copper with a thin coating of silver. Close plating involves silver foil over iron or steel. German silver actually contains no silver. It is composed of 50% copper, 25% nickel, and 25% zinc, and is often used as a base for electroplating. Paktong is a similar form of "nickel–silver" that originated in China, for which the ratios of the metals is uncertain.

Copper is also highly reactive, forming oxides or halides (salts) when exposed to air and moisture. The green or blue products of corrosion found on copper and copper alloys are mixtures of copper salts and sulfates. Copper has been used in its native state, but more often in alloys such as brass or bronze. Most copper mined today is used in electrical wire and switches, and in brass alloys.

The six platinum group metals, platinum, palladium, ruthenium, osmium, rhodium, and iridium, usually occur together in nature. These metals are not often found in artifacts. These metals are rare and have only been widely used in industry and for ornaments since the early twentieth century. Most platinum used today is as a catalyst in the systems used to control car exhaust emissions, in dentistry, and to make surgical tools, jewelry, and electrical equipment.

Iron occurs naturally in a wide variety of compounds, but mostly as simple oxide, sulfide, and carbonate minerals. It rarely occurs in its native form, and never in economic amounts.

An alloy is a mixture of two or more metals, or of a metal and a non-metal. Many minerals are natural alloys, being compounds of metals or a metal/non-metal combination. Most of these fall into the native element, sulfide and sulfosalt mineral groups.

Brass (copper + zinc) and bronze (copper + tin) are the most common and widely used alloys of copper. There are many different formulae for these alloys, and the percentages of each metal used varied according to the properties that were desired in the end product, and what was available to the metal workers in a given place. German silver is another copper-based alloy (Cu + Ni + Zn). Lattan is a copper-based alloy used for casting, but the ratios of its component metals are uncertain.

Pinchbeck is an alloy invented by Christopher Pinchbeck, a British clockmaker, in the early 1700s. It was used to make jewelry that looked like gold, but was much less expensive. The precise composition of the original pinchbeck alloy has been lost, but it was composed mostly of copper and zinc. The term pinchbeck has been applied to any inexpensive, gold-colored metal used in jewelry.

Figure 2.3

Metallic alloys like steel (buckle) and minerals like marcasite (pin and earrings) can be faceted and used in jewelry.

Pewter is a term applied to a wide range of alloys in which tin is the dominant metal, mixed with lead and sometimes copper, antimony, and/or zinc. Some pewter contains no lead at all, and is mostly tin and copper. Bronze is also an alloy of tin and copper, but it is predominantly copper.

Steel is a mixture of a metal (iron) and a non-metal (carbon). There are hundreds of formulae for different combinations of these elements and others. Jewelry made from faceted metal is often called "cut steel," even though it may be actually made of pyrite or marcasite (Figure 2.3).

Iron and nickel occur together in iron meteorites, as alloys that are over 90% iron.

Gemstones

Gem is a general term used to describe precious and semi-precious stones, usually after they have been cut and polished. In archeology, it refers only to engraved stones (cameo, intaglio, seals, etc.). The term "gem-quality" is applied to rough material that is of a quality suitable for cutting or working in some way. The real meaning of this term varies according to the material involved. The phrase "precious stone" is limited to only four names: diamond, ruby, sapphire, and emerald. Everything else then, by definition, becomes "semi-precious." The designation "precious stone" has nothing to do with quality, size or value, since it refers only to the name. It is just as possible to have a low-quality diamond as it is to have a high quality, and more valuable, topaz or zircon. The terms precious and semi-precious were developed by the jewelry and gemstone industries and are not used in mineralogy. They should not play any part in the organization of a collection.

The materials most commonly used as gems and ornamental stones are listed in Table 2.9. This is by no means a complete listing of all materials ever used in jewelry or for decorative purposes. There are many worked specimens that are one-of-a-kind, made from unexpected materials that were opportunistically obtained. These often pose problems of identification and consequently of conservation, since once a stone has been worked it loses its natural luster and form. Stones have been altered with dyes and heat for thousands of years, so it does not hold true that just because something is in an old artifact or Grandma's necklace that it cannot be dyed or otherwise not natural. Synthetics are relatively new, but imitations are as old as the stones themselves. If someone wanted a red gem, and there were no rubies available, then a garnet or spinel could be used instead. No emeralds? Use an olivine (peridot) or green sapphire. A synthetic must have the same composition and internal structure as the natural material, but an imitation just has to look like the natural stone.

Diamonds are the hardest natural substance, but they can cleave easily. They occur in every color, but shades of yellow and brown are most common. Today's faceted diamonds are cut and polished with tools embedded with tiny diamond chips or dust. Before the advent of modern methods, diamonds were used in their natural state, or roughly shaped and polished by hand. The hardness of this mineral led many early jewelers to do a minimum of work before setting diamonds in jewelry or regalia. Common imitations of diamond are colorless spinel, sapphire, zircon, topaz, quartz, and many synthetics.

Rubies and sapphires are color varieties of the mineral corundum, which is simple aluminum oxide. This mineral is second only to diamond in hardness, but is much tougher and harder to break. Rubies are, by definition, red or purplish red. The term sapphire is used for every other color.

Spinel is another simple oxide mineral. It is commonly seen today as a synthetic and may be any color. Natural red spinel was most prized as a gem, and usually was used as an imitation of ruby. Some notable pieces in the British and Russian crown jewels include large uncut spinels. These crystals are a deep red color and are distinctive because of their rough octahedral shape.

Alexandrite is a term that should be applied only to naturally dichroic specimens of the mineral chrysoberyl. This stone appears red in one type of light and green in another. The name is in honor of Crown Prince Alexander

Table 2.9 Gems and ornamental stones.

This list is organized according to the chemical composition of mineral species. The simplest, the native elements, are first, followed by progressively more complex minerals. This list only includes those species that are used as gems or ornamental materials. Organic substances, such as amber and jet, are not included and will be addressed elsewhere.

Colors: *c: colorless; pk: pink; r: red; g: green; y: yellow; o: orange; p: purple; bl: black; b: blue; br: brown; m: metallic*

Crystal systems: *isom: isometric; tetr: tetragonal; ortho: orthorhombic; hex: hexagonal; mono: monoclinic; tric: triclinic*

"Precious" stones: *four names* underlined

Group	Species	Varieties or (synonyms)	Composition	Colors	Specific gravity	Refractive index	Hardness	Cleavage/fracture
Native element	**Diamond**		C	All colors	3.52	2.417	10	Perfect cleavage in four directions
	Gold		Au	M	19.3	na	2.5–3	Hackly fracture
	Silver		Ag	M	10.5	na	2.5–3	Hackly fracture
	Platinum		Pt	M	21.5	na	4–4.5	Hackly fracture
Sulfide	**Pyrite**		FeS_2	M	5.02	na	6–6.5	Conchoidal
	Marcasite		FeS_2	M	4.89	na	6–6.5	Conchoidal
	Sphalerite	(*blende, zinc blende*)	ZnS	br,y,o,r,g,bk,c	3.9–4.1	2.37	3.5–4	Perfect cleavage in six directions
Oxide	**Chrysoberyl**	Alexandrite (cat's eye, cymophane)	$BeAl_2O_4$	r,y,g,br,o	2.71–2.75	1.745–1.755	8.5	Conchoidal, cleavage in two directions
	Corundum	Sapphire, ruby (oriental topaz, o. emerald, etc.)	Al_2O_3	All but r	4.02	1.762–1.770	9	Conchoidal, some parting
	Hematite		Fe_2O_3	r,m	5.26	na	5.5–6.5	Parting, no cleavage
	Rutile		TiO_2	r,br,y	4.2	2.61	6–6.5	One directional good cleavage
	Spinel	(balas ruby, ruby spinel, rubicelle, ceylonite, pleonaste, picotite)	$MgAl_2O_4$	All colors	3.57–3.72	1.71–1.72	8	One directional poor cleavage, conchoidal
Halide	**Fluorite**	(fluorospar)	CaF_2	All colors	3.18	1.433	4	Perfect cleavage in four directions
Carbonate	**Calcite**	(Travertine, iceland spar, mexican onyx, egyptian alabaster)	$CaCO_3$	c,w,y,br,gy,g,r,o	2.72	1.486–1.658	3	Perfect cleavage in three directions
	Magnesite		$MgCO_3$	c,w	3.0–3.2	1.509–1.700	3.5–5	Perfect cleavage in three directions

	Mineral	(common names)	Formula	Color	SG	RI	Hardness	Cleavage/Fracture
	Rhodochrosite		$MnCO_3$	pk	3.5–3.7	1.597–1.816	3.5–4	Perfect cleavage in three directions
	Aragonite		$CaCO_3$	w,c	2.95	1.530–1.686	3.5–4	Two directional good cleavage
	Azurite		$Cu_3(CO_3)_2(OH)_2$	b	3.77	1.730–1.838	3.5–4	Two directional good cleavage
	Malachite		$Cu_2CO_3(OH)_2$	gr	3.90–4.03	1.655–1.909	3.5–4	Perfect cleavage in one direction
Sulfate	**Gypsum**	(satin spar, alabaster)	$CaSO_4 2H_2O$	c,w,br,gy	2.32	1.520–1.530	2	Three directional good cleavage
Phosphate	**Variscite**	(utahlite)	$Al(PO_4)2H_2O$	y,gr,gr	2.4–2.6	1.563–1.594	4–5	Conchoidal
	Turquoise		$CuAl_6(PO_4)_4(OH)_8 4H_2O$	b,b-gr	2.6–2.8	1.61–1.65	5–6	Conchoidal to uneven fracture
	Fluorapatite	(apatite)	$Ca_5(PO_4)_3F$	g,gr,b,y,c,br,p	3.15–3.20	1.646–1.642	5	One directional poor cleavage
	Brazilianite		$NaAl_3(PO_4)_2(OH)_4$	y,gr,c	2.98	1.60–1.62	5.5	One circle perfect cleavage
Nesosilicate	*Olivine group*							
	Forsterite	(chrysolite, olivine, peridot)	Mg_2SiO_4	gr,br,y	3.34	1.654–1.690	6.5–7	Two directional poor cleavage
	Garnet group							
	Pyrope	(precious garnet, cape ruby, American ruby)	$Mg_3Al_2(SiO_4)_3$	r,p	3.60	1.74	6.5–7	Conchoidal
	Rhodolite		$(Mg,Fe)_3Al_2(SiO_4)_3$	pk,p	3.84	1.76	6.5–7	Conchoidal
	Almandine	(precious garnet, carbuncle)	$Fe_3Al_2(SiO_4)_3$	r,br	4.05	1.79	6.5–7	Conchoidal
	Spessartine		$Mn_2Al_2(SiO_4)_3$	br,o,y	4.18	1.80	6.5–7	Conchoidal
	Grossular	Tsavorite (essonite, hessonite, transvaal jade)	$Ca_3Al_2(SiO_4)_3$	gr,y,br,bk,o,pk,c	3.65	1.74	6.5–7	Conchoidal
	Andradite	Demantoid, melanite, topazolite	$Ca_3Fe_2(SiO_4)_3$	gr,bk,br,y,o	3.83	1.88	6.5–7	Conchoidal
	Uvarovite		$Ca_3Cr_2(SiO_4)3$	gr	3.77	1.87	6.5–7	Conchoidal
Nesosubsilicate	**Andalusite**	Chiastolite	Al_2SiO_5	br,c,r,g,y	3.16–3.20	1.63–1.64	7.5	–
	Kyanite		Al_2SiO_5	b,g,c,gr	3.55–3.66	1.71–1.728	5–7	–

(Continued)

Table 2.9   (Continued)

Group	Species	Varieties or (synonyms)	Composition	Colors	Specific gravity	Refractive index	Hardness	Cleavage/fracture
	Zircon	(jargoon, starlite, hyacinth, jacinth)	$ZrSiO_4$	br,r,o,y,gr,gy,b,c	4.67–4.73	1.92–1.98	7–7.5	Two poor directional cleavage, conchoidal fracture
	Topaz		$Al_2SiO_4(F,OH)_2$	All colors	3.4–3.6	1.607–1.638	8	One directional perfect cleavage
	Howlite		$Ca_2B_5(SiO_9)(OH)_5$	w	2.53–2.59	1.59	3.5	Uneven fracture
Sorosilicate	Epidote	(unakite)	$Ca_2(Al,Fe)Al_2O(SiO_4)(Si_2O_7)(OH)$	gr,y-gr,bk	3.30–3.45	1.715–1.797	6–7	Two directional good cleavage
	Zoisite	Tanzanite, thulite	$Ca_2Al_3O(SiO_4)(Si_2O_7)(OH)$	All colors but r	3.36	1.693–1.702	6.5	Two directional poor cleavage, conchoidal
	Vesuvianite	(idocrase, californite, happy camp jade)	$Ca_{10}(Mg,Fe)_2Al_4(SiO_4)_5(Si_2O_7)_2(OH)_4$	br,gr,bk,y	3.35–3.45	1.705–1.746	6.5	One directional poor cleavage
Cyclosilicate	Benitoite		$BaTi(SiO_3)_3$	b,c	3.64	1.757–1.804	6.5	Conchoidal
	Beryl	Aquamarine, emerald (smaragdite) heliodor (golden beryl), goshenite, morganite	$Be_3Al_2(SiO_3)_6$	All colors, b,g,y,c,pk	2.70–2.82 (red)	1.580–1.575 1.585–1.594 (red)	7.5–8	Poor cleavage perpendicular to long axis
	Axinite		$(Ca,Fe,Mn)_3Al_2(BO_3)(SiO_4O_{12})(OH)$	br,b,y,g,p	3.27–3.35	1.67–1.68	7	–
	Cordierite	Iolite (water sapphire, lynx sapphire)	$(Mg,Fe)_2Al_4Si_5O_{18}$	b,p-b,y,g	2.58–2.66	1.52–1.57	7–7.5	One poor directional cleavage
	Tourmaline group							
	Elbaite	(achroite, verdelite, rubellite, indicolite, siberite)	$Na(Li,Al)_3$ $Al_6B_3Si_6O_{27}(OH,F)_4$	All colors	3.0–3.25	1.615–1.655	7–7.5	Conchoidal or uneven
	Liddicoatite	(achroite, verdelite, rubellite, indicolite)	$Ca(Li,Al)_3Al_6B_3Si_6O_{27}(O,OH,F)_4$	All colors	3.0–3.25	1.621–1.637	7–7.5	Conchoidal or uneven
Inosilicate	*Pyroxene group*							
	Diopside	Cr-diopside (*violan*)	$CaMg(SiO_3)_2$	c,gr,br,y,bk	3.25–3.35	1.66–1.75	5–6	Two directional poor cleavage
	Jadeite	(jade)	$NaAl(SiO_3)_2$	All colors	3.3–3.5	1.64–1.660	6.5–7	Two directional poor cleavage

Class	Mineral	Variety	Formula	Color	Specific gravity	Refractive index	Hardness	Cleavage/Fracture
	Spodumene	Hiddenite, kunzite (triphane)	$LiAl(SiO_3)_2$	c,pk,p,gr,y,br,gy	3.18	1.660–1.676	6.5–7	Two directional poor cleavage
	Enstatite	(black star of India)	$MgSiO_3$	gy,bk,y,br	3.2–3.5	1.65–1.674	5.5	Two directional poor cleavage
Amphibole group								
	Actinolite	Nephrite (jade)	$Ca_2(Mg,Fe)_5Si_8O_{22}(OH)_2$	gr,bk,w,br	2.90–3.02	1.60–1.64	6–6.5	Two directional good cleavage
	Rhodonite		$MnSiO_3$	pk	3.4–3.7	1.716–1.747	6	Two directional good cleavage
Phyllosilicate	Serpentine	Chrysotile, tremolite, antigorite (*lizardite, williamsite, bowenite*)	$Mg_3Si_2O_5(OH)_4$ and $Ca_2Mg_5Si_8O_{22}(OH)_2$	gr,gy,bk,br	2.6–2.8	1.55–1.56	Average 4	Uneven fracture
	Talc	(soapstone, steatite)	$Mg_3(Si_2O_5)_2(OH)_2$	w,gy,br	2.7–2.8	1.539–1.589	1	One directional perfect cleavage
	Chrysocolla		$Cu_4H_4(Si_2O_5)_2(OH)_8$	b,b-gr,gr	2.0–2.4	1.50	2–4	Conchoidal
	Sepiolite	(meerschaum)	$Mg_4(OH)_2Si_6O_{15} \cdot 5H_2O$	w,gy	2	1.53	2.25	Uneven fracture
Tectosilicate	*Quartz family*							
	Quartz	(rock crystal)	SiO_2	c	2.60–2.65	1.53–1.54	7	Conchoidal fracture
	Smoky quartz	(smoky topaz)	SiO_2	br,gy	2.60–2.65	1.53–1.54	7	Conchoidal fracture
	Citrine		SiO_2	y	2.60–2.65	1.53–1.54	7	Conchoidal fracture
	Amethyst		SiO_2	p	2.60–2.65	1.53–1.54	7	Conchoidal fracture
	Rose quartz		SiO_2	pk	2.60–2.65	1.53–1.54	7	Conchoidal fracture
	Milky quartz		SiO_2	w	2.60–2.65	1.53–1.54	7	Conchoidal fracture
	Chalcedony	Agate	SiO_2	Any color, curved bands	2.60–2.65	1.53–1.54	7	Conchoidal fracture
		Carnelian	SiO_2	br,r translucent	2.60–2.65	1.53–1.54	7	Conchoidal fracture
		Chrysoprase	SiO_2	gr translucent	2.60–2.65	1.53–1.54	7	Conchoidal fracture
		Jasper	SiO_2	Any color, opaque	2.60–2.65	1.53–1.54	7	Conchoidal fracture
		Onyx	SiO_2	Any color, flat bands	2.60–2.65	1.53–1.54	7	Conchoidal fracture
	Opal		$SiO_2 \cdot nH_2O$	Any color	2.0–2.2	1.44–1.46	5.5–6.5	Conchoidal fracture
Feldspar group								
	Orthoclase	Adularia (moonstone)	$KAlSi_3O_8$	c,w,y,gy	2.56	1.518–1.526	6	Two directional good cleavage

(Continued)

Table 2.9 · (Continued)

Group	Species	Varieties or (synonyms)	Composition	Colors	Specific gravity	Refractive index	Hardness	Cleavage/fracture
	Microcline	Amazonite	$KAlSi_3O_8$	w,b-gr, gy	2.56	1.522–1.530	6	Two directional good cleavage
	Plagioclases							
	Albite	(moonstone)	$NaAlSi_3O_8$ (solid solution series)	c,w,y,gr,br,o	2.62–2.76	1.518–1.526	6	Two directional good cleavage
	Oligoclase							
	Andesine							
	Labradorite	(larvikite)						
	Bytownite							
	Anorthite		$CaAl_2Si_2O_8$					
	Sodalite		$Na_8(AlSiO_4)_6Cl_2$	b-p	2.15–2.30	1.48	5.5–6	Perfect cleavage in three directions
	Lazurite	(lapis lazuli)	$(Na,Ca)_8(AlSiO_4)_6(SO_4,S,Cl)_2$	b	2.4–2.45	1.50	5–5.5	Hackly fracture, poor cleavage
	Scapolite group							
	Marialite meionite		$Na_4(AlSi_3O_8)_3(Cl_2,CO_3,SO_4)$ $Ca_4(Al_2Si_2O_8)_3(Cl_2,CO_3,SO_4)$	c,y,pk,gr,gy	2.55–2.74	1.540–1.568	5–6	Four directional poor cleavage
	Glass	*Obsidian, tektite, moldavite* (natural)	Composition variable	gray,g,br, all colors (synthetic)	2.3–4.5	1.4–1.7	Average 5	Conchoidal fracture
Synthetics	**Glass**	*Rhinestone*	Composition variable	All colors	2.3–4.5	1.4–1.7	Average 5	conchoidal fracture
	Yttrium Aluminum Garnet	(YAG)	$Y_3Al_2Al_3O_{12}$	All colors	4.55	1.833	8.25	–
	Cubic zirconia	(CZ)	$ZrO2 + Ca$	All colors	5.6–6.0	2.15–2.18	7.5–8.5	–

of Russia, since green and red were the national colors of that country and most of the early specimens of alexandrite came from the Ural Mountains. Chrysoberyl is also one of the minerals that commonly displays chatoyancy, or the "cat's eye" effect. Usually cut as a smooth cabochon, these stones can display a band of light perpendicular to fibers of fine parallel inclusions in the stone when viewed under a strong focused light source.

Azurite, malachite, and rhodochrosite are brightly colored carbonate minerals that are most often cut as beads or cabochons, used in inlay, or to make carvings. Since they are usually slightly translucent to opaque, these materials are rarely faceted. They are relatively soft and highly susceptible to staining and chemical deterioration. They are often used with other carbonate materials, such as calcite in its many forms (marble, limestone, travertine) or aragonite. Azurite and malachite often occur together, sometimes mixed with other copper minerals, calcite, and/or quartz. Malachite sometimes occurs as botryoidal masses that, when cut, display alternating layers of light and dark green. Rhodochosite may also display alternating layers of color, from white to pink to dark rose. Magnesite is a massive white material usually associated with serpentinites. It has been used to make trade beads, fish hooks, and other small items. Magnesite can usually be distinguished from other opaque white materials by its high density.

Gypsum sometimes occurs in finely crystalline masses, which is called alabaster. This material resembles marble or fine limestone in texture and color, and has been used for similar purposes. Gypsum, however, is soluble in water, so most objects made of this material do not last if exposed to moisture in any form. Most objects identified as alabaster are actually made of some form of calcite.

Turquoise is an opaque copper phosphate that occurs in various shades of blue, blue-green, and green. Weathered specimens may appear gray, white, or brown. Like other opaque materials, turquoise is usually cut as beads, cabochons, or carved into small objects. Since turquoise is a secondary mineral, filling in cracks and small openings in pre-existing rock, it is rare to find pure specimens large enough to use for these purposes. Most fashioned turquoise includes some of the matrix, or surrounding rock, in which it was formed. This matrix may be any color, and is often useful in determining the source of the turquoise.

Olivine is a small group of rock-forming minerals, only one of which is used as a gemstone. Forsterite is the magnesium olivine, a yellow-green to green mineral found in volcanic rocks. The common name for this stone is peridot. Since volcanic rocks crystallize quickly, crystals do not have much time to form and tend to be very small. Large forsterite crystals are rare, and most peridot gems are small.

The garnets are a group of minerals having the same crystal structure, but different compositions. Only two of the garnets are commonly red, pyrope, and almandine. The other species in this group occur in all colors except blue.

Figure 2.4

This turquoise snuff bottle includes some matrix, the rock in which the blue mineral formed.

Colorless zircon has been used as an imitation of diamond, since it has a very high refractive index. Zircon gems are doubly refractive, which can give them a cloudy appearance. Looking through the top of a faceted zircon, the back facet edges will appear double. Zircons come in many colors, and this gem is often heat-treated to change or enhance the color.

Topaz crystals can be quite large, and this mineral occurs in a variety of colors. Pink, yellow and orange crystals tend to be small, but very large gems, some weighing thousands of carats, have been cut out of colorless and blue topaz. Modern clear or pale blue topaz is often irradiated and heated to cause or darken the blue color. Sometimes these stones retain radiation from this treatment.

Beryl is a simple beryllium silicate that comes in many colors, some of which have been given varietal names. Emerald is medium to dark green, aquamarine is blue, heliodor or golden beryl is yellow or orange, morganite is pink or lilac, and goshenite is colorless. Any beryl that does not fall into any of these categories is simply called beryl.

Table 2.10 Jade and other materials mistaken for it.

Gem material	Composition	Colors and translucency	Refractive index	Hardness	Specific gravity
Jadeite	$Na(Al,Fe)Si_2O_6$	**White, brown, gray, green, pink, lavender, yellow, red; opaque to translucent; often mottled**	**1.64–1.69**	**6–7**	**3.3–3.5**
Nephrite	$Ca_2(Mg,Fe)_5S_8O_{22}(OH)_2$	**Green, black, white, brown; opaque to translucent**	**1.61–1.66**	**5–6**	**3.0–3.2**
Grossular (Garnet)	Simple calcium aluminum silicate	Massive green (a.k.a. "transvaal jade")	1.54–1.55	7	2.6–2.7
Vesuvian (Idocrase)	Complex calcium aluminum silicate	Opaque to translucent green or brown (a.k.a. "Happy Camp jade")	1.49–1.69	3	2.7
Jasper	SiO_2	Opaque chalcedony (quartz), green, brown, or any other color		7	
Serpentine*	Mixture of complex iron- and magnesium-bearing silicate minerals (mostly antigorite, chrysotile, and lizardite)	Green, brown, black, gray, bluish; translucent to opaque, often mottled	1.55–1.57 (all data is for antigorite)	2.5–3.5	2.6
Steatite*	Mixture of magnesium-rich minerals, mostly talc (magnesium silicate)	White, gray, green, black, brown; opaque	2.58–1.60 (talc)	1–2 (talc)	2.6–2.8 (talc)

*These materials are rocks (mixtures of minerals). Refractive index, hardness and density for these materials are for the most common or principle constituent mineral. Properties of individual specimens may vary widely from these values.

The tourmalines are a group of 10 mineral species, only two of which are commonly used as gemstones. Names are given to colored tourmaline, regardless of which species the stones truly are. Verdelite is green, indicolite yellow, rubellite pink or red, siberite violet-red, and achroite is colorless.

Jade is the common name for gem-quality specimens of two distinctly different mineral species, jadeite and the massive variety of actinolite, called nephrite. The word jade is derived from the Spanish "*piedra de yjada*," meaning "stone of the flank." This refers to its popular use as a cure for diseases of the kidneys and liver. Other minerals that have been mistaken for jade, or used as jade imitations include green jasper (quartz), vesuvian (idocrase), massive grossular garnet, chloromelanite (a mixture of dark pyroxenes) (Table 2.10).

The original rhinestones were pieces of clear crystalline quartz found near the Rhine River. These stones were faceted and used in imitation of diamonds. They became very popular in costume jewelry, to the point where there was not enough raw material to keep up with the growing demand. Clear glass was gradually substituted, and the term rhinestone came to mean any colorless diamond imitation, regardless of its composition (see Figure 2.5).

Figure 2.5

The term rhinestone has come to mean any colorless imitation of diamond, although the original rhinestones were quartz.

Lapis lazuli is a metamorphic rock composed of three minerals, blue lazurite, white calcite, and brassy pyrite. This stone was highly prized by some cultures, both ancient and modern, because of its intense blue color. Most good-quality lapis lazuli has been mined in Afghanistan and southern Russia, although small deposits have been found elsewhere in the world. Common imitations of lapis lazuli are glass, lazulite (a phosphate mineral), and sodalite (a tectosilicate mineral similar to lazurite).

Rocks

Rocks are naturally occurring solids composed of one or more minerals. Most rocks in the Earth's crust are made up of a small group of common

Table 2.11   Comparing plutonic and volcanic rocks.

Plutonic	Volcanic	
Granite	Rhyolite	*High Si, K and Na; low Fe and Mg*
Diorite	Andesite	
Gabbro	Basalt	*Low Si, K and Na; high Fe and Mg*

minerals: quartz, calcite, gypsum, and members of the feldspar, olivine, amphibole, and pyroxene groups.

Rocks are defined according to their mode of formation, and then by their texture and composition. There are three basic types: igneous, sedimentary, and metamorphic.

Igneous rocks are those that form from a molten state. There are two types, volcanic and plutonic. Plutonic or intrusive rocks are those that form below the surface, crystallizing slowly from magma (molten rock). Grain size in igneous rocks depends upon the cooling rate, since minerals that have longer to grow will be larger than those that form quickly. Plutonic rocks cool off relatively slowly, and so tend to be coarse grained.

Volcanic or extrusive rocks are those that form at or near the surface. Volcanic rocks cool quickly and tend to be fine grained or glassy in texture. From a single mass of molten rock, both plutonic and volcanic rocks may form. So for every type of volcanic rock, there is a plutonic rock with the same elemental composition (see Table 2.11). But the minerals involved will be different, as will the textures.

Some igneous rocks are described by texture, and may have variable compositions. A pegmatite is a course-grained plutonic rock that usually consists of mostly quartz and feldspar. However, since pegmatites form in the slowest-cooling core of a pluton, they often contain rare "leftover" elements and rare minerals that do not crystallize out until the very end of the crystallization cycle. Many gem-quality mineral specimens are found in pegmatites, such as topaz, beryl, and members of the garnet and tourmaline groups.

A breccia is any rock that is composed of angular fragments in a fine-grained groundmass. A porphyry contains well-formed crystals in a fine-grained groundmass. Breccias can be volcanic or sedimentary, and porphyries can be volcanic or plutonic in origin.

Obsidian is a volcanic rock that forms when lava cools very quickly. The chemical elements in the melt "freeze" in random order. The result is obsidian or volcanic glass, which has no orderly internal structure and can be of any elemental composition.

There are two other types of natural glass. Fulgarites form when intense electrical energy causes melting and fusing in near-surface earth materials. Usually caused by lightening, fulgarites are shaped like an underground tree, branching away from the strike point. Tektites are impact glass, associated with some meteorites. They will be discussed later in the section devoted to meteorites.

Granite is a term applied to a rock having a very specific chemical and mineral composition. Granitic is a term that refers to any plutonic rock having an intergrown equigranular texture.

Some of the most common igneous minerals are quartz, potassium feldspars (orthoclase and microcline), plagioclase feldspars (albite, anorthite), micas (muscovite, biotite), olivine, and members of the amphibole and pyroxene groups. Many other minerals are found in igneous rocks, most of which occur in only very small amounts. These are called "accessory" minerals, the most common of these are corundum, pyrite, magnetite, zircon, rutile, apatite, and members of the garnet group.

Sedimentary rocks form from particles eroded from older rocks, by precipitation from solution, or by organic activity. Sedimentary rocks are described by their mineral composition, grain size, texture, and origin (Table 2.12).

Mechanical sediments are composed of particles or grains worn from other, pre-existing rocks. They are described by composition and/or particle size (see Table 2.13). The individual sediment grains can be made of anything, including minerals or other rocks. So technically there could be a sandstone made entirely of diamonds! Shale, claystone and mudstone form from very fine particles, while other mechanical sediments are mixtures of different grain sizes. Conglomerate, for example, consists of well-rounded

Table 2.12   Some common sedimentary rocks.

Mechanical	Sandstone, shale, mudstone, conglomerate
Chemical	Dripstone (cave deposits), tufa, opal, travertine
Organic	Limestone, dolomite, chert, diatomite

Table 2.13   Classification of clastic grains by size.

Particle name	Diameter
Boulders	>256 mm
Cobbles	64–256 mm
Pebbles	4–64 mm
Granules or gravel	2–4 mm
Sand (very coarse)	1–2 mm
Sand (coarse)	0.5–1 mm
Sand (medium)	0.25–0.5 mm
Sand (fine)	0.125–0.25 mm
Sand (very fine)	0.05–0.125 mm
Silt	0.005–0.05 mm
Clay	<0.005 mm

pebbles or cobbles in a finer-grained matrix. Sedimentary breccia consists of angular fragments in a fine-grained matrix.

A sediment made up of particles that fall within the sand range is called sand. If consolidated, it is sandstone. Modifiers may be added to refine the description of a particular stone. For instance, if the sand is mostly made of feldspar grains, it would be called a feldspathic sandstone. If mostly quartz, a quartz sandstone. And so on.

The term sorting describes the relative amounts of different grain sizes in a rock. A well-sorted sandstone will contain only sand-sized grains, while a poorly sorted sandstone will include a large percentage of silt, clay or larger grains.

There are a few other terms commonly used to describe sandstones. A *wacke* is a poorly sorted sandstone containing more than 10% argillaceous material (clay). *Arenites* are well-sorted sandstones having little or no clay in them. An *arkose* is a sandstone whose particles are derived from plutonic rocks and so consist largely of quartz and feldspar.

The term clay has various meanings, but in a sedimentary sense it refers to a uniform mass of clay-sized particles. Clay-sized particles are usually composed largely of clay minerals, a group of silicates having large, sheet-like molecules. Many clay minerals absorb water, changing shape and volume as a result. Mud is unconsolidated argillaceous material mixed with water.

Finer-grained sediments may form massive rocks, such as siltstone, mudstone, argillite, or claystone. If a fine-grained rock has a platy texture, it is called shale.

Conglomerate is a mechanical sediment made of rounded clasts of pebble to cobble size in a finer-grained matrix. In a sedimentary breccia the clasts are angular. In both of these types of rocks, the clasts must make up at least 25% of the volume. Rocks with fewer clasts would be classified by the matrix. For instance, a sandstone with a few rounded clasts could be called a pebbly sandstone.

Decorative conglomerates are sometimes referred to as "puddingstones." This term is also sometimes used for amygdaloidal basalt or any other specimen that contains rounded clasts or nodules of a contrasting color to the matrix.

The chemical cement that holds the grains together is also important in characterizing mechanical sediments. A calcareous cement, the most common of which is calcite, will result in a rock that is susceptible to chemical attack. A sediment in which quartz is the dominant cement will be much more stable in some environments. Other chemical cements include gypsum, some salts, and various iron oxides.

When a portion of the rock is well-cemented while the material around it is not, this can result in differential erosion as the weaker material is worn away. Concretions are masses of well-cemented sediment that often form around a core, sometimes a fossil or a fragment of rock. These structures are often spherical or rounded and occur in many different types of sedimentary rocks.

Fossils are the remains or traces of plants or animals that have been naturally preserved in the Earth's crust. Most fossils are found in mechanical sediments, although they do occur in other types of rocks.

In order for an animal or plant to become a fossil it must be buried quickly, before bacteria and scavengers can break it apart or consume it. The covering, which can be sand, mud, volcanic ash, plant sap or tar, protects the organism physically and chemically. Sometimes, fluids and minerals in the surrounding environment may interact and change the composition of the buried animal or plant.

Most organisms that survive the destructive processes of death and burial to become fossils have some kind of hard parts; shell, bones, seeds, or teeth. These strong materials resist decay and may not be easily crushed by covering sediment. Organisms having only soft tissue are rarely preserved as fossils. Organisms with hard parts first appeared about 600 million years ago, in the Cambrian era.

The earliest forms of life were simple single- and multi-celled organisms. These early forms of life are rarely found in the fossil record because there are few places on Earth where very old rocks still exist, and because these tiny organisms consisted only of soft tissue.

Trace fossils are evidence of an organism, but are not part of a plant or animal. Examples are footprints that are preserved in hardened mud, excrement (poop), nests, or filled-in channels in mud where an animal lived.

If there are open areas within a fossil, as there are between clam shells or inside a hollow bone, these will usually fill with sediment after burial. This sediment forms an *internal mold*, conforming to the details of the inside of the opening. Sometimes, if a shell has been eroded or dissolved away, this mold is the only record of an animal. An *external mold* is an impression of an organism left in the rock surrounding it.

Under certain geological conditions, a fossil may be replaced by minerals. The original hard parts and sometimes the sediment filling of the original organism is replaced, one molecule at a time, by an inorganic compound. This can happen so slowly that the form of the fossil is retained while its chemistry is being changed.

Fossils that have been replaced with minerals are called *pseudomorphs*. This word means "false form," referring to the specimen that has the form of one thing, but the composition of something else. Most fossil pseudomorphs are made of chalcedony (microcrystalline quartz).

Animals and plants that are buried quickly in soft materials that do not crush them are candidates for becoming pseudomorphs. Over time, soft tissue, bone, shell, and/or the sediment filling inside may be replaced by compounds that travel through the surrounding rock, usually dissolved in water. If this happens slowly, and without any compression or distortion of the specimen, the result will be something that has the form of the original, but the chemical composition of a different material.

The most common pseudomorphs are samples of wood that have been "petrified," replaced by the mineral quartz. Wood and other plants preserved in this way are most often buried initially by volcanic ash. Found in many places around the world, petrified wood is a popular material for lapidary artists because of its interesting color patterns and structure.

Pseudomorph names include both the original and the present materials, in this form: *(present compound)* <u>after</u> *(original material).* An example would be Quartz after Coral, where the mineral quartz has replaced the original minerals (calcium carbonate) in the coral.

Chemical sediments precipitate out of a solution, usually water, as it evaporates. These include hot spring deposits, salts that crystallize around the shores of lakes and bays, and solution cavern deposits.

Hot springs may contain lots of different minerals in solution. Upon reaching the surface, these waters cool off and the compounds held in solution will precipitate around vents or pools. The most common deposits around hot springs are composed of calcite or common opal. Both of these minerals are colorless when pure, but are often colored by other materials in the water. Oxides of iron are the most common pigments in these situations. In shades of brown, red, and yellow, iron oxide may color an entire deposit, or appear episodically, dyeing some layers and not others.

Travertine is layered calcite that forms around hot springs. These deposits are sometimes hundreds of feet deep, and may be used as decorative or building stone. "Mexican onyx" is one of the many common names used for this material.

Evaporites that form around the margins of lakes and oceans are usually made up of mixtures of soluble salts (halides) and sulfate minerals. These deposits are transitory, since they are soluble in water, and are rarely encountered in museum collections except as mineral specimens.

Solution caverns or caves often contain deposits of recrystallized calcium carbonate, usually in the form of the mineral aragonite. Stalactites, stalagmites, and other cave formations are called speleothems. Created gradually by the precipitation of aragonite from groundwater, many speleothems display a layered structure. Recent study shows that bacteria and other simple life forms may contribute to the formation of cave deposits.

Speleothems have been used for carvings and for various other decorative purposes. The use of these materials is sometimes dictated by the belief that rocks from caves have special properties due to their location underground.

Organic sediments are those that result from the activities of living things. The most common of these are the carbonate rocks, limestone and dolomite, which are largely composed of calcium carbonate and calcium magnesium carbonate, respectively. Carbonate rocks must consist of at least 50% carbonate minerals, but may also contain some detrital or pyroclastic grains.

When forming, limestone may contain both the polymorphs of calcium carbonate, calcite and aragonite. But aragonite is the least stable of the two minerals, and most older carbonate deposits will contain only calcite. Since limestone is a marine deposit that forms in quiet seas, it often contains visible fossils of marine organisms such as coral, mollusks, and foraminifera.

Limestone and travertine have a number of synonyms, including Mexican onyx and Egyptian alabaster. True alabaster is massive gypsum, and onyx is banded quartz.

Chalk is a soft, relatively porous form of limestone. The term has also been used to describe any light-colored soft material used as a writing medium. The chalk used on blackboards is usually composed mostly of gypsum, while tailor's chalk, used for marking fabric, is usually made of talc. Chalk has been used as an additive in glass, particularly in thick products that were intended for etching or engraving.

Chert is another organic marine sediment, less common than carbonate rocks, but found in huge deposits in some parts of the world. It initially consists of the skeletons of billions of tiny, single-celled animals called radiolaria. These skeletons are composed of microcrystalline quartz or chalcedony (SiO_2). Dense layers of this material accumulate on the ocean floor, where they are buried and compressed over time. The term chert is sometimes also applied to any compact, very fine-grained siliceous sediment that has resulted from precipitation or consolidation of silica gel. There may be chert lenses or very thin layers within other types of sediments, such as limestone.

Diatoms are single-celled algae that produce a hard skeleton made of hydrous silica (opal). The rock that forms from consolidated layers of diatom skeletons is called diatomite. This material has many common and commercial names, including diatomaceous earth, Fuller's earth, kieselgur, and tripolite. Diatomite is mined and used as building material, in filters, as insulation, as a mild abrasive, and as a filler in dry chemicals.

Coal is a sediment that consists of the remains of plants that have been buried, compressed, and dehydrated over time. Coal varies widely in composition and often contains clay or silt, but it is usually composed of at least 75% carbonaceous material. It is theorized that most coal formed in ancient swamps, where there was a huge biomass of plant material. Dead plants falling into an anaerobic, aquatic environment does not rot but accumulates in layers, sometimes for millions of years.

There are different types of coal, defined by their moisture content, appearance, and ability to burn at particular temperatures. Lignite or brown coal is the lowest member of the coal family. It contains up to 45% moisture. Bituminous is more dense coal, dark brown to black, with a moisture content of less than 20%. In the coal industry, there is an intermediate grade between lignite and bituminous, called sub-bituminous coal. Anthracite or hard coal is at the top of the coal scale, based on its ability to burn hot for a long time. It is black, hard, and brittle, with less than 15% moisture content. Any of these types of coal may contain some amount of sulfur and other volatile elements.

Bituminous coal baked in an oven yields a solid carbonaceous material called coke, which is used as a reducing agent in the smelting of iron. Jet is a term applied to high-quality specimens of lignite that have been used to make decorative objects and jewelry. Jet and peat, which is compressed, partially decayed plant matter, will be discussed in Chapter 4: Plants. Cannel coal is another term for hard, compact lignite. This name has been applied to material from Whitby, where most commercial jet comes from, and from Scotland. Objects made of this material date back at least to the Bronze age in Britain (2100–1700 BC).

Petroleum is a viscous mixture of hydrocarbons that is usually found in sedimentary rocks near the Earth's surface. It is the raw material from which many products are derived, including gasoline, kerosene, solvents, fertilizers, pesticides, tar, asphalt, and plastics.

Petroleum jelly or petrolatum is produced during the refining of petroleum. Vaseline is a brand of petroleum jelly originally made by Chesebrough-Pond's, Inc., and now produced by Unilever. Petroleum jelly was initially discovered in 1859 by Robert Chesebrough, who noticed the waxy substance that was found on the equipment used to drill for oil. He found that it had medicinal properties as a salve for burns and wounds. It is also used in treating leather, in cosmetics and hair dressings, as a skin conditioner and moisturizer, and to treat fungus.

Metamorphic rocks are those that have been altered in the solid state by temperature and pressure. The texture and/or composition of the original rock changes over time, but the rock never melts (otherwise it would be igneous). There are two basic types of metamorphic rocks: contact and regional.

Contact metamorphism takes place in small areas adjacent to a hot mass, like a chamber of molten rock. It can occur two ways, either through the heating of the surrounding rocks (thermal) or by a combination of heat and the injection of charged fluids from the igneous body (hydrothermal). Many ore deposits are formed hydrothermally.

Regional metamorphism is a large-scale heating and/or compression of large masses of rock, usually for very long periods of time and often at great depth. Contact metamorphism is often fairly rapid, but regional metamorphism can go on for many millions of years.

Metamorphic rocks are described by texture and/or composition. Slate, phyllite, schist, and gneiss are metamorphic rock textures, and each can have any composition. Schist is composed of thin parallel layers of small mineral grains. Phyllite is very fine-grained foliated rock, between schist and slate in grain size. Gneiss has thicker parallel layers and often larger grains. Slate is a dense, platy, very fine-grained rock that is usually derived from a fine-grained sediment such as shale or mudstone.

Slate has been used extensively as roofing material. In Asia, it may be referred to as inkstone, as it has been used to make palettes for the grinding and mixing of ink.

Rocks defined by composition may be monomineralic, like marble and quartzite, or predictable mixtures of minerals, like serpentinite and greenstone.

Marble is formed from carbonate sediments, the most common of which is limestone. It is composed mostly of calcite. Pure marble is white, but it is easily stained by impurities such as iron oxide (red or brown) or manganese oxide (black). When the grains of calcite in limestone are exposed to heat and pressure, the mineral recrystallizes, forming a dense mass of intergrown crystals. This makes marble stronger and slightly more dense than its parent rock.

Quartzite is composed mostly of quartz, usually derived from a quartz-rich parent rock like sandstone. During metamorphism, the individual quartz grains recrystallize, growing together into a strong mass.

"Soapstone" or "steatite" are names generally applied to any soft, waxy or greasy, massive metamorphic rock. The dominant mineral is usually talc, a light-colored magnesium silicate. Other phyllosilicate minerals or mixtures of minerals are used in similar ways, since their relative softness makes them attractive to carvers. Massive soft "soapstone" has also been used to make sinks, electrical switchboards, and ovens.

Figure 2.6

Steatite, soapstone and other soft rocks are often used by carvers to make decorative and useful objects, like this pipe.

Serpentinite is a highly variable metamorphic rock that is a mixture of iron- and magnesium-rich silicate minerals. Its color varies with its composition, from light gray, bluish, black, and all shades of green.

Greenstone is a low-grade metamorphic rock derived from a basic, low-silica parent rock like diabase or basalt. It gets its name from the dull greenish color of the fresh rock. Like other iron-rich rocks, when greenstone weathers it usually yields a red soil.

Granite and other granitic rocks may be partially metamorphosed or saussuritized, with some minerals changing to others, but without losing the basic structure of the rock. Individual grains are still visible in these rocks, but gneissic banding may be evident. These rocks are mentioned here because they are often used as decorate stone, or to make beads and other lapidary items. The most striking examples contain green epidote, gray quartz, and pink orthoclase feldspar. This material is sometimes known as unakite.

Table 2.14   *Some common metamorphic rocks.*

Rocks defined by texture	Schist, gneiss, phyllite, slate
Rocks defined by composition	Marble, serpentinite, quartzite, greenstone

Meteorites and Related Materials

Meteoroids are small bits and pieces of rock left over from the original material that formed the solar system. As they follow random paths through the solar system, some wander close to Earth and enter its atmosphere. Hundreds of meteoroids enter the atmosphere every day, but most are very tiny and do not survive the journey. Only the largest fragments reach the Earth's surface.

Meteors or "shooting stars" are meteoroids that fall through Earth's atmosphere. Friction between the fast-moving meteoroid and air molecules in the atmosphere produces heat, which burns the meteoroid and causes the air around it to glow.

Meteorites are meteoroids that survive their fiery flight and hit the ground. They are classified by their mineral composition and texture. Thousands of meteorites have been identified on Earth and there are undoubtedly many more yet to be discovered.

Each meteorite is given a unique name, based on its location on Earth. They are classified by their mineral composition and texture. And each is designated as either a fall or a find, with associated dates. A "fall" is a meteorite that was seen falling to Earth and then found. A "find" is a meteorite that was found, but was not seen falling to Earth.

There are two basic types: iron meteorites and stony meteorites. Iron meteorites are fairly easy to recognize because they are composed of more than 90% iron. They attract a magnet, and are very dense. Stony meteorites, or chondrites, can look like an ordinary rock.

Chondrites or stony meteorites are the most common type of meteorite and are some of the oldest rocks in the solar system. They are made of materials similar to rocks in the crusts of the terrestrial planets, such as Earth and Mars.

Chondrites contain many tiny balls of silicate minerals called chondrules. These are not found in rocks formed on Earth. Chondrules are often visible in a fresh broken or sawn surface as light-colored round or oval particles.

Carbonaceous chondrites are rare stony meteorites that contain complex carbon compounds from which they get their name. Some contain water and amino acids, the building blocks of life. Carbonaceous chondrites are believed to be samples of our solar system's earliest rocks, unchanged after nearly 4.6 billion years.

Achondrites are rare stony meteorites that have few or no chondrules. These rocks may be chunks of the crusts of larger bodies, such as other planets. Meteorites that originated on the Moon and Mars fall into this category.

Iron meteorites consist mainly of iron and nickel. They resemble material thought to lie deep in the cores of some planets, including Earth. This suggests that iron meteorites may be chunks from the core of a larger body that broke apart.

Slicing, etching, and polishing an iron meteorite reveals a delicate interlocking pattern of crystals. This is called a Widmanstätten structure, and it is the unique "fingerprint" of each meteorite. These patterns can only form in low gravity environments and are not found in rocks on Earth.

The stony-iron meteorites are intermediate between chondrites and irons. These very rare meteorites are equal mixtures of iron/nickel alloys and silicate minerals. Pallasites are striking examples of this type of meteorites, consisting of green olivine crystals in a matrix of metallic iron. Another type of stony-iron meteorite, called mesosiderites, contain pyroxene and plagioclase feldspars, minerals that are common on Earth.

Some meteoroids land with such force that they leave a depression or crater. These impact features, technically called astroblemes, may be round or elliptical, depending on the angle at which the meteoroid hit the ground. There are astroblemes all over the Earth. Recent impact sites are easy to spot, but older craters have been subjected to millions of years of erosion and burial, and are harder to identify.

Some meteoroids shatter upon impact, while others remain intact. Those that break when they hit the ground may be found in fragments around the site of impact. Some of these "fragments" may weigh a couple of tons! All of the meteorites from a single fall are given the same name. Thus, the many hundreds of meteorites that have been found at Meteor Crater in Arizona are called by the name Canyon Diablo.

When a large meteoroid strikes the Earth, the shock and heat caused by the impact can liquefy pieces of the Earth's crust. The resulting blobs of molten surface rock are thrown into the atmosphere. They quickly cool and solidify into glass as they fall back to the ground. These are called tektites, and may be found by the thousands scattered around some major impact sites. Tektites are not meteorites since they did not originate in space.

In Collections

There are traditional methods used for organizing geological collections that are determined by the way these specimens are used. As geological specimens may be very large and/or heavy, some pieces may have to be stored separately from the main collection. There are also other considerations, such as environmental susceptibilities or toxicity of certain species, that may affect storage decisions.

If a collection is to be used in a non-traditional way, or for specific purposes, then there is no reason why it should not be organized to facilitate that use. Collections should not, however, be reorganized every time a new project comes along. The main things to consider are the safety of the collection and ease of retrieval, of both information and specimens.

With few exceptions, minerals and rocks should be stored in a dry, cool place. The few specimens that are susceptible to light, moisture or other factors can be isolated if necessary. Cabinets containing toxic or radioactive specimens can be marked individually, or all cabinets in a collection can be marked.

Most mineral collections contain potentially harmful species or forms. Toxic species may be the primary components in a specimen, but they may also occur as deterioration products. An example of this is melanterite, which is a common by-product of the decomposition of pyrite and marcasite. This highly poisonous sulfate of iron occurs as a white powder or crust on decomposed specimens.

Naturally toxic substances may also be included in compounds such as paints, ceramic glazes, and dyes. Natural poisons have long been used as insecticides in collections that contain materials susceptible to attack by pests. The most common among these compounds are arsenolite (arsenic trioxide) and mercury.

The potential hazards associated with exposure to some mineral species in personal and institutional mineral collections can be minimized through a combination of good housekeeping, appropriate storage methods, good hygiene, and common sense. If all specimens are treated with respect and handled using methods appropriate for each species, the risk to humans can be minimized. Many of the mineral species that are hazardous are rare and occur in very small amounts. This reduces the potential for exposure or contact with toxic amounts.

There are three types of toxicity in minerals. Each of these, as listed here, is progressively worse than the one before it. Species that are radioactive are the most hazardous, being also poisonous and toxic as dust.

Substances that are toxic as dust are hazardous in situations where they are in the form of airborne dust. This can occur in many situations, including natural outcrops, some manufacturing processes, in the laboratory, and during some lapidary work. Dust can accumulate in mineral collections as a result of the deterioration or alteration of some species. Dust can also form during specimen handling or if it is improperly stored or packed. Any mineral dust inhaled over a long period of time is likely to cause respiratory damage, regardless of the species involved.

The species that are the most hazardous to humans and other animals as poisons are those that have a toxic effect on the body and that are soluble in water or mild acid. Some species, like realgar, contain a potentially toxic element (arsenic), but have such a low solubility potential that their toxicity as a poison is considered to be low under normal circumstances.

Poisons usually enter a body through the mouth or nose, but some substances may be absorbed through the skin. Susceptibility to poisons depends on an organism's individual characteristics, such as age, mass, past history, general health, and body chemistry. Some toxins, such as lead, mercury, and arsenic, can accumulate in the body and may cause problems over a long period of time.

Radioactive minerals emit natural radiation, which can be hazardous to organisms. They are also poisonous and toxic as dust. Radioactive materials can be found in a variety of collections, but most are associated with minerals, rocks, and fossils. If handled and stored appropriately, hazards from radiation can be minimized.

Radiation is a term that usually refers to invisible particles or waves of high energy. When these particles or waves encounter another material, they can strip or "bounce" electrons from atoms, causing those atoms to change.

There are three basic types of natural radiation: alpha, beta, and gamma. An alpha particle consists of two protons and two neutrons. This is the same as the nucleus of a helium atom. Since it has no electrons, it is actually an ionized or charge helium atom, with a positive charge of $+2$. Alpha particles are relatively big and cannot penetrate most materials and do not travel far. They are very strong, however, and can cause major changes in whatever they do encounter. Beta particles are loose electrons, and have a negative charge of -1. Beta radiation travels farther and faster than alpha particles, but it can be slowed or stopped by simple insulators like wood, glass, or plastic. Gamma particles are high-energy photons, or electromagnetic waves. These particles are neutral (no charge), they move very fast, and can pass through most materials.

Radiation hazard can be reduced by simply limiting the amount of time of exposure, by increasing the distance from the source (specimen), and by

Table 2.15   Some toxic minerals.

Species	Composition	Mineral group	Toxic elements	Type of toxin
Arsenic	As	Native element	As	Dust
Lead	Pb	Native element	Pb	Poisonous
Mercury	Hg	Native element	Hg	Poisonous
Sulfur	S	Native element	S	Dust
Arsenopyrite	FeAsS	Sulfide	As	Dust
Cinnabar	HgS	Sulfide	Hg	Poisonous
Cobaltite	CoAsS	Sulfide	Co, As	Dust
Galena	PbS	Sulfide	Pb	Dust
Glaucodot	(Co,Fe)AsS	Sulfide	Co, As	Dust
Greenockite	CdS	Sulfide	Cd	Poisonous
Linneaite	$Co^{2+}Co^{3+}_2S_4$	Sulfide	Co	Dust
Metacinnabar	HgS	Sulfide	Hg	Poisonous
Orpiment	As_2S_3	Sulfide	As	Dust
Realgar	AsS	Sulfide	As	Dust
Skutterudite	$CoAs_{2-3}$	Sulfide	Co, As	Dust
Arsenolite	As_2O_3	Oxide	As	Poisonous
Claudetite	As_2O_3	Oxide	As	Poisonous
Curite	$Pb_2U_5O_{17}\cdot4H_2O$	Oxide	U, Pt	Radioactive
Massicot	PbO	Oxide	Pb	Poisonous
Minium	$Pb^{+2}_2Pb^{+2}O_4$	Oxide	Pb	Poisonous
Tellurite	TeO_2	Oxide	Te	Poisonous
Thorianite	ThO_2	Oxide	Th	Radioactive
Uraninite	UO_2	Oxide	U	Radioactive
Calomel	Hg_2Cl_2	Halide	Hg	Poisonous
Cryolite	Na_3AlF_6	Halide	Na	Poisonous
Cerussite	$PbCO_3$	Carbonate	Pb	Poisonous
Phosgenite	$Pb_2(CO_3)Cl_2$	Carbonate	Pb	Poisonous
Sphaerocobaltite	$CoCO_3$	Carbonate	Co	Poisonous
Witherite	$BaCO_3$	Carbonate	Ba	Poisonous
Borax	$Na_2B_4O_5(OH)_4\cdot8H_2O$	Borate	B	Poisonous
Colemanite	$Ca_2B_6O_{11}\cdot5H_2O$	Borate	B, Ca	Poisonous
Anglesite	$PbSO_4$	Sulfate	Pb	Poisonous
Chalcanthite	$CuSO_4\cdot5H_2O$	Sulfate	Cu	Poisonous
Linarite	$PbCu(SO_4)(OH)_2$	Sulfate	Pb, Cu	Poisonous
Melanterite	$FeSO_4\cdot7H_2O$	Sulfate	Fe	Poisonous
Crocoite	$PbCrO_4$	Chromate	Cr, Pb	Poisonous
Autunite	$Ca(UO_2)_2(PO_4)_2\cdot10-12H_2O$	Phosphate	U	Radioactive
Erythrite	$Co_3(AsO_4)_2\cdot8H_2O$	Phosphate	Co, As	Poisonous

(Continued)

Table 2.15   (Continued)

Species	Composition	Mineral group	Toxic elements	Type of toxin
Metazeunerite	$Cu(UO_2)_2(AsO_4)_2\cdot 8H_2O$	Phosphate	U, As	Radioactive
Mimetite	$Pb_5(AsO_4)_3Cl$	Phosphate	As, Pb	Poisonous
Pyromorphite	$Pb_5(PO_4)_3Cl$	Phosphate	Pb	Poisonous
Scorodite	$FeAsO_4\cdot 2H_2O$	Phosphate	As	Poisonous
Torbernite	$Cu(UO_2)_2(PO_4)_2\cdot 8-12H_2O$	Phosphate	U	Radioactive
Vanadinite	$Pb_5(VO_4)Cl$	Phosphate	Pb	Poisonous
Zeunerite	$Cu(UO_2)_2(AsO_4)_2\cdot 10-16H_2O$	Phosphate	U, As	Radioactive
Wulfenite	$PbMoO_4$	Molybdate	Pb, Mo	Poisonous
Carnotite	$K_3(UO_3)_3V_3O_8\cdot 3H_2O$	Vanadium oxysalt	U	Radioactive
Cuprosklodowskite	$(H_3O)_2Cu(UO_2)_2(SiO_4)_2\cdot 2H_2O$	Nesosilicate	U	Radioactive
Sklodowskite	$(H_3O)_2Mg(UO_2)_2(SiO_4)_2\cdot 2H_2O$	Nesosilicate	U	Radioactive
Actinolite	$Ca_2(Mg,Fe)_5S_8O_{22}(OH)_2$	Inosilicate	–	Dust
Ferrogedrite	$(Fe,Mg)_5Al_2(Si_6Al_2)O_{22}(OH)_2$	Inosilicate	–	Dust
Riebeckite	$Na_2(Fe^{+2},Mg)_3Fe^{+3}_2Si_8O_{22}(OH)_2$	Inosilicate	–	Dust
Tremolite	$Ca_2(Mg,Fe)_5Si_8O_{22}(OH)_2$	Inosilicate	–	Dust
Anthophyllite	$(Fe,Mg)_7Si_8O_{22}(OH)_2$	Phyllosilicate	–	Dust
Chrysotile	$Mg_3Si_2O_5(OH)_4$	Phyllosilicate	–	Dust
Grunerite	$(Fe,Mg)_7Si_8O_{22}(OH)_2$	Phyllosilicate	–	Dust
Erionite	$(K_2,Ca,Na_2)_2Al_4(Si_{14}O_{36})\cdot 15H_2O$	Tectosilicate	–	Dust

providing shielding. The effects of radioactivity decrease with distance. So keep these materials away from places where people spend a lot of time. Specimens in exhibits should be placed as far back in the display as possible, and there should be a substantial barrier of glass or Plexiglas between them and the public.

Cases and drawers containing radioactive materials should be clearly marked. There should be posted safety rules that limit and specify what types of interactions are allowed with these specimens. Contact with these specimens should be limited to hands. Keep radioactive materials away from the eyes, mucous membranes, and reproductive organs (don't carry them around in your pocket). Anyone handling these materials should wash their hands immediately afterwards.

Radiation is cumulative, so the more radioactive materials stored in one area, the hotter that area will be. It is best to scatter the radioactive materials throughout the collection. This will occur naturally if a mineral collection is stored according to Dana's order. Most radioactive mineral species occur within the oxide, phosphate, and nesosilicate groups.

One of the daughter products of natural radiation is radon gas. In order to allow this gas to dissipate, it is important to ventilate storage areas and/or cabinets that contain radioactive materials. This can be done simply by leaving the doors off cabinets overnight, or by creating vents at the bottom of a cabinet door. Radon is heavier than air, so it will settle in the bottom of a cabinet or exhibit case.

Radioactive materials are poisonous as dust and if ingested. They should never be handled by children or anyone with health problems that may affect the immune system.

Private individuals may own natural radioactive materials, as long as they do not refine or process it.

A list of some of the toxic species most often found in mineral collections is shown in Table 2.15. This is not a list of all potentially hazardous species, but it includes most of the common toxic minerals.

3

Introduction to Organics and Organisms

Some Organic Compounds

Organisms are composed of mixtures of organic and inorganic compounds. The inorganic materials have been addressed in the Chapter 2. The following is a brief introduction to organic compounds.

Carbon atoms form bonds readily with hydrogen, oxygen, and nitrogen. Carbon also may combine with halogen elements (fluorine, chlorine, bromine, iodine), with phosphorus and sulfur, and, less often, with other elements.

Hydrocarbons are those molecules that contain only carbon and hydrogen. This term is also used sometimes to describe any simple organic molecule, possibly with additional elements such as nitrogen, phosphorus, or oxygen.

There are four basic kinds of organic molecules that exist in large quantities in organisms or living systems: carbohydrates, lipids, proteins, and nucleotides. These combine with water, which makes up between 50 and 95% of the volume of most cells.

Carbohydrates are sugars and multi-sugar molecules. They are classified according to how many sugar molecules they have: monosaccharide, disaccharide, or polysaccharide, having one, two, and many, respectively. Carbohydrates are the main energy storage molecule in living systems, mostly in the form of cellulose and starch. Some of them also serve other purposes, such as energy transport and structural support in cells.

Cellulose is a polysaccharide, a polymer made of glucose molecules. It is the principal structural molecule in all plants. It makes up the fibrous part of the plant's cell walls. Cellulose is flexible in young plants, which allows their cells to grow. In dead plant cells, it is usually the only compound left after dehydration. Wood is about 50% cellulose, while cotton is pure cellulose.

Chitin is another polysaccharide, but unlike cellulose, its sugars are combined with nitrogen-bearing molecules. Tough and chemically resistant, it makes up the exoskeletons of insects and other arthropods, and the cell walls of many fungi.

Lipids are organic compounds that are insoluble in water, including waxes and fats. Oil and fat are generally the same thing. At room temperature, oil is liquid, and fat is solid. Oils are derived from plants and animals, while fats are animal products.

Nucleotides are large molecules that combine into the nucleic acids (DNA and RNA), which carry genetic information.

Amino acids are simple organic molecules that all have a similar general formula, containing carbon, hydrogen, oxygen, nitrogen, and occasionally sulfur. They are the biochemical building blocks that form the structures called proteins. There are over 100 amino acids known, only 20 common ones are found in most animal tissue. The amino acids found in plants and microorganisms are often rare compounds. Some of the basic 20 amino acids cannot be synthesized inside an animal's body and must be taken in as food.

Proteins are composed of linear chains of amino acids. A protein may contain any combination of the 20 amino acids that are found in natural organic substances. Some proteins may contain thousands of amino acids. Many proteins are specialized, such as enzymes, hormones, antibodies, and those whose job is to store or transport energy or other compounds.

Enzymes are specialized proteins that act as biological catalysts. They can accelerate chemical reactions without being changed themselves. Most enzymatic reactions occur within a narrow temperature range, from 30 to 40°C. Each enzyme usually only reacts with only a small number of closely related compounds. Some require the presence of additional small non-protein molecules (coenzymes).

The collagens are a group of common, relatively simple fibrous proteins. They are over 1400 amino acids long, in three chains that are twisted into a tight helix. Approximately one-fourth to one-third of all protein in an organism is usually collagen, and it is the most common protein in vertebrate animals.

Collagen is a major structural element in connective tissues: skin, tendons, muscle, and internal organs. It combines with inorganic compounds in bones and teeth. Cartilage is collagen mixed in an amorphous gel. Dentine, which makes up the bulk of a tooth, is a mixture of collagen and hydroxyapatite (a mineral), and water.

Keratin is another group of fibrous proteins. These compounds are major components of hair, skin, wool, horns, hooves, fingernails, claws, and feather quills. These proteins contain a lot of cysteine, one of the few amino acids that has sulfur in it.

Conchiolin is a fibrous protein similar to keratin that is found in mollusk shells, where it is mixed with calcium carbonate.

Tannins are astringent compounds found in plants. These large molecules bond readily with proteins. Catechols are condensed tannins. These compounds are extracted from tree bark and other plant sources and used in tanning leather and in medicine.

There are, of course, thousands of other organic and inorganic compounds found in natural materials. Some others are listed in Appendix B, the glossary.

Classification of Organisms

An organism is a living entity composed of one or more cells. The simplest organisms, like bacteria or amoebas, consist of just one cell. More complex organisms may consist of billions of specialized cells that work together in a cooperative unit. All organisms take in energy, excrete waste, reproduce, and respond to changes in their environment.

Scientists have described and classified organisms in a number of different ways. Early descriptions were based solely on appearance and simple physical attributes. As more sophisticated tools have been developed for characterizing species, additional information contributes to the body of knowledge about all life on Earth. Since molecular and genetic data have become available for many forms of life, these has been a movement to reorganize the traditional classification systems that have been in use for many years.

The system commonly in use today is known as the Linnaean system of taxonomic classification, named for Carolus Linnaeus (1707–1778), the Swedish scientist who developed it. In this system, each organism has a unique, two-part name. Similar organisms were clumped together under a single name, but divided from each other at lower levels. The species designation is the lowest level of classification, and kingdom the highest: kingdom, phylum, class, order, family, genus, species. The binomial of each organism is the genus and species. Written *Genus species*, with only the genus capitalized, and both words either <u>underlined</u> or *italicized* (but never <u>*both*</u>).

Linnaeus divided all organisms into two kingdoms, Plant and Animal. This system persisted for several hundred years, even though increasing numbers of organisms did not fit well within either of these categories. In 1969, Dr. Robert Whittaker of Cornell University proposed a five-kingdom system of classification (see Table 3.1).

Prokaryotes have cells with no nucleus, and "floating" DNA. Eukaryotes have cells with a membrane or cell wall, and a nucleus.

Table 3.1 Five-kingdom system of classification (after Whittaker, 1969, in Campbell et al., 1999).

Kingdom	Characteristics	Examples
Monera	One celled, prokaryotic	Bacteria
Protista	One to multicelled, eukaryotic	Algae, *Amoeba, Paramecium*
Fungi	Multicellular, absorptive nutrition, eukaryotic	Mold, mushrooms
Plantae	Multicellular, photosynthetic nutrition, eukaryotic	Green plants
Animalia	Multicellular, ingestive nutrition, eukaryotic	Animals

Table 3.2 *Eight-kingdom system of classification (after Campbell et al., 1999).*

Kingdom	Characteristics	Examples
Bacteria	One celled, prokaryotic	Bacteria
Archaea	One celled, prokaryotic	
Archaezoa	One celled, eukaryotic	*Giardia*
Protista	One to multicelled, eukaryotic	*Amoeba, Paramecium*
Chromista	One to multicelled, eukaryotic	Brown and golden algae, diatoms
Fungi	Multicellular, absorptive nutrition, eukaryotic	Mold, mushrooms
Plantae	Multicellular, photosynthetic nutrition, eukaryotic	Green plants
Animalia	Multicellular, ingestive nutrition, eukaryotic	Animals

Table 3.3 *Three domain system of classification (after Campbell et al., 1999).*

Domain	Kingdom	Examples
Bacteria	Bacteria	Proteobacteria, gram-positive bacteria, cyanobacteria, spirochetes, chlamydias
Archaea	Archaea	Methanogens, halophiles, thermophiles*
Eukarya	Archaezoa	Diplomonads (*Giardia*), trichomonads, microsporidians
Eukarya	Euglenozoa	Euglenoids, kenetoplastids
Eukarya	Alveolata	Dinoflagellates, foraminifera, slime molds, ciliates
Eukarya	Stramenopila	Diatoms, golden algae, brown algae, water mold
Eukarya	Rhodophyta	Red algae
Eukarya	Plantae	Green algae**, green plants
Eukarya	Fungi	Mold, mushrooms
Eukarya	Animalia	Animals

* The Archaea are divided into three main groups, based on the habitats in which they are found. Methanogens are anaerobes that cannot live in the presence of oxygen. As a source of energy, they used hydrogen (H_2) to reduce carbon dioxide (CO_2) into methane (CH_4). These organisms live in oxygen-free environments, like swamps and the guts of animals. Extreme halophiles live in salt-rich environments, and extreme thermophiles thrive in hot water

** The position of green algae relative to other forms of algae and plants is unknown at this time. It is generally agreed that green algae and plants share a common ancestor

The Kingdom Protista gradually became the dumping ground for organisms that did not fit well within any other category. Systematists using genetic and chemical data have proposed further divisions of the Kingdoms Monera and Protista as shown in Tables 3.2 and 3.3. Table 3.3 shows the introduction of another level of classification, the "superkingdom" or domain, and the further division of the former Kingdom Protista.

Type Specimens

Type specimens are the designated standard for a given name. There are types for family, genus and species. A certain species may be designated as the type (ideal standard) for a family or genus. Types fall into several categories:

- *Holotype:* the single specimen designated (and figured) in the literature as the standard for a given species.
- *Paratype:* any number of other specimens that are part of the original type series, also should be figured.
- *Syntypes:* any number of specimens that are collectively the standard.
- *Hapantotype:* directly related individuals representing distinct life stages; the equivalent of a holotype.
- *Lectotype:* a single specimens designated as the standard for a given species after that species has already been established and described.

Obsolete terms that may be found on type or related specimens include:

- *Allotype:* a single specimen designated as the opposite sex equivalent of the holotype.
- *Cotype:* formerly referred to either syntypes or paratypes.
- *Genotype:* the holotype of a name that is also designed as the standard for a genus.
- *Topotype:* specimen that came from the type locality of the species, or that may be an undocumented member of the original type series.

Illustrated specimens that are not designated as primary types may be called vouchers or hypotypes. These are important specimens, although not as much so as primary types of the same species.

In mineralogy, the same terms are used, but with different meaning. The holotype of a mineral species is the specimen from which the characterizing data was obtained, such as unit cell dimensions and shape, chemical formula, etc. Type specimens rarely exist for species defined before 1800. Since most modern analytical methods are, at least in part, destructive, sometimes the only existing sample is destroyed or processed in order to obtain the data needed to define a new species.

Type collections should be maintained separately from a general collection, or at least in secure storage. Scientifically, they are the most important specimens in a collection. The type collection should include a reference for each type specimen. Specimens that have been cited more than once in the literature should be stored under the first name and citation. Type collections can be organized phylogenetically, or chronologically by date of publication. A collection of related publications is useful, and may be kept with the specimens or separately.

4

Plants

Introduction

Plant Classification

Plants can be divided into eleven divisions, according to basic factors such as methods of reproduction, energy sources, and physical structure (see Table 4.1). The division is a modification of the Linnaean classification system, being between kingdom and phylum.

Table 4.1   Divisions of plants.

Division	Common name	Approximate number of species	Characteristics
Bryophyta	Bryophytes, liverworts, hornworts, mosses	31,600	No specialized vascular tissues and no real roots; must absorb moisture from their above-ground environment.
Psilophyta	Whisk ferns	<5	Vascular plants with no seeds
Lycophyta	Club mosses	1000	Vascular plants with no seeds
Sphenophyta	Horsetails	15	Vascular plants with no seeds
Pterophyta	Ferns	12,000	Vascular plants with no seeds
Coniferophyta	Conifers	550	Vascular plants with unprotected seeds and no flowers (gymnosperms)
Cycadophyta	Cycads	100	Vascular plants with unprotected seeds and no flowers (gymnosperms)
Ginkgophyta	Ginkgos	1	Vascular plants with unprotected seeds and no flowers (gymnosperms)
Gnetophyta	Gnetophytes	70	Vascular plants with unprotected seeds and no flowers (gymnosperms)
Anthophyta	Flowering plants (angiosperms)	235,000	Vascular plants with protected seeds (angiosperms)

*all extinct.

The angiosperms or flowering plants can be further divided into *monocots* and *dicots*. Monocot seeds have one cotyledon or seed leaf, and dicots have two. Monocots include lilies, iris, palms, and grasses. Dicots include most non-coniferous trees and shrubs. In monocots, the vascular cells are arranged in bundles throughout the ground or body tissue of the stem. Dicots have the vascular tissues arranged in a ring inside the stem. The veins in monocot leaves are parallel, while those in dicots branch out from a stalk or *petiole* that connects the leaf to a branch. Monocot flowers usually have petals and other parts in multiples of 3, while dicots' parts are in multiples of 4 or 5.

Plant Structure

There are two basic systems in a plant: the shoot system, which includes above-ground elements such as leaves, stems, buds, and flowers and fruit (if there are any); and the root system, the underground parts, including roots, tubers, and rhizomes (Figure 4.1).

Figure 4.1

Parts of a plant. This is a generic diagram and does not represent a particular type of plant.

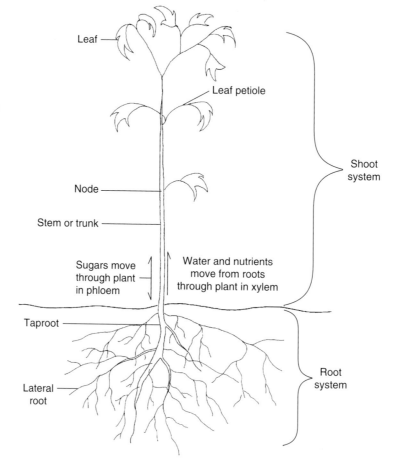

There are three types of tissue that make up all of these plant parts. The dermal cells are the densely-packed outer layer, which varies in thickness in different plants. The cells in this layer may secrete a waxy coating or cuticle that helps reduce the amount of water lost through a plant's exposed surfaces. The ground tissue is the body of the plant. And vascular tissue is made up of the specialized cells that transport water, minerals, food, and hormones throughout the plant.

Vascular cells are divided into xylem, which transport water and minerals from roots to the upper plant, and phloem, which takes food (sugars) from the leaves to the rest of the plant. These two types of cells are usually arranged in parallel, concentric form, with the phloem on the outside.

Photosynthesis is the process by which plants convert the energy in sunlight into food (sugar). A simple chemical equation for this process is shown in Figure 4.2.

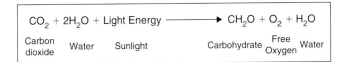

$$CO_2 + 2H_2O + \text{Light Energy} \longrightarrow CH_2O + O_2 + H_2O$$

Carbon dioxide   Water   Sunlight   Carbohydrate   Free Oxygen   Water

Figure 4.2

Conversion of sunlight into plant energy.

Chlorophyll is one of the compounds that allows this cycle to work. It is a photosynthetic pigment that absorbs light energy and helps convert it to chemical energy. There are other pigments that work during photosynthesis, depending on the type of organism involved. The carotenoids are another group of these light-processing pigments. These yellow and red compounds can be seen in some plant tissues, like carrot roots and tomato skin, and in leaves that are no longer photosynthesizing (fall color).

Most of a plant's photosynthesis occurs in the leaves. Energy-producing leaves tend to be large, thin, and arranged so that they can all get some sunlight. Leaves may also be adapted for specialized purposes, such as defense, prevention of water loss, and attraction of pollinators or prey.

Stems support the plant, usually above the ground, and contain the various specialized tissues that transport nutrients and moisture. Some stem structures are prostrate or below ground, like corms and rhizomes, which store energy (food). Wood is the term used to describe dense, often large stems of some plants.

Bark is the multi-layered outer portion of the stems and roots of woody plants. While the word is used most often in referring to just the epidermis of a stem, bark actually includes all layers of the plant from the outside down to and including the vascular cambium. The vascular cambium is the only part of a stem that grows. Its undifferentiated cells divide rapidly, producing secondary phloem cells toward the outside of the plant and secondary xylem cells toward the inside (Figure 4.3).

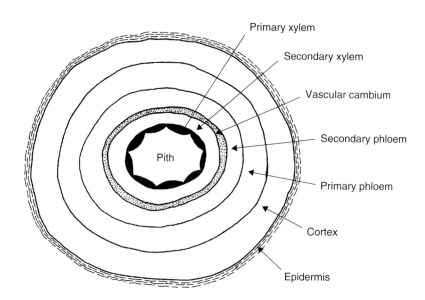

Figure 4.3

Cross-section of a mature woody plant.

The cortex or cork is the layer within the bark between the epidermis and the phloem. This layer protects the plant against disease and parasites, and may contain tannins and other chemicals.

Roots in general grow downward, toward water, and away from light. They absorb and transport moisture, store food, and anchor the plant in the ground.

Flowers are reproductive structures in flowering plants (hence the name). They are extremely diverse and are often the most useful diagnostic feature of a specimen. Fruit, like apples and peaches, encloses fertilized seeds.

Algae and fungi were originally clumped together with the plants, when the classification of organisms began simply with plants and animals. Algae and fungi are now classified within their own kingdoms (see Chapter 3). Most algae produce energy by photosynthesis, but fungi are saprophytes, obtaining their energy from adjacent materials.

Lichens, which contain both algae and fungus, have been used decoratively and some provide sources of dyes.

Fossil Plant Materials

Amber is the fossilized resin (sap) from plants. Fossilization occurs when a specimen of plant resin is buried and gradually becomes compressed and partially dehydrated. Partially fossilized resin is called copal, which is less dense and softer than true amber.

Modern plant resins are often substituted for true amber, and it is often diffi-cult to tell the difference. Some trees and shrubs will produce copious amounts of resin if wounded, so people will purposefully cut into the outside of a plant. Kauri gum is probably the most common resin collected this way. When the resin begins to flow, insects and sometimes small animals are inserted onto its sticky surface, where they will later be covered by more sap. In order to detect these inclusion-filled fakes, it is often necessary to identify the animals included in them to determine whether they are ancient or living species.

Amber can be found in rocks dating back to the Mesozoic era, about 80 million years ago. There undoubtedly were deposits of plant resin before that time, but they have failed to survive to this day. This may be due to the gradual breakdown of the hydrocarbons that constitute most amber, as well as its dehydration after burial.

Amber can be formed by any plant that produces sap or resin. It is not specific to pine trees, as is commonly believed. The amber found in the Baltic region of Eastern Europe was indeed formed in a huge pine forest that covered that area about 10 million years ago, during the Miocene Epoch. Much of today's commercial amber is mined in Mexico and the Dominican Republic. These deposits are older than the European amber, and were formed by large shrubs in the Pea family.

Some amber has been given common or commercial names based on the locality from which it comes. For example, Burmite is from Myanmar (formerly Burma), Rumanite comes from the Carpathian region of Romania, and Simetite is from the Simeto River area in Sicily.

Amber is soft, has a low melting point, and a very low density. Most amber will float in saturated salt water. It may be transparent, translucent or opaque, and varies in color. Most often it is yellow or brown, but specimens of red, blue, and green are known. Inclusions of insects, plant parts, dust, and other debris are sometimes found in amber formed from resin that was extruded onto the outside of a plant. There is lots of amber, however, that formed on the inside of plants, and this material rarely carries inclusions. Amber is very important to paleontologists because it preserves organisms, both plant and animal, that are far too delicate to be preserved by the normal fossilization processes of burial and dehydration.

The cloudiness in some amber specimens is due to the presence of many very tiny air bubbles. In an effort to produce the more commercially desirable transparent amber, this material is often "cleared" by heating. This has the effect of driving off the air bubbles, and may achieve a better-looking product. At the same time, however, water is also driven off, leaving a more brittle, and sometimes less lustrous material. Heating done too quickly or at too high a temperature can also result in the formation of flat ovoid structures within the amber. These "flying saucers" are often exploited by dealers as natural inclusions.

Amber fragments and cuttings are sometimes heated and compressed into a solid mass, which is then worked into beads or other items. The commercial name for this material is amberoid or ambroid.

Coal is the compressed and dehydrated fossilized remains of plants. These materials are classified by some as sediments, even though they are composed largely of organic compounds. Coal is discussed in detail as an organic sediment in Chapter 2.

Jet is the common name given to black, high-quality, homogeneous specimens of lignite coal. Fossilized plant material, coal consists of a complex mixture of hydrocarbon compounds, water, and small amounts of other elements, usually sulfur. It is very soft and has a very low density. As it is coal, it is also flammable.

Jet has been used to make a wide variety of items, mostly small household objects and jewelry, usually beads or memorial carvings. It is soft and easy to work, and the raw material is relatively inexpensive and plentiful. Jet became very popular in England after the death of Queen Victoria's husband Prince Albert. Inexpensive memorial jewelry and other items were made in great numbers in England, and distributed worldwide. The popularity of black jewelry led to the use of black beads as decoration on clothing and household items. Due to the softness of jet, many artists chose to use instead beads made of shiny black glass known as "French jet." Jet, because it is coal, contains a certain amount of moisture and may absorb more if given the opportunity. Some jet objects will discolor adjacent fabrics and lose their luster over time, usually due to the absorption of moisture.

Bog oak is wood that has been buried, usually in an anaerobic environment such as a bog or swamp. In Ireland this material is popular for carvings, often with a Celtic theme. It is used as an imitation of jet, although it is usually not black, but a dull dark brown.

Peat is a deposit of partially decayed plant material. It forms in swamps, marshes, and other wetlands. Like coal, the decomposition of dead plant matter is inhibited by the lack of oxygen. Layers of dead plants, trees, fungus, and moss may build up very quickly, depending on the climate and amount of water present. Most modern peat deposits are at or very close to the ground surface, and date from the end of the last great ice age, about 10,000 years ago.

Peat has been used as a building material, both structurally in walls, and as insulation. It is a common household fuel in many parts of the world, sometimes in combination with animal dung. It can be cut from the ground, often in areas where peat is still actively forming. This is common practice in places where there are few trees or other sources of fuel.

Products

This section contains a discussion of some of the products produced from plants. Some of these materials are not species-specific, and are produced from whatever plants are available and suitable for the prescribed purpose.

Wood

Wood is a general term that usually refers to the rigid stems and branches of some vascular plants, usually shrubs and trees. It is composed of cellulose, hemicellulose, and lignin. The latter two compounds are the glue that cements fiber cells together. Lignin is a large polymer molecule that makes up 17–30% of most wood by volume. When paper is produced from wood pulp, the lignin is often intentionally removed. Lignin photo-oxidizes, producing acidic compounds that can attack the cellulose in the finished paper. Lignin-free paper lasts longer and is less susceptible to light damage.

Wood contains water inside its cells and in between cells. When wood is cut (dead), it first loses the free water, and then, more slowly, the cell wall water. This all causes 3-dimensional shrinkage. Ideally, wood should be "seasoned," or dried slowly to the point of equilibrium (free water is gone, but there is no loss of cell wall water). If wood is dried too quickly, it may split or crack, because the outer portion is drying and contracting at a different rate from the middle. The outside compresses the more moist inside, which causes the outer part to break. These same reactions can take place if seasoned wood is saturated and then dried too quickly.

Wood is the general term applied to stems and branches of a wide variety of gymnosperms and angiosperms. It is used without processing other than shaping, and as the raw material for products such as paper.

Wood is generally divided into two categories, hardwoods, from deciduous trees, and softwoods, from conifers (see Table 4.2). Some species fall into a vague middle range of medium-hard woods. These include Douglas fir, eucalyptus or gum, mahogany, and walnut.

While each type of wood has specific characteristics that make it appropriate for certain uses, the choice of wood is often opportunistic. In other words, a craftsman uses what is available. Some exotic woods, like mahogany and ebony, have special characters that make them so desirable that they have been used as a trade item. Only a few of these will be discussed here.

Mahogany is any of the hardwoods in the family Meliaceae. These trees are found in the Caribbean, Central and South America, Asia, and Africa. The wood resists termite attack, is easy to work, and has a beautiful reddish hue when polished. Its water resistance made it attractive to ship builders, who used it whenever it was available in sufficient amounts.

Ebony is a dense, hard, fine-grained wood from several species of the genus *Diospyros*, which also includes persimmons. While the name ebony is often given to any black, heavy wood, true ebony may not be completely black. Some forms are black with lighter-colored streaks or spots. Ebony was used for making furniture and carvings. It was also used to make parts of musical instruments, including the black keys on piano and organ keyboards

Table 4.2 Soft and hard woods.

	Group	Genus	Parts used	Uses
Soft woods	Pines	*Pinus*	Wood, cones, needles	Lumber, paper, food, decoration
	Larch	*Latrix*	Wood	Lumber
	Spruce	*Picea*	Wood	Lumber
	Hemlock	*Tsuga*	Wood	Lumber
	Fir	*Abies*	Wood	Lumber
	Redwood and Sequoia	*Sequoia*	Wood	Lumber, insect repellant
	Cedar	*Chamaecyparis, Thuja, Libocedrus*	Wood, bark	Lumber, insect repellant
	Cypress	*Taxodium*	Wood	Lumber
Medium-hard woods	Douglas fir	*Pseudotsuga*	Wood, cones	Lumber, paper, decoration
	Mahogany	Family Meliaceae	Wood	Furniture, ship-building
	Walnut	*Juglans*	Wood	Lumber, food
	Gum or eucalyptus	*Eucalyptus*	Wood	Lumber
Hard woods	Willows	*Salix*	Wood, narrow stems, bark	Lumber, medicine
	Aspen, poplar, cottonwood	*Populus*	Wood	Lumber, carvings (Kachina)
	Hickory	*Carya*	Wood	Lumber, sports equipment, tool handles
	Birch	*Betula*	Wood	Lumber, sports equipment, tool handles
	Alder	*Alnus*	Wood	Lumber
	Beech	*Fagus*	Wood	Lumber
	Chestnut	*Castanea*	Wood, nuts	Lumber, food
	Oak	*Quercus*	Wood, acorns	Lumber, food
	Elm	*Ulmus*	Wood	Lumber
	Sassafras	*Sassafras*	Wood, bark	Lumber, bark tea
	Sycamore	*Platanus*	Wood	Lumber
	Cherry	*Prunus*	Wood, fruit	Lumber, food
	Holly	*Ilex*	Wood, berries	Lumber, decoration
	Maple	*Acer*	Wood	Lumber
	Ash	*Fraxinus*	Wood	Lumber, sports equipment, tool handles
	Ebony	*Diospyros*	Wood	Furniture, decoration

and fingerboards and cheek rests for violins. In the same genus, the wood of the persimmon (*D. virginiana*) is light cream colored. Similar to ebony in strength and hardness, it has been used to make golf club heads.

African blackwood is another hard black wood that is commonly used in musical instruments. This wood has a higher natural sheen than ebony, and is the preferred choice for making the tubes for oboes, clarinets, and other woodwinds.

Wood splints are made by delaminating wood, separating it along the internal growth rings. A tree is cut down and the bark removed. The body of the log is then pounded with a heavy mallet or other object, along its entire length. This will crush the tiny layer of spongy growth within each tree ring, allowing the outer layer of wood to be removed. After pounding the log, the surface of the wood is scored with a knife, lengthwise with the grain. The splint can then be peeled up, coiled, and dried. Sometimes only a part of a log would be processed in this way. This is a long and labor-intensive process, but a single tree can produce a great many feet of splints.

Before use, the splints are cleaned and scraped to remove the porous, soft layers on either side. Once dried and coiled, splints can last for years before use. Like many basket-making materials, splints are soaked in water prior to use.

Wood splints tend to be flat or flat on one side and slightly convex on the other. They are used to make mats, baskets, and furniture, usually in combination with other, more rigid materials.

Bamboo is often used in the same ways that wood is, for furniture and as a building material. But bamboo is actually in the Poaceae, or grass family. Two genera, *Bambusa* and *Phyllostachys*, produce bamboo that is used for construction, weaving, papermaking, and for food.

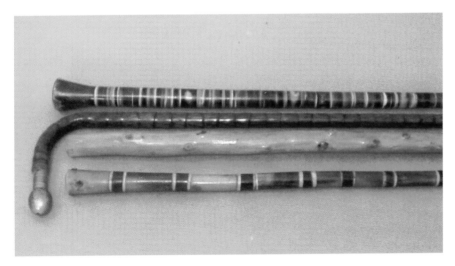

Figure 4.4

Walking sticks may be made of a single stem, or may be composites of plant and other materials. From the top these are made of stacked rings of horn, cane, wood, and horn–wood.

Bark

Bark cloth has been made from the inner bark of some trees, mostly in tropical areas such as Africa and the South Pacific. Trees used for this include the paper mulberry, breadfruit, and some species of fig. The inner bark is stripped from branches or the tree trunk, soaked in water, and beaten until the fibers are compressed and flexible. Bark cloth is used for making clothing, decorative objects, and household items.

Kapa or tapa cloth is made from mulberry tree bark. Kapa is specific to Hawaii, while tapa is made throughout Polynesia. The differences arise from the methods used to prepare the bark, and the uses to which it is subsequently put.

Bark of birch and other trees has been used to make canoes and shallow-draft boats in many parts of the world. Large pieces of bark are usually stretched over a wooden framework, and the seams are sealed with plant resin or pitch.

The cork oak, *Quercus suber*, produces a thick bark that has been used mostly in the form of plugs in bottles. Since cork is light-weight, porous, and soft, it is sometimes used for other purposes, such as linings in humidors, wall-coverings, and chair seats. Cork floats, and has been used to support fishing nets and other things in the water. Early life-jackets or belts were composed all or in part of cork.

Cinnamon is the inner bark of a small evergreen tree, *Cinnomomum zeylanicum* or *C. verum*, which is in the laurel family. Cassia (*C. aromaticum*) and camphor (*C. camphora*) are other members of this genus. The bark, leaves, and sometimes whole stems from these trees are also used as a spice. Cassia is sometimes called bastard cinnamon because it is produced in greater quantities, but is less aromatic than true cinnamon. All of these spices have been combined with resin and vegetable soils to produce fragrant oils and incense. Cinnamon and other similar fragrant bark powders have been used medicinally to treat many ailments, from kidney disease to snakebite.

Quinine is an alkaloid compound used to treat malaria and other feverish ailments. It is a product of the bark of the *Cinchona* tree, a large evergreen originally found in South America. The bark alone is called Peruvian bark, and is used in powdered form to treat fevers.

Willow bark is a source of acetylsalicylic acid or aspirin, which is used to treat headaches and fever. This is just one of the many medicinal compounds derived from plants.

Paper

Papermaking has evolved over the years as technology advanced, as different natural materials became available, and as the needs of various civilizations changed. The earliest known plant-derived paper was invented in Egypt, in about 3000 BC. Stems of a type of marsh grass, *Cyperous papyrus*, were cut into long strips, which were then layered at right angles. The resulting mat was then pounded thin and left to dry. Since that time, other cultures used plant products like thin bark and some animal products, like skin and woven silk, on which to write. The inventor of paper made from mixed plant fibers is generally agreed to have been Ts'ai Lun, an official at the Chinese court in 105 AD. Until that time, silk fabric was used as a writing surface. But this was expensive and took a lot of time to make. Ts'ai Lun made his paper of rags, old fish nets, China grass, and hemp, all shredded together, mixed with water, and collected in a flat sieve. Papermaking spread throughout Asia and the Middle East, and flax was added to the list of possible ingredients.

At the time of Gutenberg's first Bible publication in 1456, Europeans were writing on parchment and vellum. It took three hundred sheep skins to make one Bible, so even with the invention of printing, the mass production of books was not possible until changes were made. Efforts were made to improve the process of creating paper from linen rags, and "vegetable parchment" became popular. For the next 400 years, paper was made from recycled cotton and linen. Rags became so scarce that they were smuggled from one country to another, and people were buried in shrouds of wool rather than linen.

Eventually, through experimentation with lots of plant materials, it was found in the mid-1800s that soft wood pulp was a very efficient and economical paper material.

Modern paper often contains chemicals that enhance its appearance, reduce its pH (acidify), and give it specific physical properties. Many of these additives can affect the way paper reacts to light, humidity, and other environmental factors.

Fabric and Cordage

Plant fibers have been used for thousands of years to make cordage, fabric, and other useful products. Depending on the species, plant fibers consist mostly of cellulose and water. Other components present may include lignin, carbohydrates, hemicellulose, pectins, wax, and tannins.

Bast is the inner bark of a plant, composed of the phloem and other fibrous cells. Hard fiber, which comes from leaves, is used mostly for cordage (rope, twine, cord) and the rough fabric used for making sacks and other containers. Soft fiber, which comes from plant stems, is used to make thread and finer fabrics like linen, cotton, and woven hemp.

Cordage and fabric are made from natural plant fibers that come from different parts of various plants. Table 4.3 lists some of the most common plant fibers used to make fabric and cordage.

Cotton fiber is made of the epidermal hairs from seeds of members of genus *Gossypium*. These fibers consist of hollow cylindrical tubes that are 15–22 μm in diameter, narrowing at one end. The walls of a cotton fiber are made of 90–96% cellulose, mixed with about 5% water and small amounts of pectins, and other impurities. When dried, these tubes are flat and naturally curl or twist like a ribbon. Untreated cotton has from 150 to 300 twists per inch. The fibers are from 0.5 to over 2 inches long, and are extremely thin, from 0.0005 to 0.0009 inches in diameter.

Table 4.3   Common plant fibers.

Common name	Generic name	Parts used	Uses
Cotton	*Gossypium* sp. (mallow family)	Seed fiber	Thread, cotton cloth, rope
Jute	*Corchorus* sp.	Bast (inner bark)	Hessian (rough cloth), twine, rope
Abaca or Manila hemp	*Musa textilis* (banana family)	Leaves	Cloth, mats, baskets
Sisal	*Agave sisalana*	Leaves	Cloth, mats, baskets
Nettles	*Urtica dioica*	Bast (whole stems)	Thread, cloth
Hemp	*Cannabis* sp.	Bast (whole stems)	Thread, cloth
Flax	*Linum usitatissimum*	Bast (whole stems)	Thread, cloth (linen, batiste, cambric, lawn)

Table 4.4   Mixed cotton fabrics.

Common name	Composition	Uses
Airplane fabric	Cotton + cellulose acetate	Airplane wings and bodies, uniforms, ski-wear
Balloon cloth	Vulcanized cotton + oil	Balloons, airplanes, gliders, tents
Book cloth	Cotton + starch and/or clay	Book bindings
Buckram	Cotton + starch or sizing	Hats, bookbinding, coat lining
Polished cotton	Cotton + resin	Clothing, household uses

The process of mercerization was invented by John Mercer in 1844. It involves soaking cotton in an 18% solution of NaOH (sodium hydroxide), which causes the fibers to swell and the cellulose to relax. Afterwards, the fibers retain their increased diameter and are less convoluted.

Cotton has been successfully combined with other materials to create fabrics for specific purposes. Table 4.4 lists some of these fabrics. Cotton fabric has also been given various names depending on the coarseness or fineness of the weave, and its intended use. These include calico, canvas, batiste, cheesecloth, muslin, organdy, cotton gabardine, gingham, lawn, voile, terrycloth, and cotton flannel.

Cotton fabrics were often used as the basis for needlepoint, embroidery, and other stitched arts. Cotton canvas has been used for paintings.

Oil cloth is canvas that has been impregnated with linseed oil, or covered with a thick layer of oil paint. These cloths were used for water-proof clothing and as floor coverings. Linoleum followed, as an inexpensive flexible water-resistant floor covering. First manufactured in the mid-1800s in England, linoleum consists of an organic binder (linseed oil and resin), inorganic filler (pigment and limestone), and organic filler (wood dust and ground cork).

Flax has been used to make thread and fabric since Neolithic times. Cotton cloth was first produced in India in about 1500 BC. Since cotton fibers come from the seed, and flax from the plant stem, the individual fibers are shaped very differently. Often, the only way to tell cotton from linen cloth is by microscopic examination of the fibers. Cotton looks like thin, flat ribbon, and flax fibers look segmented, like bamboo.

The generic name for flax, *Linum usitatissimum*, in which the species name means "most useful." This refers to its uses as a source of fiber and oil. The bast fibers from the stems of flax plants are prepared by retting. During this process, fiber bundles are loosened from bast cells by the decomposition of the pectin "glue" that holds the cells together. This is accomplished by wetting the plant stems in the presence of bacteria (*Clostridium* sp.), or by dew retting outdoors. Dew retting involves laying out the plants in a damp field and waiting for nature, in the form of water and fungus, to do the work. This can take weeks or months, but it is virtually labor-free. Sometimes the fibers that have been treated this way retain some of the fungus, which causes dark threads among the finished product. Wetting in a vat with bacteria is more labor intensive, but it goes a lot faster. Most modern commercial retting is done with chemicals.

Figure 4.5

This fine lace and fabric are linen, which is made from flax.

Like cotton, there are many different linen fabrics made from the basic flax fiber. Most of these are defined only by the type of weave and the fineness of the fiber, such as cambric and damask. The word linen is usually applied only to unbleached plain weave material. Some names are applied to similar fabrics made of cotton and linen. An example of this is canvas, a plainly woven fabric of varying weight made from hard-twisted yarn. Canvas may be made from hemp, cotton, jute, or flax (linen). Most fine fabrics, particularly of European or American manufacture, are made from flax. Since its invention in the 1600s, most lace has also been made of flax thread.

The common name for *Boehmeria nivea* is China grass. Processed by retting, like flax and hemp, this member of the nettle family yields single fiber cells that are 2½–25 inches long, the longest of all single plant fiber cells. They actually average 5–6 inches in length, but this is still significantly different from other plant fibers.

Jute is made from the bast fibers from *Corchorus olitorus* or *C. capsullaris*, also called Jew's mallow. The roots of these plants are used as food in Southeast Asia, and root ends, or jute cuttings, are used to make paper.

The bast is prepared by retting, but the end product is not separated down to individual fibers. After processing, the bast is left in its original form, in long bundles that are usually brown from the tannins present in these plants. The bast fibers are from 4 to 7 feet long and large, with a diameter of 20–25 mm.

Jute is used to make coarse fabrics such as burlap, in furniture webbing, and to make carpet. It is an ingredient in linoleum, where it is coated with ground cork and boiled in linseed oil.

Sisal and henequin are both made from the white inner fibers of *Agave* leaves. They are made from different species of *Agave*, but the process is basically the same. Material produced in Mexico is called henequin, and that from Indonesia and East Africa is called sisal.

This material is most often used to make twine and rope, but not for maritime use, since it decomposes in salt water. It is also used in brushes and as a substitute for horsehair in stuffing upholstery.

Hemp is made from the bast fibers of *Cannabis sativa*. This is a larger plant than flax, and produces much coarser fibers. Abaca or Manila hemp is very different from plain hemp. Abaca is made from *Musa textilis*, commonly called the fiber banana plant. The core fibers of the leaf sheaths of this plant are resistant to salt water, which makes them useful for rope and fabric to be used at sea. It is also used to make handicrafts such as hats and household items. Paper made from abaca has a wide variety of uses, including paper currency (i.e. Japanese yen notes), sausage casings, industrial filters, and tea bags. The finest grade abaca is woven into a cloth called pinukpok.

Coir is fiber that has been beaten and combed from the rough brown outer husk of the coconut. This material can be used in a very rough state, but it is lighter colored and stronger if retted first. Coir is highly resistant to wear and decay, even when wet for long periods of time.

Coir fibers vary in thickness, and can be up to 10 inches in length. Short, coarse fibers are used to make brushes, long fibers to make rope and woven matting, and short curly fibers are used as packing material and upholstery stuffing. Due to its resistance to decay and its strength, coir is used to make cordage and fenders for ships, including the longest and most important cables and rigging. Coir is also used to make wall and floor coverings, brooms, brushes, rugs, and mats.

Woven and Dried Plant Materials

Basket-making and other forms of plant material weaving were probably the precursors to the invention of textiles. Simple weaving of flexible materials became more refined over time, and some woven objects took on an artistic quality separate from their utilitarian usefulness. A basket is a container made of woven materials. Most common basket-making materials are derived from plants, and may include any and all parts of a plant, from the roots, to the smallest twigs. Basket design is usually dictated by what materials are available, and the intended use of the finished product.

Plant materials are often softened in water before woven into baskets or other objects. Repeated soaking and drying can cause the plant fibers to separate and fray. This can happen during construction, or after, in a basket is used to hold wet materials or if it is cleaned with water. The most common plant materials used to make baskets and other woven objects are wood and bark strips, grasses, rushes, thin twigs, vines, thin roots, and leaves. The only prerequisite for basket materials is that they be flexible enough for weaving. Consistent thickness is also important for anything but the coarsest of baskets. Some baskets are constructed over a frame of wood or other stiff materials. Decorations such as feathers, leather, or dyed plant materials may also be added, depending upon the intended use of the basket.

Some baskets are made of clumps of bound leaves or pine needles, woven into place with long flexible vines or thin leaf strips. Thin strips of bark or wood are also commonly used, although the preparation of these materials may add considerably to the work it takes to produce a finished basket.

Baskets and wicker-work are often found in historical and anthropological collections. Baskets can be made from any natural flexible material. Popular plant materials used in basket-making include grasses, reeds, bark, straw, thin strips of wood, vines, and pine needles. Wicker is a term used to describe furniture and other items made of interlaced branches (usually willow).

Objects that consist of or contain dried plant materials are susceptible to damage from light, insects, and moisture. As these items have lost moisture over time, they are not as flexible or strong as they were when first made. They must be handled carefully and many require physical support to retain their shapes and integrity.

Raffia fibers are derived from the leaves of the raffia palm (*Raphia farinifera*). Peeled from both sides of the palm, the fibers are dried in the sun. The fibers are used for a variety of handicrafts and decorations, including hats, baskets, ribbons, and mats of various sizes. Raffia is often dyed and combined with other stronger materials like wood or vines. Hula or grass skirts are often made from raffia.

Pineapple fiber or Pina is strong white silky fiber taken from the leaves of the pineapple plant. It is used as thread, in making fishing nets, and to wrap and sew cigars. Since the leaf fibers are somewhat short, they are separated and tied together to form thread. The finest thread is used in making Pina cloth, which is used to make the "Barong Tagalog," the national costume of the Philippines. It is also used to make household linens, handkerchiefs, and other items of clothing. Coarser Pina fibers are used mostly for cordage and, when crushed, as a raw material for paper.

Straw is the general term for those parts of a cereal plant left over after the grains or seeds have been removed. It consists largely of the dry stalk or stem, and some leaves. During the harvest of such crops as wheat, rye, barley, corn, or oats, straw is usually whatever is left behind in the field. It has historically been used in a variety of ways, and was regarded as an important product of the harvest.

Straw is used as loose bedding for domestic animals. It is used as stuffing in mattresses and furniture. In construction, it is used to make thatched roofs, and is mixed into mortar or mud bricks to give them strength. The combination of mud and straw has been practiced for thousands of years, in many areas of the world. A mixture of mud or clay and straw is called cob, and the resultant bricks may be of any size.

Loose or in bales, it is used as building insulation. It is spread on the ground or wrapped around plants as protection against cold and pests. It is used to be a popular packing material, and is still favored by some wine shippers. Straw rope has been made in various thicknesses, and is used mostly in thatching and packing.

Straw from a wide variety of plants, not just those that produce cereal grains, is commonly used in many cultures to make woven items such as mats, hats, floor covering, and baskets. Straw decorations are often placed on thatched roofs. These rick ornaments are usually in the form of animals, made of straw that has been bunched and tied into shape. They may be just for decoration, or they may identify the thatcher who made the roof.

There are many forms of harvest-related items that are made of straw, including crosses and corn dollies. Traditionally these are made of the last plants harvested, and are kept inside the home until the following spring. To return the spirit of the harvest to the soil, these woven straw items are supposed to be plowed back into the ground in the first furrow cut in the spring. Corn dollies come in many forms, and may be made of any kind of straw or dried grain plants (see Figures 4.6 and 4.7).

Linen straw is finely-woven or braided straw that is finished or treated to imitate fine linen fabric. Fine decorative patterns have been made of straw applied to wood or fabric, and then coated with lacquer or resin. This art is practiced today in Russia, Belarus, and parts of Eastern Europe (see Figure 4.8).

Plant fibers, like cotton and jute, must be processed before using. There are many forms of plant materials that can be used with little or no preliminary work. These include materials that are woven just as they come from the plant, such as vines, bark strips and flexible branches, or saplings.

As the name implies, bentwood objects or structures are made from plant materials that have been bent or twisted into a certain shape. These include

Figure 4.6

This corn dolly angel is a symbol of the harvest, and would be kept in the house for good luck.

Figure 4.7

A corn dolly from the previous harvest would be returned to the soil and plowed into the first furrows dug in the spring.

Figure 4.8

This wooden box is decorated with tiny straw pieces that are cut by hand and then glued. The finished piece is lacquered to hold the design in place.

various forms of furniture, trellises and other garden structures, and things made as decorations.

The materials used for these purposes vary widely, since the only prerequisites are flexibility and availability. Saplings, offshoots, vines, and flexible branches are most common. The creation of bent wood objects must take place while the materials are still green and flexible, so harvesting and manufacture usually follow within a day. Re-wetting may be used to keep the materials flexible longer.

Some bentwood projects are done over a period of time, as materials become available, and some objects may include more than one type of wood. Trees commonly used as sources for bentwood include ash, aspen, bald cypress, birch, cottonwood, box elder, dogwood, red cedar, maple, hickory, and different species of fruit trees. Some vines, such as honeysuckle, wisteria, and rattan vine (*Berchemia scandens*) are also used.

Wicker is a general term applied to anything woven from natural materials. It is usually used in reference to furniture made of thin woven plant materials, sometimes in combination with rattan or wood. Common materials include willow, seagrass, corn stalks, palm frond ribs, and thin wood splints.

Rattan refers to a climbing palm that grows in the jungles of Southeast Asia. This unusual plant looks like a vine, and may reach lengths of several hundred feet without ever achieving a diameter of more than 2 inches. The rattan plant is supple when fresh and bends easily. Historically, it has been used to construct bridges and scaffolds in Asia, where it is called the "wood of steel."

Bamboo is a grass, in the Poaceae family. The stems of bamboo are called culms. They are jointed, with regularly spaced nodes, from which sprout single leaves and branchlets.

There are about one thousand species of bamboo, some of which can reach huge size. In some cases it grows to the height of trees and may have a diameter of 30 cms and more. Bamboo can be seasoned, like the wood from trees, and it has been used in the construction of houses and other structures, and to make furniture. Smaller pieces are used to make furniture or woven together to make mats for flooring or window-covering. Green bamboo can be split lengthwise and flattened, then dried to create a hard, strong material that can be used like wood or even paper.

In order to produce square bamboo canes for construction, the young culms may be placed inside a square tube. As the plant grows, the culm will fill the available space, forming a long cane that has a square cross-section. The tubes must be adjusted as the fast-growing plant matures, and it is removed after the culm has reached the desired size.

Plant materials were the earliest materials used as brushes and brooms, and are still favored for some applications. A bunch of reeds or straw tied around a stick is a useful tool, easily made and easily replaced when worn out. Like baskets and other objects made of plant materials, brooms were usually made of whatever was available. So there is no definitive broom-making material.

Most modern brooms are made of either plant materials or synthetics. The old round broom shape gave way to the more efficient flat broom, which was invented by the Shakers in the early 1800s. The modern "corn" broom is made of the stems of sorghum, which is also called Guinea corn or millet. The seeds of this plant are used to make bread, or as food for livestock. The tan or yellow stems are used to make brushes and brooms.

Brushes have been made from both plant and animal materials. Fine brushes, for writing or painting, are usually made of animal hair. Toothbrushes and short-bristle cleaning brushes are most often made of stiff plant materials, like small twigs or stems.

Plants used as food or medicine are often dried so they can be stored and used months or even years after harvest. Plant materials used for decorative purposes are also dried, sometimes before being used, and sometimes after they have been incorporated into an object. Bouquets or wreaths may contain green and dry elements when they are created.

Wreaths and other decorative objects made from woven or interlaced branches or vines can be made with a wide variety of materials, since they are not expected to have much strength or to last for more than a few years, if that. Grapevines, which are unsuitable for larger, stronger projects such as bentwood furniture or trellises, are commonly used for wreaths and decorations.

Wreaths often consist of a base, woven out of vine or thin branches, and other materials added for visual interest. The latter may be other plant products, like leaves, cones, berries, flowers, grasses, or seeds. They may also include animal parts, like feathers, or artificial items like silk flowers or fabric forms.

Wreaths are seldom intended to last more than a year or two. If the base structure is well-constructed, it may outlast the decorations applied to it, which can be renewed over time. Since plant materials tend to shrink as they dry out, wreaths may shed or fall apart completely as they age.

Some plant materials may be found as part of preserved bouquets, which are sometimes protected under a glass dome or in a frame, behind glass. These may include flowers, grass, seeds, pods, cones, fruit, stems, leaves, and seed heads. This latter type of structure includes cattails and thistles, in which thousands of seeds are held together in an interesting natural shape. Pressed flowers or seeds may be incorporated into handmade paper, or preserved flat under glass, often in interesting arrangements.

Seeds, cones, and other small plant parts are often made into jewelry or other items of personal decoration, sometimes sewn to fabric. Necklaces made of local seeds or pods are commonly made for the tourist trade.

Decorative plant materials are sometimes coated or sprayed with consolidants or resin. This serves to hold the fragile parts together, and to protect

the whole thing from moisture. Over time, these coatings may soften and attract dust, or they may darken and become brittle.

Cattails are tall, prolific reeds in the genus *Typha*. These plants produce large cylindrical seed heads and straight, thick stems. The seed down or fluff that comes from the cattail heads has been used as a filler in mattresses and pillows, and as insulation in clothing. A poultice made with the seeds has been used to stop bleeding and as a remedy for toothache. The roots are edible, and the stems are sometimes used as a source of plant fiber. The stems have also been used to make arrows and the rigid structures on which some baskets are made. Cattail heads have been used as torches, but without being first soaked in oil or wax, they are not effective as lights and tend to smolder.

Besides cattails, a few plants have been effectively used as torches and fuel for specialized lamps. The rushlight or rush candle is made from rushes common in wet fields or bogs. These plants have a tall pithy stem and few or no leaves. The stems are collected, and soaked in water to facilitate the removal of the tough outer layer. The inner bark and the pith are left intact, and the stem is laid out to dry. The dried stems are dipped repeatedly in a mixture of whatever candle-making fat or wax is available, usually a combination of animal fats and beeswax. The resulting reed candles are several feet long and usually are held in a lamp especially designed for this purpose. As these reeds burn best at an angle, rather than in a vertical position like most candles, a rush lamp supports the rush candle at about a 45° angle.

Gourds are the fruit of some members of the Cucurbitaceae or cucumber family. Fresh, some gourds may be used as food. When dried and cleaned, gourds can be used as containers or incorporated into artwork. With or without a water-resistant coating, like plant latex or animal fat, gourds have been used as floats for fishing nets and even for small children. Gourds have been made into rattles and simple wind instruments. Some gourds are prized for their unusual shapes and brilliant colors.

Figure 4.10

This Hopi rattle is a hollow gourd, painted as a Chaveyo (ogre). This object also includes wood and feathers.

In the making of snuff bottles and other small items, gourds and other fruits can be placed in wooden or metal molds while they were still growing. The inside of these molds are carved in reverse so that the positive designs will be impressed into the adult fruit. Objects created in this way were often lacquered or decorated after they were removed from the mold. Other fruits molded in this way include tangerines, oranges, and lemons.

Luffa is a genus of tropical and subtropical gourds. Several species of these plants produce large fruits which are eaten as a vegetable in Asia and Africa. Mature fruit like this may be processed to remove the soft tissue, leaving a network of open cells. The finished product resembles a marine sponge, and may be used in the same ways. These vegetable sponges are called loofas or loofahs.

The quest for imitations of ivory have led to the use of "vegetable ivory," the hard white nuts produced by various tropical trees. The most common of these are the doum palm (*Hyphanae thebaica*) and the tagua (*Phytelephas macrocarpa*). These nuts have a brown fibrous rind, but the meat inside is homogeneous white or yellowish white. Softer than ivory, these nuts are easy to carve, and are popular for making small items such as netsuke, buttons, beads, and jewelry.

Figure 4.11

These imitation ivory chickens are carved from tagua nut (left) and a large fish vertebra (right).

Plant Fluids

Some plants produce fluids that have been used in their natural states, as everything from calking to food, and processed to create lacquers, resins, and water-proofing.

Latex is a term used to describe the milky white sap of various tropical plants that is the parent material of rubber and gutta-percha. Rubber is the sap from a number of different tropical plants, mostly in the genera *Ficus* and *Hevea*. This fluid is viscous and unstable, its properties changing quickly with changes in temperature and moisture.

Rubber has been given a number of different names over the years, depending on its use, and by whom. The French called it caoutchouc, based on a Brazilian native word "cahuchu," meaning "tree that weeps." Columbus called it "goma de un arbol," or "gum of the tree" after having seen Haitian natives playing with balls made of natural rubber. Gum-elastic was a common name for it in the 1800s. The name rubber or India rubber comes from the discovery in the late 1700s that elastic plant sap could be used to rub out the marks of a pencil or charcoal. Vegetable leather is another, less common, name that probably refers to the texture and color of a flattened piece of raw rubber.

Hard rubber has a variety of names, some of which may denote differences in composition or plants of origin. These include ebonite, bone rubber, gutta-percha, and vulcanite. Gutta-percha is technically a product of Asia, from different plants than those that produce rubber, but these terms are often used interchangeably for any rigid rubber material.

Early uses of rubber mostly involved the weather-proofing of fabric or leather. This must have been frustrating, since these coatings melted in hot sunlight. Charles Macintosh was a Scottish chemist who found that by combining rubber with naphtha, he got a more stable compound that would not melt if it got warm. Clothing made from fabric coated with this compound was called a Macintosh.

Vulcanization of soft or India rubber was discovered by Charles Goodyear in 1839. He was followed by Nelson Goodyear, who patented the vulcanization of hard rubber in 1851. These processes involve the treatment of natural rubber with heat, sulfur, and various metallic compounds. The resultant material is stronger and more stable than raw rubber, while still retaining the desirable properties of elasticity and flexibility. It is also resistant to heat and does not melt like raw rubber or gutta percha.

Vulcanized rubber can be carved, or, more importantly, molded into almost any shape. The uses for this versatile, water-proof, flexible material increased with time. These included household and decorative objects, apparel, personal items, insulation, and equipment and materials for use in medicine, the military, and industry. Vulcanized rubber also goes under the commercial names: vulcanite and ebonite.

Gutta-percha (with or without the hyphen) is the hardened latex from a number of different trees found in Borneo, Sri Lanka, and Malaya. The name comes from the Malayan words for juice (gutta) and tree (percha). This viscous plant sap hardens quickly and, after vulcanization, looks and behaves like hard rubber. The term gutta percha has also been used to describe unvulcanized hard rubber, regardless of its origin.

When the demand for the raw gutta percha material increased in the mid-1800s, hundreds of thousands of trees were felled for the harvest of their sap because the natives did not realize that they could obtain continuous supplies of this material without killing the source trees. Early gutta percha often contained foreign material, such as bark, leaves, and dirt because it was sold in large blocks by weight. These "extras" were added to increase the size and weight of the blocks created for export. This foreign material may or may not have been completely removed prior to heating and molding, and may account for the brittleness and irregular coloration of some objects made of this material.

Gutta percha objects were created from raw, untreated latex that was melted and molded, or from vulcanized gutta percha, which has most of the same properties as hard rubber. Molded gutta-percha was made into a staggering diversity of objects, including golf balls, jewelry, thread, tool and weapon handles, condoms, water pipes, buttons, and in dentistry as a base for dentures, as fillings, and as artificial teeth. The thread was woven into waterproof blankets, tents, and other fabrics, mostly for use by the military.

Rubber has been imitated for many years, but particularly after World War I, when the demand for rubber grew much faster than could be accommodated by the world's supply of the natural material. Companies in the USA and Europe worked hard to create products that had the same elastic and water-resistant properties as natural rubber. Beginning in the 1930s, products like latex, filatex, lycra, neoprene, and lastex, the "miracle yarn," came on the market.

Readers interested in learning more about rubber and gutta percha are referred to Mike Woshner's excellent book on the uses of these materials in the Civil War era (1999).

Oil, Resin and Wax

Plant resins and distillates from a wide variety of plants have been used as coatings and to impregnate porous materials. The purpose of these activities was usually to provide an object or material with water resistance and, sometimes, added strength.

Some useful oils, like turpentine, are produced as the by-products of other manufacturing or processing. Oil of turpentine is produced as a by-product of paper-making (sulfur turpentine), from treatment of otherwise unusable wood, like stumps and slash left from logging (wood turpentine), or from the distillation of tree resin (gum turpentine). Most, but not all, turpentine is made from pine tree materials.

Turpentine has medicinal uses, both topical, as for lice, and internal, to destroy parasites. It is a solvent and a common ingredient in paint and varnish.

When turpentine has been distilled from plant resin, the remaining residue is rosin, which is used to increase surface friction. Rosin may also be derived directly from plants, if the natural resin is dehydrated. The common uses of rosin are in soldering flux, and as a surface treatment on stringed musical instruments. Athletes also use rosin to enhance the grip of hands and feet in many fields, from gymnastics to ballet.

Another hard resin is mastic, which comes from an evergreen shrub in North Africa and the Mediterranean. Mastic is used as a flavoring in liquor, candy, and chewing gum. Small objects and jewelry were created from it, but few of these items survive today due to the softness of resin and its low melting point.

Plant fluids have also been used to produce compounds that are used in making protective coatings, consolidants, and glues.

Lacquer or shellac was sometimes layered to produce a material that could be carved or molded. Popular examples of this process are the red Asian "cinnabar" ware and "union" cases used for early photographs. Most cinnabar-ware actually contains no cinnabar, although this toxic sulfide of mercury was originally used as a coloring agent. Some of this lacquer-ware is composed entirely of many layers of lacquer, but most has a base of wood or metal.

Black or dark brown daguerreo-type cases were very popular in the mid-1800s, and most consist of molded resin compounds combined with sawdust and pigment. Often identified as gutta percha or hard rubber, these composition cases are more brittle than those materials. If chipped, the fresh surface of rubber or gutta percha will appear homogeneous and smooth, while the composition will be porous, mottled, and coarse.

Resin "compositions" were also used to make molded decorative and household objects. These compounds were used for the covers of books, picture frames, buttons, and lots of other small objects. Most of these items were black, but sometimes they were made white, as an imitation of ivory. These items are brittle and flammable and were the precursors to modern plastics.

In order to produce harder, tougher materials, inventors combined plant resins with other plant and animal fluids, and inorganic materials such as diatomaceous earth, and pulverized glass, porcelain, or stone. The resultant compositions could take much more abuse than earlier molded resin compounds, and were made into everything from door knobs to billiard balls.

Celluloid, which was patented in the USA in 1870, is a combination of pyroxylin, camphor, and cellulose fiber. It could be molded under pressure, and could be made in any color. Later experiments revealed that certain additives increased its flexibility and luster. Most early celluloid was used to make small household and decorative objects, often in a white or cream color to imitate ivory. With the invention of motion pictures, celluloid became commonly used as film.

Celluloid combines synthetic and natural materials. Its successor, Bakelite, is originally completely synthetic, composed of carbolic acid mixed with formaldehyde. Later forms of bakelite also included cellulose fiber and natural pigments.

Many types of plants can produce oil from seeds, fruit, leaves, roots, and stems. Some of these oils, like those made from olives, flax (linseed), poppies, and walnuts. Some of these were mixed with dry pigments to make early oil paints.

There are several species known as the tallow tree. In western Africa, *Pentadesma butyracea* is called the tallow tree or the butter-and-tallow tree because the oil derived from its fruit is used like butter. In India, the tallow tree is *Vateria indica*, the seeds of which produce an oily wax. The tallow tree of China is *Sapium sebiferum*, in the family Euphorbiaceae. The waxy oil from the seeds of this tree is used to make candles.

Jojoba oil was first produced as a possible substitute for the spermaceti oil or wax derived from sperm whales. Jojoba oil is pressed from the seeds of the jojoba tree (*Simmondsia chinensis*), which is a member of the Euphorbiaceae family. This oil is very stable and resistant to oxidation. Its uses are mostly cosmetic, in shampoos, lotions, and sun block lotions. It is also used as a lubricant, as a polish, and mixed with other oils and wax in water-resistant coatings and candles.

Wax is a general term for compounds that share certain physical properties. There are many natural sources of wax, both animal and plant, and some are produced synthetically, mostly from petroleum. Natural waxes are complex compounds of fatty acids and other organic molecules. Each wax is unique, with properties specific to its source.

Vegetable or plant waxes are obtained from a variety of plant groups, some from external coatings, and some from internal secretions. These natural waxes are sometimes mixed with other compounds, including plant and animal oils and synthetic wax. Vegetable waxes have a wide range of uses, including precision casting, coatings on paper, fabric, fruit, and candy, in cosmetics, polishes, pharmaceuticals, and as a base for chewing gum. These compounds are resistant to electrical current and water, which makes them useful as coatings on wire and electrical devices.

Candelilla wax or cerote is a scaly coating on the stems and leaves of some members of the genus *Euphorbia* that grow in the hot, dry Chihuahuan desert of northern Mexico and the southwestern USA. The waxy coating protects the plant from dehydration in the fierce sun and wind. To remove the wax, the entire plant is boiled in water, with mild sulfuric acid added. The wax is skimmed from the surface of the liquid and dried.

Carnauba and ouricuri are waxes collected from the leaves of South American palm trees, mostly in Brazil. The palm leaves are cut and dried in the sun. They are then beaten to remove the wax particles. The palms that produce these waxes grow slowly, and only a certain number of leaves can be taken each year without killing the tree.

Rice wax or rice bran wax is a by-product of the milling of rice. It is commonly used as a coating on food for sale, in chocolate, and as a base for lipstick and other cosmetics.

Esparto wax is a by-product of the processing of a Mediterranean plant known as esparto grass, needle grass, or Halfah grass (*Stipa tenacissima*). This perennial grass is used for making high-quality paper. This wax is only produced in small quantities and is rarely used outside Europe.

Japan wax is actually more of a stiff vegetable oil. It is extracted from the fruit and seeds of various Asian species of *Rhus* and *Toxicodendron*. This substance is inexpensive and extensively used in lotions, cosmetics, and to make candles, even though it oxidizes readily and turns rancid as it ages.

Montan and ozocerite are two wax compounds found associated with fossilized plant material. Historically, these compounds have been found in coal deposits and exploited without much processing. They are now produced as by-products of the processing of lignite and sub-bituminous coal.

Perfume and Other Scented Things

Plant and animal products have been combined into a wide variety of scented forms. The purposes for this vary from disguising unpleasant odors, to attracting a mate, or to just liking the smell.

Perfume is the most concentrated form of a liquid scent. Toilet water and cologne are dilute variations. Potpourri is a mixture of naturally-scented plant parts, usually flower petals, seeds, leaves, and bark. Incense is a substance that gives off a scent when heated. These are usually plant resins, either used in their natural state or combined with other substances to increase or change the smell.

Plant-derived scents may come from any part of a plant; flower, bark, wood, seeds, leaves, root, or sap. Most natural scents are volatile and have a definite life-span. Objects that may have held scent at one time rarely do so after many months have passed.

While perfumes may be simple or complex, they all consist of three principle ingredients: the main scent, secondary or blender scents, and a fixative. The main scent is usually potent, and is balanced by the secondary scents added to it. The fixative is a compound that holds the whole thing together. Some fixatives work best for certain scents. The example, the best fixative for lavender scent is orris root.

Jojoba oil is derived from the seeds of the jojoba tree (*Simmondsia chinensis*), which is grown commercially in Mexico, Arizona, and Southern California.

This oil is very stable and lasts for a long time without oxidizing. It was originally promoted as a substitute for spermaceti, the oil derived from whales. Most of its uses are cosmetic, in soap, shampoo, sun-tan lotions, and skin cream. Mixed with other compounds, it is useful in lubricants, candles, polish for wood and leather, and as moisture-resistant coatings.

Frankincense or olibanum is an aromatic resin that is used as incense. It is the dried milky sap of trees in the genus *Boswellia*. Myrrh is the dried sap of trees in the genus *Commiphora*. Both of these genera are in the family Burseraceae, which also includes olives. Myrrh is used in perfumes and as incense. Both frankincense and myrrh were used as trade items, and their most popular uses were as incense at funerals and as additives in wine.

Tar and Asphalt

Tar is a dark-colored viscous fluid that results from the decomposition of wood, coal, or petroleum. It is produced commercially, usually as a product of the processing of coal into coke.

Asphalt is a natural dark-colored solid made of complex hydrocarbons. This material occurs in solid form, sometimes called asphaltum or gilsonite, or in liquid form when heated. The latter may form pools at the ground surface, like those at La Brea in Los Angeles, California. Asphalt is most often found at or near the Earth's surface, the result of the natural break-down of petroleum. It is sometimes concentrated in porous rock.

Historically, asphalt has been mined for use as mortar for building and paving stones, as a water-proof road surface and lining for ditches and ponds, and as calking for ships. Both asphalt and tar have been used to seal or calk boat hulls, shingles, and fabric. In medicine, they have been used to seal wounds and as a disinfectant. Tar is used to flavor candy and as an ingredient in dandruff shampoo and cosmetics.

Creosote is the common name applied to variety of products, including coal tar, coal tar pitch, wood creosote, and coal tar creosote. These materials are created by the high temperature treatment of hardwoods or coal, or from the sap of the creosote bush (*Larrea tridentata*). Some of these compounds are used medicinally, as disinfectants or laxatives, and to treat skin diseases. They are also used as coatings to prevent the decomposition of wood, as insecticides, and fungicides.

Dyes

Many plants produce compounds that can be used to stain or dye other materials. These coloring agents may come from bark, root, flower, fruit, seed, or the entire plant. Lichens, algae, and fungus have also been used to produce dyes. The hue and quality of the colors produced may be consistent for a

Figure 4.12

This Iriquois mask is made of a mixture of plant and animal materials: wood, pigments, horse hair, corn husks, copper, and a feather.

particular plant, or may vary according to the season, amount of moisture present, and the health and age of the plant (see Table 4.5).

Most vegetable dyes are applied to natural animal or plant fibers that have already been spun into yarn or thread. Some, like henna (*Lawsonia inermis*) are used as dyes for hair, leather, paper, and wood, and may be used as pigments for painting on various materials, including skin. Henna is commonly used for body decorations and temporary "henna tattoos."

Mordant is a compound that is combined with dye to make it "fast" or less likely to fade. Some mordants contain metallic salts that can change or enhance the dye color. Compounds commonly used as mordants include alum, Glauber's salts, tannic acid, tin (stannous chloride), and copperas (iron sulfate).

Table 4.5   Examples of plant materials and mordants used to produce dye (after Lesch, 1970).

Resultant color	Plant common name	Plant part used	Mordant
Red or pink	Bloodroot	Root	Tin
	Crabapple	Fruit	Alum
	Cudbear (lichen)	Whole lichen mass	Alum
	Lavender + rosemary	Infusion of leaves and stems	Alum
Purple	Purple grapes	Fruit	Tin
	Elderberry	Fruit (berries)	Alum
	Blackberry	Fruit (berries)	Tin
Brown or tan	Oak	Acorns (seeds)	Alum
	Black walnut	Nut hulls	Alum
	Coffee	Beans (seeds)	Alum
Orange or rust brown	Henna	Leaves	Tin
	Madder	Root	Chrome
Yellow	Red onion	Outer skin of root	Chrome
	Turmeric	Whole plant	Alum
	Yellow onion	Outer skin of root	Alum
Green	Indigo	Whole plant	Chrome
	Privet	Leaves and twigs	Copperas
Blue	Elderberry	Fruit (berries)	Chrome or tin
	Indigo	Whole plant	Alum

Plant Materials in Collections

Plants and plant products appear in museum collections in many forms. Environmental and storage conditions that are ideal for a botanical specimen are generally good for products made from parts of the same plant. Composite objects, however, must be considered for all the different materials they contain, and an environmental compromise reached that will be the best for the thing as a whole. Sometimes the best treatment for a composite object is to take it apart so that the different materials can be stored separately.

Botanical Specimens

Traditional botanical specimens are plants that have been pressed, dried, and mounted on a standard-sized sheet of high-quality, acid-free paper. Most herbaria use paper that is specifically made for this purpose. Seeds and small plant parts are contained in seed packets, which are folded out of high-rag, acid-free paper. These may be attached to the larger botanical sheets to which they are related, or stored separately.

Some botanical specimens may be wet-preserved, stored in a solution of 70% ethanol (alcohol) mixed with water. These are usually bulky or woody materials that do not lend themselves to pressing, such as tubers, thick stems, bark, or succulents.

As colors and textures of plants usually change as the specimen dries, and the general shape may be altered by pressing, photographs or accurate drawings are an important part of any botanical collection. The appearance of the living plant is an important part of the data on a specimen. Photos may also record the environment in which the plant was found, and what other species were present.

Wood specimens made consist of slices, cores, or other cut samples of varying sizes. Bark is also kept as part of a specimen, although often separately.

Created Objects

Historical, library, and anthropological collections contain plant materials in many forms. Most common are the many forms of wood, fabric, and paper.

Baskets and other items made from woven plant materials are usually not intended to last for many years, and are often made quickly. In collections, these objects often arrive showing signs of wear or other damage, which makes them even more susceptible to damage from water or pests.

Items made of rubber or gutta-percha may be difficult to identify. They are generally dark in color and may show mold marks. Natural, unvulcanized latex objects often show signs of deterioration, such as shrinkage, embrittlement, and distortion. Vulcanized latex may have a sulfurous odor, particularly if the environment is warm and moist. This material may become brittle with age, particularly if it has been exposed to repeated changes in temperature. High-sulfur vulcanized latex may also secrete enough sulfur to affect surrounding objects in a collection.

Most plant materials and plant products are highly susceptible to damage from moisture and pests. Dried plant materials are generally highly flammable. Some objects made of plant materials are coated with varnish, resin, or other coatings to protect them from moisture and pests. These compounds may increase the flammability of the object.

Figure 4.13

This Hopi Aholi kachina is made from the soft root of the cottonwood tree, and is decorated with wool, feathers, and fabric.

5

Invertebrate Animals

Introduction to Animals and Classification

All animals are members of the Kingdom Animalia, which is also sometimes called Kingdom Metazoa. All members of the Animalia are multicellular and heterotrophic, meaning they rely directly or indirectly on other organisms for their nourishment. Most animals ingest food and digest it in an internal cavity.

Most animals are capable of complex and relatively rapid movement compared to plants and other organisms. Most reproduce sexually, by means of differentiated eggs and sperm. Most animals are diploid, meaning that the cells of adults contain two copies of genetic material.

Animal cells lack the rigid cell walls that characterize plant cells. The bodies of most animals (all except sponges) are made up of cells organized into tissues, each tissue specialized to some degree to perform specific functions. In most cases, tissues are organized into even more specialized organs.

The development of most animals is characterized by distinctive stages, including a zygote, formed by the product of the first few division of cells following fertilization; a blastula, which is a hollow ball of cells formed by the developing zygote; and a gastrula, which is formed when the blastula folds in on itself to form a double-walled structure with an opening to the outside, the blastopore.

Somewhere around 9 or 10 million species of animals inhabit the Earth. The exact number will probably never be known. And, since the origin of life on Earth, uncounted millions of species have come and gone, only a small number of which left behind evidence of their passing.

Animals range in size from no more than a single cell to complex organisms weighing many tons, such as blue whales and giant squid. The majority of all animals inhabit the world's oceans, with fewer in fresh water and even fewer on land.

Animals are separated into thirty-five phyla, only the more common of which will be discussed here (see Table 5.1). All but the Chordata are invertebrates, animals that have no vertebral column (backbone) nor a notochord, the primitive beginnings of one. Invertebrates inhabit all types of water, they fly, they burrow, and they crawl on the ground. About 98% of all living animals

Table 5.1

Some invertebrate phyla.

Phylum	Examples	Notes
Porifera	Sponges	Porous body, no tissue or organs; sessile; mostly marine, a few freshwater
Cnidaria (Coelenterata)	Jellyfish, corals, sea anemones, hydrozoans	Two body layers, stinging cells, mostly marine, a few freshwater
Platyhelminthes	Flatworms, planaria, tapeworms	Incomplete digestive systems; freshwater and marine; many are parasites
Nematoda	Roundworms, nematodes, hookworms, plant parasites	Round worm-like body, complete digestive systems; terrestrial, freshwater and marine; many are parasites
Mollusca	Clams, snails, slugs, cephalopods, chitons	Soft body, most with hard outer shell; marine, freshwater and terrestrial
Annelida	Segmented worms, leeches	Body segmentation, complex organ systems; marine, freshwater and terrestrial, some are parasites
Arthropoda	Insects, spiders, trilobites*, ticks, scorpions, centipedes, crustaceans, eurypterids*	Jointed appendages, hard exoskeleton; largest and most diverse group; freshwater, marine and terrestrial
Bryozoa	Bryozoa "moss animals"	Sessile, colonial, freshwater and marine
Brachiopoda	Lamp shells	Marine, most resemble clams
Echinodermata	Starfish, urchins, crinoids, sand dollars, sea cucumbers	Spiny-skinned, pentaradial (five-part) symmetry; marine, most are sedentary or sessile
Chordata	Tunicates, fish, amphibians, reptiles, birds, mammals	Dorsal hollow nerve chord, notochord; marine, freshwater and terrestrial

* All extinct.

are invertebrates, estimated at between 3 and 15 million species, as opposed to only 47,000 species of vertebrates.

Porifera

The sponges are simple animals without internal organs or lots of specialized cells. They live attached to the floor of the ocean or, in a few cases, in streams or lakes. Sponges suck water and nutrients in through body pores and expel it again after nutrients have been filtered out. Support for the body tissues is provided by spicules, tiny hard structures made of either calcium carbonate or silica. In some sponges, the spicules are fused together into a lattice, while in others they are unfused and random. Sponges in the class Demospongiae may also have a tough support structure made of the fibrous protein spongin. Cleaned and dried, these are the commercial sponges used for washing. Glass sponges are those that have a fused silica skeleton, a lattice made of siliceous spicules. These delicate structures were sometimes collected as curiosities and carry common names like "Venus' flower basket."

Cnidaria or Coelenterates

The only members of this group of interest here are the corals, which are a large group of invertebrates that live singly or in colonies. The hard corals construct elaborate, rigid calcareous exoskeletons, which can build up over generations, forming coral reefs. Soft corals are solitary, more flexible animals that have calcareous particles in their cell walls.

The exoskeletons of hard colonial corals provide support and protection for the soft-bodied animals that live in them (see Figure 5.1). When these animals die, whatever organic pigments were present fade, leaving behind the calcareous structures. Dried corals may contain inorganic pigments such as iron oxide that provide color, but most hard corals are white or gray.

Decorative coral is usually one of the hard corals. They are described by color, rather than by species, and live in tropical and temperate seas. The traditional orange or red "precious" coral is native to the Mediterranean and has been severely over-collected for hundreds of years. Most red coral on today's market is dyed coral from the Pacific Ocean. Black coral is a branching, tropical type that is also rare. There are a number of corals that are collected and sold today as black coral, but it is often merely dark-colored coral that has been dyed black.

Figure 5.1

Live corals like this one are colonies of many animals living together, supported by their hard calcareous exoskeleton.

Mollusca

The mollusks are a huge, diverse group of animals that share certain characteristics. They have a soft body that is divided into three basic parts. The head-foot mass contains sensory and motor organs, the visceral mass contains the digestive, reproductive, and excretory organs, and the mantle is the outer mass which surrounds the viscera and, in some animals, secretes the shell. The radula is a movable toothed strip of hard chiton that can be pushed out of the animal's mouth and used to scrape food off surfaces and draw it back toward the digestive tract or gut. Some species use the radula to attack other animals, scraping holes in their shells or rasping soft tissue so it can be easily digested.

Many groups of mollusks produce hard outer shells that protect and support the soft-bodied animals within. These shells have a layered structure, and are composed mostly of calcium carbonate. Figure 5.3 shows the basic structure of mollusk shell. In some groups, there is a chitinous covering over the shell, called the periostracum. This brown fibrous layer dries and often wears away after the animal dies. Some gastropods also carry an operculum, a hard plate of shell material that can be used to seal up the aperture or shell opening, protecting the soft-bodied animal within. Opercula are usually flat or ribbed on the inner surface and convex and smooth on the outside.

Figure 5.2

The artist who created this carving took advantage of the natural branched shape of the coral from which it is made.

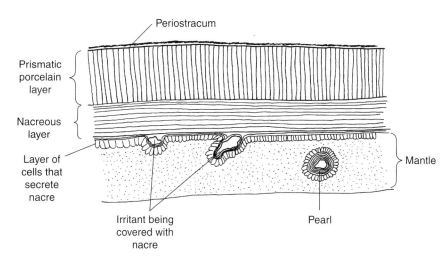

Periostracum

Prismatic
porcelain
layer

Nacreous
layer

Layer of
cells that
secrete
nacre

Irritant being
covered with
nacre

Pearl

Mantle

Figure 5.3

Structure of mollusk shell.

There are seven classes of living mollusks, only the four most common of which will be covered here. The class Bivalvia includes over 7500 species of two-shelled mollusks. These animals, which are also called pelecypods, carry two calcareous shells that meet at a hinge, where they are attached with flexible ligaments. There are large muscles attached to the inside of each shell, which allow the animal to open and close them at will. Some bivalves, like scallops, can move their shells apart and together fast enough to propel themselves through the water. Some bivalves can move about or dig burrows for themselves using their strong foot muscle. Others, like mussels and oysters, are sessile, attached to a substrate during their whole adult lives.

Gastropods are the largest group of mollusks, with over 38,000 species known. This diverse group includes animals with shells and without shells that live in seawater, freshwater, and on land. Gastropods without shells include terrestrial and marine slugs. Gastropod shells are coiled, beginning with the protoconch, the larval beginnings of the shell. The animal secretes shell continuously throughout its life, depositing it along the leading edge of the aperture. As the body grows, it needs more room, and so creates a progressively larger home for itself. Some gastropods, like the ear shells or abalone (genus *Haliotis*) and limpets (like genera *Acmaea* and *Fissurella*) have a very wide aperture.

Cephalopods are the smartest and most complex of the mollusks. This group includes squid, octopus, cuttlefish, and chambered nautilus. The ammonites were an extremely diverse and successful group of cephalopods that roamed the world's oceans for millions of years until their extinction at the end of the Cretaceous period, about 65 million years ago.

Arthropods

Arthropods are invertebrates having a hard exoskeleton, a segmented body, and jointed appendages. The body is generally divided into three segments, the head, the thorax, and the abdomen. In some cases, two of these segments are fused. Pairs of specialized appendages grow from various body segments. These include legs, wings, mouth parts, and antennae. The outer skeleton is composed mostly of chiton, a polymer made of glucose molecules combined with nitrogen-bearing molecules.

Most arthropods lay eggs, which hatch into larvae. Some are viviparous, like scorpions, and bear live young. As most arthropods grow, they shed or molt their outer skin covering a number of times before becoming adults. There are some groups that metamorphose from larva to adult inside a cocoon or pupa of their own making.

The phylum Arthropoda contains more species than any other group of organisms. There are over one million species described, and undoubtedly many more to be discovered. The phylum is divided into three subphyla: trilobites, all of which are extinct, Chelicerata, which have no jaws or antennae, and Mandibulata, which have jaws and antennae.

Trilobites were a highly diverse group of marine arthropods that lived throughout the world's oceans from the Cambrian to the Permian, about 520 to 245 million years ago. They swam or skimmed over the bottom of the sea, lay on the sea floor, or plowed through the sand and mud. These animals are common in paleontological collections. Large specimens or slabs containing interesting specimens are sometimes used as decorations. Small individuals are sometimes mounted in jewelry.

Chelicerata include horseshoe crabs, sea spiders, scorpions, ticks, mites, and spiders. This group also includes the eurypterids or "sea scorpions" that became extinct in the Late Devonian, about 360 million years ago. This group is characterized by a cephalothorax, which is a fusion of head and thorax segments, and an abdomen. The cephalothorax usually carries six pairs of appendages. The first pair is chelicera, which take the place of jaws. The second pair are called pedipalps, which can be used for walking, chewing, or grasping. The rest of the appendages are walking legs. Most members of the Chelicerata are terrestrial, but some groups, like the horseshoe crabs, live only in the water.

The Mandibulata is by far the largest group of arthropods, since it contains the insects. Animals in this group have two or three body segments, one or two pairs of antennae, and one pair of mandibles. The subphylum Mandibulata is divided into six classes, the largest two of which are the Hexapoda (insects) and Crustacea (crustaceans).

Insects are typified by three main body segments, which are themselves further segmented, antennae, mandibles, three pairs of legs, two pairs of wings, and compound eyes. There is incredible diversity in this huge group and body types and sizes vary greatly.

Insects are of interest as specimens in collections, but also as pests and agents of deterioration in collections of all kinds. They also contribute body parts, like wings, and chemicals to the manufacture of objects and materials found in collections.

The class Insecta is divided into three subclasses, the Archaeognatha, which are the bristletails; the Zygentomas, which includes primitive wingless insects like silverfish, and the Pterygota, which includes everybody else, who all have wings. The Pterygota is, in turn, divided into two groups according to how and where the wings develop. The Exopteryogota develop wings on the outside of the body during the gradual metamorphosis from the immature larvae to adult. When these insects hatch from an egg, they look like miniature adults, only without wings. As they grow, they shed their exoskeleton a number of times, as it becomes too small for the expanding body. Each of these steps is called an instar. The animal in these growth stages is called a nymph on land, or a naiad in the water. The Exopteryogota includes grasshoppers, crickets, cockroaches, earwigs, termites, dragonflies, true bugs, lice, and scale insects.

Butterflies, moths, flies, beetles, bees, wasps, ants, fleas, and some other groups belong to the Endopterygota. In these insects, the wings develop inside the larva, and metamorphosis from larva to adult is relatively abrupt. The larva or caterpillar that hatches from the egg molts as it grows in a series of instars. At the last molt stage, the caterpillar becomes a pupa, usually inside a woven cocoon or a hardened exoskeletal pupal case. During this last stage, the insect develops adult features, like wings and legs, which are mature and usable immediately upon its emergence from its protective housing.

Butterflies, and to a lesser extent moths, have been collected for their wings, which are used in many types of decorative objects and adornments. Some of these insects are captively bred or cultured so that the wings of the adults can be collected and used (Figure 5.4).

The infamous aphrodisiac or passion-stimulator called Spanish Fly is not made of flies, but rather of dried and crushed beetles from several different genera. The resulting powder contains cantharidin, a compound that causes a strong burning sensation when taken orally or if rubbed on the skin. The increased blood flow caused by this irritation can prolong sexual stimulation. Similar effects have been obtained with mixtures of sugar, paprika, ginseng, licorice root, and various peppers.

The Crustacea is the second largest group within the Arthropods. This diverse group includes lobsters, crabs, shrimp, sow bugs, barnacles, and many other forms. Over 38,000 species of crustacea are known and there are probably many more yet to be discovered. Most Crustacea have a hard chitinous exoskeleton, three body segments, two pairs of antennae, and gills for breathing. Most

Figure 5.4

Butterfly wings have been used to decorate fabrics, wood, and many other types of materials.

have a telson, a terminal segment on the back of the abdomen that often resembles a tail. Except for barnacles, which are sessile, crustaceans can move about freely, walking, swimming, or crawling, mostly in water.

Crustaceans are good to eat, and many species of vertebrates, including whales, fish, and people, include them in their diets. They are important links in the food chains in many different marine and terrestrial habitats.

Products

Silk

A number of insects and other invertebrates create thin fibers, for a variety of reasons. Spiders make webs for support and to capture and encase their prey. Some bivalve mollusks create byssal threads that anchor the animal's shell to rocks or other substrate.

Silk fabric and thread are derived from the cocoons that some insects make as part of their metamorphosis from caterpillar to butterfly or moth. Most commercial silk is created by *Bombyx mori*, a small moth that was originally native to Asia. These animals no longer live in the wild, and in cultured populations they have lost their ability to fly.

Tussah is silk made from the cocoon of the wild silkworm, *Antheraea pernyi* or *A. melitta*. The latter animals tend to produce silk that is coarser and of lower quality than that produced by *B. mori*.

When the internal clock inside a caterpillar (i.e. hormones) tells it that the time is right, it creates a pupa or cocoon made of silk filaments secreted by two glands on its head. The tiny threads are combined, as they form, with a gummy substance that glues them together.

The gummy glue holding the cocoon together consists of sericin, which is brittle and hard when dry, but which dissolves in boiling water. The filaments are made of fibroin, which is strong and elastic, and unaffected by hot water. The processing of silk depends on these factors, that the glue will dissolve and the silk fibers will be undamaged by boiling water.

Unhatched cocoons are boiled to dissolve the gum holding them together. This has the unfortunate effect of killing the animal inside. One cocoon can yield from 300 to 1600 yards of fiber.

There is still some gum present on the silk fibers when they are spun and woven. This is removed during another "degumming boiling." The total weight loss from dissolved sericin glue is about 20%.

The innermost and outer layers of the cocoon are regarded as waste material, as are inferior cocoons, or those that already hatched. This material is degummed and carded, yielding short-fiber silk that is called "schappe." The degumming process of these fibers often involves fermentation in manure.

Silk fabric has many names, depending on its weight, weave, and intended use. Some of these are velvet, brocade, chiffon, crepe, crepe de chine, damask, faille, gauze, georgette, jacquard, moire, satin, taffeta, and tulle. Fabrics having the appearance of silk, but made from other natural or man-made fibers, may also bear these names. But originally and rightly, these names are only applied to silk fabric.

Tussah or wild silk is obtained from caterpillars that are not cultivated, living naturally on mulberry, cherry, or oak trees. The cocoons are gathered by and processed by hand, resulting in an uneven and irregular product. Tussah is tan or brownish, depending on where the caterpillar had been living and what it had been eating. Tussah is often mixed with other fibers to produce hybrid fabrics.

Shellac, Dye and Wax

The Coccoidea is a large family of insects that live by sucking fluids from living plants. Some of these insects, most of which are very small, secrete resinous cocoons on the tree stems and branches on which they feed. This resin is called sticklac, and is harvested by collecting the affected plant parts. The resin-coated branches are dried and pulverized, run through a sieve, and washed. The end product is called seedlac, which is then further processed to produce shellac. Shellac is used as an insulating coating on electrical equipment and wire, as an adhesive, to make early phonograph records and cylinders, and as a surface polish and sealer for wood and metal.

Although many members of the Coccoidea produce resin, the most commercially important is *Laccifer lacca*, also known as the lac insect. The bright red pigment present in the body of *Laccifer lacca* has been used as a dye, mostly for use on leather, wool, and silk. In India, it is used as a cosmetic pigment. In order to obtain both dye and resin, the sticklac must be harvested before the insects emerge from their cocoons, since it is only in their pre-emergent state that the dye is present. This and other lac-producing insects are cultured on host trees as a continuous source of sticklac and lac pigment.

Some other members of the Coccoidea produce waxy secretions that are collected, concentrated, and used for a variety of purposes. These waxes have several names, including Chinese insect wax and Japanese insect wax. Both lac and insect wax are produced largely in China, India, and southeast Asia.

Cochineal is the name used for red dye made from either the lac insects mentioned previously, or from related insects that parasitize prickly pear and other cactus species in Mexico and Central America. These insects are all small, and it takes about 70,000 of them to produce 1 pound of cochineal.

The tissue of some mollusks can be used to produce rich and intense dyes. Purple, red, and blue dyes are historically the most popular products of these invertebrates, almost all of which are members of the Muricidae, the murex family of marine snails.

Beeswax is the compound made by bees to form their structural nests. Many species of bees produce wax, but most commercially produced beeswax is made by *Apis mellifera*, the common honeybee. Ghedda is a general term for wax produced by other types of bees, particularly those from Asia.

The wax is created by young bees who secrete it from glands on their abdomens. The insect scrapes the small platelets of wax off and chews them into a soft mass, adding enzymes and moisture. The masticated wax is added to the comb, and chewed into place.

The composition of beeswax varies by insect species and by what the bees have been eating. Beeswax has a low melting point, and is often cast into useful or decorative shapes. Combined with resins, it was used as a water-proofing and adhesive. It has been used as a coating on paintings and furniture, to enhance the appearance of and to protect the surfaces from moisture. It was used as a water-repellent and adhesive in ships and boats. Beeswax has been applied to fabric, cordage, and hair to add luster and increase water-resistance, and as a base for cosmetic and medicinal creams and lotions. Beeswax was the primary and best available material for making candles until the invention of paraffin wax, which is a by-product of the distillation of petroleum.

Shell

Some mollusks produce a hard exoskeleton that is composed of calcium carbonate, sometimes mixed with conchiolin, a schleroprotein. Either or both of the two common polymorphs of calcium carbonate may exist in one shell (calcite and aragonite). The composition and structure of the shell varies according to the species of animal, its age, and health.

Mollusk shells consist of two structural parts, the outer porcelain layer, in which the crystals of calcium carbonate are aligned perpendicular to the outside of the shell, and the thinner inner nacre, in which the crystals are laid down parallel to the inside of the shell (see Figure 5.3).

When the animal is alive, the shell may be covered with a layer of fibrous tissue known as the periostracum. This layer may be very thin and translucent, or thick and dark. It is composed of chitin, a polysaccharide that also makes up the exoskeletons of insects and other arthropods.

Mollusks are harvested for their meat and, in some cases, for shell and pearls. Shells have been used whole, as decorative objects and as currency. Money shells in tropical regions are most often cowries, members of the genus *Cypraea*, and were common forms of currency in Asia, Southeast Asia, and parts of Africa. Tribes that inhabited coastal areas in both North and South America collected shells that would be used whole or cut into various shapes as trade items. This currency, sometimes called wampum, is sometimes found in burials and other sites hundreds of miles from the sea.

Figure 5.5

Shell brooch is made from the shiny inner nacreous layer of shell. The layered texture of the nacre is clearly visible.

Once the meat has been extracted, mollusk shells are usually discarded. Huge middens or piles of clam, oyster, and other shells disclose the appetite people have for these animals. Shells have sometimes been processed, either fresh or from middens, to provide calcium carbonate for a variety of purposes. Calcium carbonate has a huge number of practical uses in medicine, food production, chemicals, cosmetics, building materials, and many more.

Since shell is composed mostly of calcium carbonate, it is relatively easy to cut and grind into useful shapes. Although it is not as hard as stone, bone or ivory, shell is often used in preference to these materials because it may be easier to get, easier to work, and lighter in weight. And sometimes the attractive colors or shape of some shells may have influenced artisans to choose them over other, hardier materials.

Native American artists created small round discs of shell that were drilled in the center and used as beads or bead separators. These are called heishi, a word that originally meant "shell." A shell is first cut or broken into small flat tiles, and a hole is drilled in the center of each. They are then strung tightly together on wire or cord. The entire strand is then ground against a stone or a turning wheel until the discs are round. Modern heishi are made in many different materials and are often produced by machine.

Puka shells originated in Hawaii, where the flat broken tops of worn *Conus* shells were used as decorations or beads. Beach worn cone shells were often found as concave round fragments with a natural central hole where the spire had broken off. The Hawaiians took this a step further by creating their own pukas out of cone and other mollusk shells that were not quite so worn, but that were the right size and shape to be used as beads. A round shell, usually slightly concave, is drilled in the center and strung as beads. The word puka means "hole" in Hawaiian.

The layered structure of shell has made it popular with artists producing cameos, layered carvings that usually take advantage of differently colored layers in a material. In shell cameos, the design is usually carved from the white outer porcelain layer, with the background cut down into the more strongly colored nacre below. Most shell cameos are made from large gastropods in the genus *Cassis*, which are called helmet shells. Moderate to large-sized cameos tend to retain some of the natural curvature of the shell. This is one way to distinguish shell cameos from those made of stone or other materials, which tend to be flat (Figure 5.6).

Shells have also been etched to create patterns in the different layers. Early artists would create a design on the shell using tar or wax, and then etch the unprotected areas using acidic plant fluids. The coating would then be removed, leaving a raised pattern or design. Modern etching is done with acids or sand-blasting.

Shells have been used as tools, sometimes in their original form and sometimes with modifications. Large bivalves or snail shells are useful as scoops,

Figure 5.6

Shell cameo designs are usually carved from the white porcelain shell layer against a background of the darker nacreous layer underneath.

scrapers, bowls, hoes, shovels, and lamps (floating oil type). Really big shells, like those of the giant clam *Tridacna gigas* have been used for more exotic purposes, such as bathroom sinks or church fonts.

Some large gastropods have been used as trumpets or horns. A hole was ground or cut at the small end of a big coiled shell to give the trumpeter an opening into which he could blow. The resulting sound depended on the size and shape of the shell, and the strength of the blower. A variety of shells have been used in this way, mostly from the genera *Cassis, Bursa, Charonia*, and *Strombus*.

Arrangements of shells in a frame, or merely glued to a backing are popular craft items. These have been as art by home crafters for hundreds of years, and are also sold as tourist items. Sea shell figurines and other three-dimensional composite objects are also popular souvenirs from areas of the world where shells are readily available.

The nacre, or smooth inner layer of mollusk shells, is sometimes brightly colored and attractive. Some invertebrate animals have been hunted to near-extinction for their brilliant nacre. An example of this is the Paua shell,

Figure 5.7

Large items are made from the thickest parts of a shell. This large bivalve has been marked for cutting, and will be used for many different items.

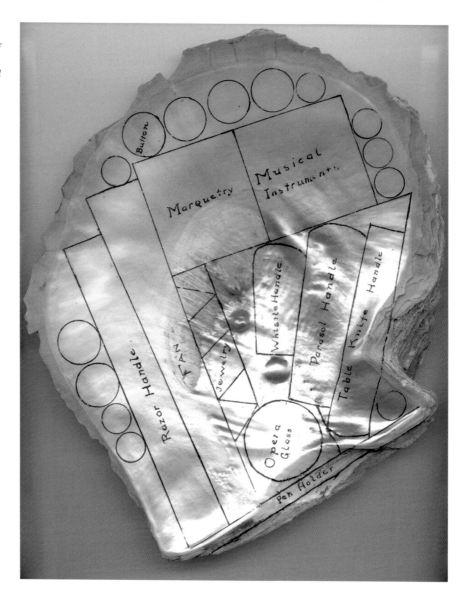

Haliotis iris, which has a beautiful dark blue iridescent nacre. Cut into various shapes, these shells are made into jewelry and as inlay.

Shell has been cut into a huge variety of forms that are intended to be used with the shiny nacre uppermost. Sometimes the nacre is used alone, but some of the porcelain layer is often retained to give an object strength. "Mother of Pearl" is the name given to objects that are made from the nacreous layer of shell, whether it includes the porcelain or not (Figure 5.7).

The opercula is a plate of shell material that some gastropods use to close up the shell opening like a trap door. These plates are usually round, and may be white or carry the same pigments as the main part of the shell. Opercula usually become separated from the rest of the animal when it dies and the tissues holding it in place decompose. Brightly colored opercula have been used as decorations, often because they look like eyes.

Pearls

Pearls are growths that form inside the shells of mollusks, usually in response to the presence of a parasite or other irritant. They are composed of layers of nacre that the animal secretes over the foreign body. Pearls tend to be the same color as the nacre inside the shell. Sometimes pearls are loose, forming in the mantle cavity, and sometimes they become attached to the inside of the shell. These latter pearls are called blisters and may contain rotten organic matter or a smaller, loose pearl.

Natural or oriental pearls are produced naturally by bivalves, such as oysters and clams, and by a few gastropods, such as abalone. Cultured pearls are induced by the introduction of foreign objects into the mantle cavity. Modern cultured pearls are usually "seeded" with a sphere made from the shell of Mississippi River mussels (family Unionidae). The culturing process involves prying open the shell and inserting both the seed or nucleus that will become the core of the new pearl, and a piece of "donated" mantle tissue from another oyster.

Mabe pearls are based on a hemispherical nucleus that is inserted through a hole drilled in the outside of the oyster's shell and glued into place. The animal inside will secrete nacre over this round knob which, when harvested, will yield a large pearl that is flat on one side. Mabes and other blister pearls can only be harvested by killing the oyster, since they must be cut out of the shell.

The longer a cultured pearl stays in the oyster, the more layers of nacre there will be. If a pearl is harvested too soon after the nucleus is deposited, the layers of lustrous nacre may be so thin that they wear away when the pearl is used in jewelry.

Cultured freshwater pearls are produced by placing a tiny piece of mantle tissue inside the shell. Some bivalves can take many of these tissue "seeds" at the same time, unlike marine oysters, which will usually only make one or two pearls at a time.

Cultured and natural pearls can usually be distinguished from each other with the use of a medical x-ray. Cultured pearls will show a core bead of flat layered shell with thin layers of nacre around it, while natural pearls will be concentric throughout.

Pearls are usually described in terms of their shape, color, and diameter. Descriptions of larger pearls also often include weight measurements. Pearl weight is expressed in terms of carats, grains, or momme (see Appendix C: Measurements). Like other beads, pearls are often sold by the strand instead of individually. Strands may be bundled into bunches having a minimum weight, like 1 kg.

In Collections

In museum collections, most invertebrates will be encountered as natural history specimens, which are divided into dry and wet-preserved. Those animals having a shell or tough exoskeleton, like starfish, shelled mollusks, and lobsters, may be dried after death. The tissue may be removed, but it is often left inside the shell or carapace to shrivel and dry. Wet-preserved specimens are usually "fixed" in a solution of formalin or some other preservative to prevent the tissues from deteriorating quickly after death. After a brief period, the specimen is usually removed from the toxic fixing solution, rinsed, and placed in a storage solution of 70% ethanol (alcohol) mixed with water.

Shells that have been used decoratively or that have been in amateur or private collections have often been cleaned and treated to enhance their appearance. This usually involves the removal of the fibrous periostracum layer, and

Figure 5.8

This lampshade holds a landscape of dried flowers and grass, and a real butterfly, all between two layers of plastic.

cleaning with soap and/or bleach. The lip of the aperture, which may be rough or broken, is often filed down by collectors who want a more perfect shell.

Shells, pearls, and other invertebrates may be found in art and anthropology collections as worked objects, or as part of composite objects. The nacreous layer of mollusk shells is commonly referred to as Mother-of-Pearl, and may be found as inlay in objects made of wood and stone, and as small decorative and utilitarian objects such as buttons, jewelry, tool handles, and small carvings. Pearls are used most often in jewelry, drilled through so that they can be strung like beads. They are also used as decoration on fabric and *objects d'art.*

Coral has been used to make cameos, beads, and other forms of jewelry. In some parts of the world, the belief that coral, particularly the red forms, contain a natural spirit, leads to its use as a charm. Items made for this purpose may include coral branches that have only been polished, but not reshaped. This is due to the belief that if the natural form is altered too much, the beneficial spirit within the coral will depart. Coral was often used to make items for children, such as small bead bracelets or necklaces and teething toys, since it was believed in some cultures that this material was a charm to protect against witches.

Invertebrates are common as fossils, and are found in rocks dating back almost to the beginning of life on Earth. Most animals that survive the fossilization process do so because their bodies include some hard part(s), such as a shell, exoskeleton, endoskeleton, or teeth. Some completely soft invertebrates, however, have been fossilized as impressions. These include jellyfish, insects, eggs, and larvae.

6

Vertebrate Animals

Introduction to Animals and Their Classification

Vertebrates are those animals that have a backbone or a notochord, a primitive spine. Compared to the other animal phyla, there are relatively few species in the Phylum Chordata, only about 50,000. As humans and most of the animals associated with them are in this group, it is of interest beyond mere numbers.

There are three subphyla within the Chordata. The first two are tunicates and amphioxus, both primitive, headless animals that will not be discussed here. The third group is the most highly developed and complex, the vertebrates or craniates (they have heads). The vertebrates have a segmented body, a cranium enclosing the brain, a heart, and a notochord or vertebral column. Other characteristics are not consistent, but most vertebrate species have bones of some kind, skin, at least two pairs of trunk appendages, and separate sexes.

Within the Phylum Chordata, the subphylum vertebrata is divided into seven classes of animals (Table 6.1).

Amphibians live in water and on land, with members of some groups going from one environment to another at some point in their lives. Most amphibian eggs are externally fertilized, and their development involves growth stages in water and on land. There are some groups, however, that are exclusively aquatic or terrestrial. Amphibians lay non-amniotic eggs that have no protective shell or strong outer membrane.

There are three orders within the class Amphibia. Order Anura is the largest of these, with over 5000 living species. This group includes frogs and toads. The order Urodela includes the 510 species of salamanders and their relatives. The smallest group is order Apoda, the caecilians, which are legless, blind, worm-like animals that borrow in the soil.

Most amphibians lay eggs in water. The hatchlings or larvae breathe in water with exterior gills. They gradually metamorphose into adults, at which point they leave the water to live on land. During the larva-to-adult transition, the gills are replaced by lungs, and four legs and eyelids develop.

Table 6.1   Classes of vertebrate animals.

Class	Examples	Notes
Agnatha	Hagfish, lampreys, slime eels	The lowest animals having vertebrate characteristics; marine eel-shaped jawless scavengers and parasites with notochord and cartilaginous fins and skeleton
Chondrichthyes	Sharks and rays	Jawed fish with tough skin and scales, skeleton of cartilage, some lay eggs, some give live birth
Osteichthyes	All other jawed fish	Jawed fish with skeleton of bone ± cartilage, most have skin scales and teeth, externally fertilized eggs
Amphibia	Frogs, toads, salamanders	Cold-blooded four-legged animals that spend part of their lives breathing in water and part on land, some lay eggs, some give live birth
Reptilia	Snakes, lizards, alligators, dinosaurs*, turtles	Terrestrial cold-blooded animals with scaly skin, four legs, breathe only in air, some lay eggs, some give live birth
Aves	Birds	Warm-blooded toothless animals with feathers, two wings and two legs, internal fertilization of shelled eggs
Mammalia	Poodles, ponies, porcupines, people	Warm-blooded animals with hair, two or four limbs, most give birth to live young, a few lay eggs

* All extinct.

Except as specimens in natural history collections, amphibians produce little in the way of materials used by artists or in the manufacture of practical objects.

Reptiles differ from the amphibians in that their eggs have a shell or outer membrane (amniotes). Most reptiles are carnivorous and lay external eggs that were fertilized internally. Some lizards, chameleons, and skinks bear live young, as do all boas, vipers, and garter snakes. All reptiles breathe with lungs, even though some spend most of their time in the water.

Reptiles are divided into four orders. The order Crocodylia includes crocodiles, alligators, and their relatives. The order Testudines includes the turtles and tortoises. The order Rhynchocephalia is represented by only two species, the tuataras of New Zealand. The largest order by far is the Squamata, which has over 7000 species of lizards, snakes, and their relatives.

Turtles, tortoises, and terrapins have both an endoskeleton of bone and an exoskeleton. The exoskeleton consists of a two-part case made of keratin. The upper portion of this structure is the carapace, which is connected to the plastron on the underside of the animal by a bony bridge. Tortoises are terrestrial, while the other members of the order Testudines spend most of their time in the water (Figure 6.1).

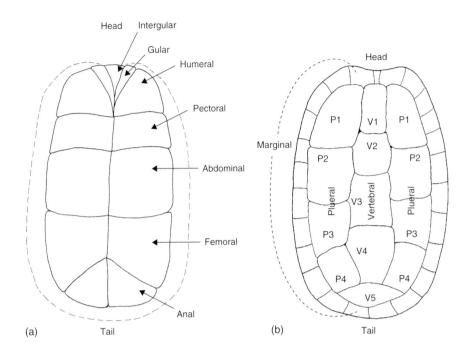

Figure 6.1

Arrangement of skutes on turtle: (a) plastron and (b) carapace.

Some reptiles have been hunted to the point of extinction for their meat, skin, and carapaces. The seven species of sea turtle are caught both at sea and on land, where they must return to lay their eggs.

Birds are warm-blooded vertebrates that lay shelled eggs, have feathers on their skin, two wings, and two legs. No living species have teeth, although some extinct birds may have had them.

Birds can be divided into two basic groups at a level between class and order, called "super orders." The Paleognathae is the smaller of the two groups, containing mostly the flightless birds and the Tinamiformes of South America. The Neognathe includes all other birds.

The Paleognathae super order includes only two orders, with few species. The Neognathae includes 26 orders, among which the Passeriformes is the largest, with over 5000 species worldwide. Table 6.2 lists the orders of birds, with some examples of each and an approximate number of living species. These numbers are approximate, since this list was compiled from several sources that did not completely agree.

Mammals are the source of much of the material of interest here, and so will be covered in more detail than the other groups. These are warm-blooded animals that have hair, and who feed their young with milk. There are three basic groups within this class: the monotremes or Metatheria, that lay eggs; the marsupials, that give live birth to underdeveloped young who are then nurtured in a pouch; and the placentals or Eutheria, whose young are

Figure 6.2

These modern jewelry items are made from feathers.

nurtured in the mother's body through a placenta. Most mammals fall into this last category. Table 6.3 lists the orders within the class Mammalia, and gives some examples of each.

Mammals live in freshwater, in seawater, on land, and underground. Some can fly or glide. Carnivores are those who eat nothing but other animals. These occur within a number of the mammalian orders, and include dogs, cats, and some whales, bats, and dolphins. The insectivores live on insects. This group includes aardvarks and other anteaters, and some bats. Herbivores are those animals that live entirely on plants and algae. These include most hoofed animals (horses, cattle, pigs, deer, etc.), most rodents, and the Lagomorphs (rabbits and such). The omnivores will eat anything, meats or plants. This group includes most bears, raccoons, skunks, and, of course, people.

Table 6.2 Orders of birds.

	Examples	Approximate number of living species
Order Paleognathae		
Struthioniformes	Ostrich, emu, cassowary, kiwi, rhea	12
Tinamiformes	Tinamous	45
Order Neognathae		
Anseriformes	Swans, geese, ducks	150
Galliformes	Grouse, partridge, pheasant, quail, turkeys	256
Sphenisciformes	Penguins	16
Gaviiformes	Loons	5
Podicipediformes	Grebes	20
Procellariiformes	Albatrosses, shearwaters, petrels	93
Pelecaniformes	Pelicans, boobies, gannets, cormorants, frigatebirds	57
Ciconiiformes	Herons, bitterns, storks, ibises, flamingoes	115
Accipitriformes	Vultures, condors, ospreys, hawks, eagles, kites	226
Falconiformes	Falcons	60
Turniciformes	Buttonquail	15
Gruiformes	Cranes, rails, bustards	196
Charadriiformes	Plovers, stilts, avocets, snipes, gulls, terns, auks	305
Pterocliformes	Sandgrouse	16
Columbiformes	Dodos, pigeons, doves	300
Psittaciformes	Cockatoos, parrots	330
Cuculiformes	Cuckoos	151
Strigiformes	Owls	134
Caprimulgiformes	Nightjars, oilbirds	96
Apodiformes	Swifts	403
Trochiliformes	Hummingbirds	325
Coliiformes	Mousebirds	6
Trogoniformes	Quetzals, trogons	35
Coraciiformes	Kingfishers, rollers, hornbills, hoopoes	192
Piciformes	Toucans, woodpeckers	376
Passeriformes	Wrens, larks, swallows, thrushes, creepers, tits, chickadees, bluebirds, crows, jays, starlings, sparrows, finches, warblers, cardinals	5200

Body Parts

Among the vast diversity of vertebrate animals, there are certain body elements that many have in common, such as skin and bones. The following is a general discussion of those body parts that have historically been used to make things, either in their natural state, or processed somehow.

Table 6.3   *Orders within the class mammalia.*

Order	Examples	# Genera*	# Species*	% of all mammal species	Geographic range**
Monotremata	Echidna and Platypus	2	3	<1%	Australia
Marsupiala	Opossum, ringtail, bandicoot, koala, wombat, kangaroo, wallaby, tasmanian devil	70	239	6%	North and South America, Australia, Asia
Insectivora	Hedgehog, mole, shrew	71	434	11%	Worldwide
Dermoptera	Flying lemur, coluga	1	2	<1%	South-east Asia
Chiroptera	Bats	173	859	22%	Worldwide
Primates	Lemur, loris, marmoset, monkey, ape, human	43	148	4%	Worldwide
Edentata	Anteater, sloth, armadillo	14	31	<1%	North, Central, and South America
Pholidota	Pangolin, Scaly Anteater	1	8	<1%	Africa, South East Asia
Tubulidentata	Aardvark	1	1	<1%	Africa
Lagomorpha	Hare, rabbit, pika	9	64	2%	Worldwide
Rodentia	Beavers, squirrel, chipmunk, marmot, porcupine, chinchillas, capybara, gopher, rat, mouse, vole, gerbil, hamster, guinea pig, nutria	340	1605	41%	Worldwide
Carnivora	Wolf, dog, jackal, fox, bear, cat, raccoon, weasel, otter, skunk, badger, mongoose, hyena	110	252	6%	Worldwide
Pinnipedia	Sea lion, seal, walrus	16	34	<1%	All oceans + Lake Baikal
Mysticeti	Right whale, grey whale, rorqual	5	10	<1%	All oceans
Odontoceti	Beaked whales, beluga whales, narwhal, sperm whale, dolphin, porpoise	32	64	2%	All oceans, and some rivers and estuaries
Sirenia	Manatees and dugongs	2	4	<1%	Subtropical Atlantic and Indo-Pacific coasts and rivers
Proboscidae	Elephant, hyrax	5	13	<1%	Africa, Middle East, India
Perissodactyla	Horse, zebra, tapir, rhinoceros	6	16	< 1%	Worldwide
Artiodactyla	Pig, peccary, hippopotamus, camel, deer, elk, moose, caribou, giraffe, cattle, sheep, goat, antelope	67	172	4%	Worldwide

* These numbers were acquired from several different sources and should be considered approximate.
** Ranges include introduced species.

Skin

Skin is the outer covering of animals that have an inner skeleton, such as mammals, reptiles, amphibians, birds, and fish. Skin, or integument, is the largest organ of a body. It performs many functions, not the least of which is the containment and protection of the other organs and processes inside the animal.

Skin varies greatly from one species to the next, but there are some general characteristics that all skin shares. It has a layered structure of specialized cells, and can contain hair follicles, pigments, scales, blood vessels, nerves, and glands.

The outermost layer of the skin is the epidermis. The cells in this layer may be hard or cornified. Some animals have specialized epidermal cells in the form of scales, feathers, and hair. Other epidermal growths include hooves, nails, claws, horns (not antlers), and beaks. Epidermal cells of all kinds are molted or shed and renewed by the growth of new cells from below. Epidermal structures such as hair and feathers may be rooted in the underlying dermis and fatty layers (see Figure 6.3).

Under the epidermis is the dermis, which holds blood vessels, nerves, pigments, and glands. The boundary between the epidermis and dermis is the germinative layer, where new cells are continuously created. Below the dermis is a layer of fatty tissue. This subcutaneous fat serves as insulation and varies in thickness according from species to species.

Leather is the preserved skin of an animal. Skin that has been merely dried is stiff and subject to mold when wet. Skins were sometimes included in dried or smoked meats, and were also used to make glue or sizing.

Parchment is the cured skin of a goat or sheep. Vellum is a finer version of parchment, made from the thin skin of young animals, usually kids, lambs, or calves, cured and sometimes bleached.

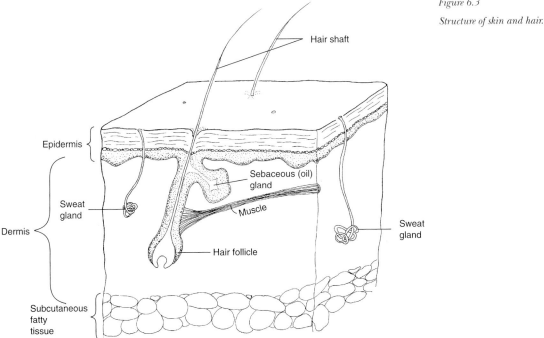

Figure 6.3

Structure of skin and hair.

The skin of sharks and rays is rough and scaly. It is dried and used as an abrasive, like sandpaper. In some Asian cultures, it has been used to decorate the handles of weapons and tools, and in making small decorative objects like snuff bottles and opium cases. If tanned like leather, shark skin can be pliable and tough, making it suitable for shoes, boots, and other objects. Shagreen is shark or ray skin that is bumpy with placoid scales. This material is often dyed and used to make coin purses, game pieces, and other small objects.

The tough skin of some reptiles, like alligators, crocodiles, and armadillos, may be tanned and used to make personal items such as shoes and purses. Skin and other body parts of these animals are also used to make novelty and household items, such as baskets, hats, and backscratchers.

Hair and Fur

Hair is a filamentous appendage that originates in the skin of mammals. It is a characteristic of mammals, although some species have very little of it, or none at some stages of life. Plant "hairs" are fine fibers, unrelated to animal hair. Hair insulates a body against hot or cold. Pigmented hair gives an animal its outward appearance and may provide camouflage. Some animals shed and grow specially pigmented hair according to the season. A rabbit or weasel that is brown during the summer may grow a white coat for winter. The pigments in hair may also change or disappear with age.

The average hair is composed of about 90% keratin, a fibrous protein, and about 10% water. Each hair consists of two or three layers. The outer layer is a sheath called the cuticle, which is thin and colorless. It is made up of overlapping scales in layers. Inside the cuticle are the long spindle-shaped cells of the cortex, which makes up the bulk of the hair. These cells also contain whatever pigments are present in the hair. The innermost layer, which is only present in large thick hair, is the medulla or pith.

The root of the hair is held in a pocket in the skin, called a follicle. The hair root is fed by blood vessels that traverse the dermal and fatty skin layers. Figure 6.4 shows the relationships among the various parts of the hair and the layers of surrounding skin.

Wool fibers are hair that is covered with tiny, lustrous scales. Oils are secreted along the hairs from glands adjacent to the hair follicles. These oils travel up the hair shaft and give the fleece its natural waterproofing. In sheep, this "wool grease" is lanolin. Wool hairs are soft, wavy and flexible (Table 6.4). Beard hairs are longer, more flexible, and are found only in the outside coat.

Sheep's wool fibers are classified by their diameter: fine (17–23 μm), medium (23–33 μm), coarse (33–42 μm), and "mixed carpet" wool (20–50 μm). Luster wool is mostly beard hairs with a medulla, and scales that are close to the stem.

Figure 6.4

This necklace is made of woven human hair and ivory decorations. Jewelry like this was often made in memory of particular person, sometimes from their own hair.

Woolens are fabrics made from woolen yarn, and there are many types, depending on the weave and weight of the material. These fabrics may contain other materials in small amounts. Worsted is woolen fabric made from good-quality wool fibers that are all roughly of the same length. Felt is matted or compressed hair or wool.

Commercial fabrics made from sheep's wool have a variety of names, depending on the weave pattern and the weight of the fabric. These include cavalry twill, challis, felt, flannel, gabardine, khaki, tweed, serge, sharkskin, velour. Cassimere is a fabric made of sheep's wool, not cashmere. It is of moderate weight and used most often for making men's suits.

Wool or hair can be harvested from a live animal by brushing or by collecting tufts as they are shed. Wool can also be harvested by shearing or shaving

Figure 6.5

Hair jewelry is usually from long, dark hairs from humans or horses.

Table 6.4 Sources of wool and fleece.

Common name	Source animal	Range
Mohair	Angora goat	
Cashmere	Cashmere goat	Tibet, India, Iran, Iraq, SW China
Goat hair	Domestic goats (many varieties)	Domesticated worldwide
Wool	Sheep (many varieties)	Domesticated worldwide
Cow hair	Domestic cattle (many varieties)	Most comes from Russia
Angora	Angora rabbit	Domesticated worldwide
Cat hair	Domestic cat (many varieties)	Domesticated worldwide
Camel hair	Bactrian (two-hump) camel	Asia
Alpaca	Alpaca	Andes Mountains
Guanaco	Guanaco or Huanaco	Argentina
Llama	Llama	Western South America
Vicuna	Vicuna	South America
Qiviut	Musk Ox	Arctic

the animal. This is usually done in the spring, when the need for a heavy coat is past, but before the animal naturally sheds its wool. Pulled wool comes from the pelt of a dead animal, and fleece is wool shorn from a living animal.

Llamas, alpacas, guanaco, and vicuna are camellids, South American relatives of modern camels. There are two hybrids also. The huarizo comes from a llama father and an alpaca mother. The misti or paco-llama is the offspring of an alpaca father and a llama mother. Llamas are the most common animal in this group. They are creatures of high altitudes, but have been domesticated as pack animals elsewhere. An adult llama weighs about 250 pounds, and is about a third the size of a camel.

The llama's thick coat has two layers. The outer hairs are coarse and long, while the downy undercoat is very fine. Colors range from white to brown and black. Some animals are pied, or multi-colored.

Vicunas are smaller than llamas, and adults weigh only about 100 pounds. Hairs from this animal are the finest or thinnest known, about 1/2000 inches in diameter. Like other camel relatives, the vicuna has a layered coat. The innermost hairs are extremely soft, elastic, and have a strongly cohesive outer surface. This last property makes these fibers resistant to dyes, stains, and water. As these animals are small, and their hair so fine, it takes fleece from about forty vicuna to make one coat.

Camel hair is only taken from the Bactrian or two-humped camel, and never from the Dromedary, or one-humped camel. Bactrians are native to southern China and Russia, through Mongolia, Tibet, and parts of the Middle East. Camel hair comes in three quality levels. The best is called noil, and it consists of the soft, downy short hair closest to the hide. The second type is the intermediate growth that covers most of the body. It is this fiber that is used for making most camel hair fabric. The third type is the outer, coarse hairs that are tough and wiry. These fibers are from 4 to 10 inches long, are used to make coarse fabric, twine, and rope. Camels naturally shed their hair in clumps, and are not shorn like sheep.

The term horsehair can refer to either the long coarse hairs of a horse's mane and tail or the shorter, more lustrous body hair. The most common uses of horsehair is as upholstery stuffing and as padding in coats and other heavy garments. Long horsehair has been woven into ladies' hats, which were usually dark in color.

Cow hair has been used to make coarse yarns for blankets and rugs. It has also been used to make felt, often mixed with other fibers.

Angora and Cashmere goats produce long, lustrous hair that is highly prized as fiber. Mohair is produced by the Angora goat, which has been domesticated worldwide. The fibers average about 9 inches in length, and are very strong and lustrous. Having more than twice the strength of sheep's wool fibers, mohair is very resistant to wear and was often used for rope and cordage. Modern uses of this material are usually limited to high-quality clothing and felt hats. Cashmere goats produce fiber that is very similar to sheep's wool in appearance, but it is softer and stronger.

Other types of goats also produce usable fibers, but of much lower quality. This material is called common or ordinary goat hair or meadow goat hair.

The Musk Ox is a large arctic animal related to goats and cattle. It gets it name from the strong musky smell of the male, which is particularly pungent during the mating season. The heavy fur of the musk ox has an outer layer of long guard hairs that may reach the ground. The under coat, which is called qiviut or qiviuq, is extremely fine and highly prized for its insulating qualities. Qiviut is collected by combing.

Rabbit hair is also collected by combing and is usually mixed with other fibers in yarn and fabric. It can add smoothness and luster to other lower-quality materials. The Angora rabbit is the most favored for its long, soft hair.

Quills and bristles are still, thick specialized hairs carried by some animals. Bristles are short stiff hairs with a large medulla, the optional core or third layer in the hair's cortex. Bristles on the face are often sensors, but quills, like those of the porcupine, are for defense.

Figure 6.6

The quills of this North American porcupine (Erithzon dorsatum) *are actually specialized hairs that grow in the animal's skin.*

Porcupines are a group of large rodents whose epidermis produces a dense growth of barbed quills. The tiny barbs are microscopic, at the end of a stiff, straight shaft that can be raised when the animal is threatened. Porcupines cannot throw their quills, but they do shed them like ordinary hair, sometimes into the skin of a predator. Quills, like other types of hair, grow back when they are lost.

In some species, the porcupine's skin may be covered with thousands of quills. Depending on the diameter of the quill shaft, there can be as many as 150 to the square inch of skin.

Porcupine quills have been used as sewing pins and needles, as fasteners for cloth and leather, and as decoration. Quills readily accept dye, and have been used to create rich patterns on clothing and personal items.

Fur or pelage is the body hair of some mammals. The term is also used to describe dressed or tanned animal pelts with the hair intact and items made from these materials.

Figure 6.7

Big cats like cheetah (Acinonyx jubatus) have been hunted extensively for their beautiful fur.

Table 6.5   Some fur-bearing animals.

Common name	Order	Family	Domesticated or farmed
Mole	Insectivora	Talpidae	
Rabbits and hares	Lagomorpha	Leporidae	x
Chinchilla	Rodentia	Muridae	x
Muskrat	Rodentia	Muridae	
Beaver	Rodentia	Castoridae	
Marmot	Rodentia	Sciuridae	
Squirrel	Rodentia	Sciuridae	
Coypu (nutria)	Rodentia	Echimyidae	
Buffalo	Artiodactyla	Bovidae	x
Seals	Carnivora	Phocidae and Otariidae	
Raccoon	Carnivora	Procyonidae	
Big cats (leopard, tiger, lion, cheetah, ocelot, panther, lynx)	Carnivora	Felidae	
Badger	Carnivora	Mustelidae	
Ermine	Carnivora	Mustelidae	
Mink	Carnivora	Mustelidae	x
Otter	Carnivora	Mustelidae	
Sable	Carnivora	Mustelidae	
Fox	Carnivora	Canidae	x
Bear	Carnivora	Ursidae	
Skunk	Carnivora	Mephitidae	

Historically, fur has been prepared and used as garments and other protection from cold and moisture. In each culture, indigenous animals were hunted and killed for their fur, so the list of animals used in this way is a long one. Table 6.5 is by no means a complete catalog of these species, but presents the common and representative groups. Some of these animals have been domesticated specifically for their fur, while others have been driven to the point of extinction by fur hunters.

Fur or hair fibers have often been mixed with other materials, like wool, linen, or silk, to create hybrid yarns or fabrics.

Feathers

The feather is one of the great engineering marvels of the natural world. They are low in density, but can be very strong. Feathers are composed of keratin, a fibrous structural protein that is also the main constituent in hair, wool, fingernails, and hooves. Feathers grow from the epidermis, just like hair.

Birds, which are warm-blooded animals in the class Aves, are the only animals that have feathers. There are six different types of feathers, which are classified according to their shape, purpose, and where they are found on the bird.

The outer contour or vane feathers have a classic "feather" shape; a shaft with flat opposing vanes (see Figure 6.8). There are two classes of contour feathers, the symmetrical body feathers, and the asymmetrical flight feathers that fill out the wings and tail.

The feather shaft consist of two parts (Figure 6.9). The hollow lower part below the vane, which attaches to the bird's skin, is the calamus. At the base of this hollow tube is an opening called the inferior umbilicus. This is the passage through which blood vessels feed the growing feather. When the feather reaches maturity, this opening dries up and closes off. The solid upper part of the feather, from which the vanes grow, is the rachis.

The vanes consist of individual, parallel branches called barbs. The barbs each look like a tiny feather, with two rows of tiny barbed branches called barbules. The barbules on adjacent barbs interlock, which gives the feather vane its flexible strength. In non-flying birds like the emu and ostrich, the barbules are not hooked together, resulting in contour feathers that appear fluffy, rather than flat and sleek.

Some contour feathers include an additional structure, a smaller rachis that emerges from the shaft below the vanes. This afterfeather or aftershaft has branching barbs, but no barbules, so it is downy or fluffy. This type of feather is seen most often in the family Phasianidae (pheasants and grouse).

Semi-plumes have characteristics of both down and contour feathers. They tend to be short, with some downy barbs. They lie directly beneath the contour feathers, giving both support and insulation.

Pinfeathers or filoplumes are even simpler, having a thin quill with a small tuft of barbs at the end. These small feathers have a sensory corpuscle at the base, which gives the bird a sense of touch throughout its plumage. Filoplumes let the bird feel how its feathers are moving and where they are so that it can make adjustments during flight.

Down feathers consist of many very thin, fine branches on a narrow rachis. They are the insulation under the larger, stronger contour feathers, and are the only feathers present on very young birds.

Powder feathers grow continuously, usually on the breast or belly of the bird. The barbs of these downy feathers break down, disintegrating into a fine powder. This dust may help the bird with preening and waterproofing of other, larger feathers. Birds in the family Ardeidae, which includes herons and bitterns, have the most powder feathers, although they do appear mixed in with normal down in many other bird species.

Figure 6.8

Feather types: (a) flight feather, (b) filoplume, (c) bristle, (d) down, and (e) body contour feather.

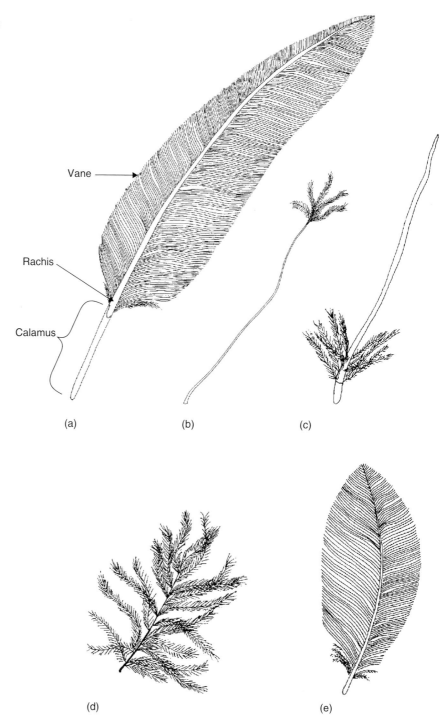

Vane

Rachis

Calamus

(a)

(b)

(c)

(d)

(e)

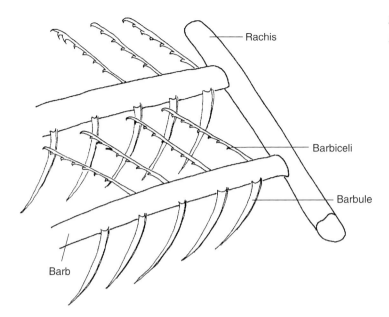

Rachis

Barbiceli

Barbule

Barb

Figure 6.9

Interlocking feather parts.

Not all birds have bristle feathers, which consist of a rachis with no barbs. These hair-like feathers are found mostly around the eyes, nose, and mouth. They are common in birds that feed on flying insects, and may enhance the senses of the bird, just the way whiskers do on a dog or cat.

Birds moult at least once each year, shedding old feathers and growing new ones to replace them. Most flying birds tend to shed feathers in symmetrical pairs, one from each side at a time, so that they can still fly while new feathers are growing. But some species, like ducks, geese, and other water birds, may be grounded during mounting due to the loss of too many contour feathers.

The causes of color in feathers may be structural, compositional (pigment), or a combination of both. Refraction and reflection of light from the orderly arrangement of barbs and barbules in some species produces structural colors of blue, green, silvery white, or multi-hued iridescence. Most feathers, however, are colored by pigments like the melanins (black, gray, brown), porphyrins (brown, red, some green), and carotenoids (red and yellow). In some cases, the visible colors of a feather are caused by a combination of pigments and surface structure. These are usually yellow-green, blue-green, or iridescent.

The feather is thought to have evolved from the scaly skin of reptiles. Long scales with frayed outer edges may gradually have developed into more and more complex and useful structures, and may eventually have become feathers. Feathers are rare in the fossil record. They are found as fragments in amber, in very fine-grained, low-energy sediments, and as impressions or external molds. The most famous of these is the *Archaeopteryx*, a flying bird-like reptile found in the Solnhofen Limestone deposit in Germany. This was the first fossil ever found that showed both the skeletal characteristics of reptiles and feathers of a bird.

Many types of birds have been killed for their feathers throughout human history, a practice which has caused the extinction or near-extinction of many species. Some birds have been raised commercially as a source of feathers. These include ostriches, pheasants, rheas, parrots, egrets, herons, macaws, emus, geese, ducks, and peacocks. Some of these birds are also raised for their meat and eggs. Table 6.6 describes some of the birds most often sought for their feathers. Male birds tend to have the brightest, largest, showiest feathers and so are most often targeted by collectors. A complete list of birds that have been killed for their feathers would probably be a list of all bird species.

Figure 6.10

*The snowy egret (*Egretta thula*) and its relatives have long flight feathers and plumes that have been popular decorations on hats and clothing for hundreds of years.*

Table 6.6 Feather sources.

Long plumes and tail feathers	Colorful or patterned flight and body feathers	Neutral-colored feather trim	Down	Whole or partial body with feathers
Heron	Pheasants	Ducks	Ducks	Various songbirds
Peafowl	Partridge	Geese	Geese	Hummingbirds
Egret	Ducks	Doves		Parrots
Ostrich	Orioles	Quail		Owls
Marabou and	Jays	Pigeons		
other storks	Tanagers	Chickens		
Rhea	Grebes	Turkeys		
Pheasant	Ibis	Owls		
Swallows	Flamingo	Terns		
Birds of paradise	Kingfishers	Gulls		
Lyre bird	Parrots	Pelicans		
Emu	Macaws			
Swans	Eagles			
	Hawks			

Feathers can be gathered from a captured live bird, which is then either retained as an ongoing source of feathers or released. Feathers dropped during molting can be collected, but these are often worn and, if they are not very fresh, will probably show the effects of insect predation or chemical erosion.

Feathers in museum collections are often part of composite objects, since few items are ever made of nothing but feathers. Hats, hair ornaments, and fans are common feathered objects (Figure 6.10). Less common are baskets with feather decoration, like those of the Pomo Indians of Northern California, and capes and headdresses covered with a dense layer of feathers, like those created by the native Hawaiians. Many cultures used feathers in religious or spiritual objects, in trophies of the hunt, and in symbols of authority or power. These may take the form of clothing, personal decoration, or ceremonial objects.

Most feathers are used singly or in small groups. The feathers of different birds were often combined to create a desired effect. Sometimes whole or partial wings or tails would be incorporated into a decoration. In extreme cases, entire birds may be supported by a large hat.

Down feathers are used in stuffing pillows, mattresses, and clothing. Most of this type of feather is harvested from domestic ducks and geese.

Figure 6.11

Feathers from birds of prey, like this bald eagle (Haliaeetus leucocephalus) *have been used as trophies and in religious and ceremonial items.*

Bone and Antler

Bones are the elements of the internal skeletons of vertebrate animals. They provide mechanical strength and structural support for the organism. The composition of bone varies among different species, bone type, and age. Generally, bones consist of a mixture of inorganics (minerals), water, and an organic matrix.

There are two types of bony tissue: cancellous or spongy bone and cortical or compact bone. Cortical bone is denser and more highly ordered than the randomly woven cancellous bone tissue. Cancellous bone is open-celled and porous, with from 30% to over 90% porosity.

The minerals in bone change as an animal ages. Juvenile or immature bone contains amorphous calcium phosphate or the mineral brushite ($CaHPO_4 \cdot 2H_2O$). Mature bone contains the mineral hydroxyapatite ($Ca_5(PO_4)_3(OH)$), but with some modifications. There tends to be some internal crystal disorder within bone apatite, and the carbonate radical may substitute for phosphate. Calcium deficiency and other health problems may affect the composition and properties of bone.

The organic matrix in bone is mostly collagen, which consists of three polypeptide (alpha) chains of amino acids coiled in a triple helix. Collagen consists mostly of the amino acids glycine, proline, and hydroxyptoline. The collagen in different types of body tissues are made of different alpha chains. Type I collagen is in skin, bone, dentin, and tendons. Type II collagen is in cartilage.

Besides collagen, other compounds make up 2% to 5% of the total organic matrix of bone. These include proteins that promote mineral deposition and regulate the size, orientation and growth rate of bone mineral. There are also lipids in bone cell membranes and carbohydrates.

Bone has been used as tools, weapons, and in some decorative objects. It can be broken or cut into desired shapes, and ground into a sharp point. In some cases, entire skulls, feet, or other groups of bones have been used to create an object. Bone is present in specimens that have undergone taxidermy, and in some skins. Hides intended for use as rugs or wall trophies are sometimes left with the head and/or feet intact, including the bones.

Small pieces of bone have been used to make jewelry, buttons, and other personal items, often in imitation of ivory. Domestic animals that are used as food or beasts of burden are the source of most commercial bone. These include cattle, camel, and water buffalo. Scrimshaw is an art form in which designs are scratched a light-colored material, and then ink or paint is rubbed into the lines. The raw material used is often ivory (teeth) or bone.

The males of some mammal species have a bone called the baculum within the penis. Also called the penis bone, penile bone, or *os penis*, it is an aid to copulation and its size and shape are specific to each species. Animals that have such a bone include rats, dogs, and walruses. These bones are used as fertility charms and objects of curiosity.

Bone char is the ash produced by burning animal bones. It is used in some ceramics and as a whitening agent in some foods. It is also used in home aquarium filters.

Bone meal is ground up or crushed animal bone. It is put into fertilizer, soil enrichments, and dietary supplements as a source of calcium and phosphorus.

Antlers are cranial bone growths that occur within the Cervidae, or deer family (Figure 6.12). Only the males of most species carry antlers, with the exception of caribou and reindeer, where they appear on both males and females. Antlers are used by these animals for defense and for display, which

Figure 6.12

This elk (Cervus elaphus) and other members of the Cervidae (deer family) annually grow and shed antlers.

is a combination of impressing the opposite sex and rivals, and for species recognition.

Antlers are grown and shed annually from two points on the front or side of the skull. During the growing season, an antler is covered with skin and fine hair. Blood vessels feed the bony mass, which grows from the ends and around the surface. As an antler nears its maximum size, the blood supply is gradually cut off and the "velvet" coating dries and sloughs off. After a short time, a sinus opens between the basal burr on the skull and the bottom of the antler. The antler is then dropped, and a scar forms on the pedicle.

Antler bone is similar to skeletal bone in composition, but its rapid rate of growth produces a coarse structure with compact, hard material only around the outside and at the tine tips. The older an animal gets, the larger and more complex its antlers become. Antler growth is also affected by climate and available food, since the rapid growth of this much bone can tax an animal's metabolism.

Teeth

A tooth consists of three basic parts, the crown, which is exposed, the neck, which is at the gum line, and the root, which is embedded in the gum and jaw. The crown may be completely or partially covered with a harder substance known as enamel. The bulk of the tooth is composed of dentine, which surrounds and protects the inner pulp cavity. Pulp is vascular tissue that contains nerves and blood vessels, fed from below through a narrow channel in the dentine called the root canal. The root of the tooth is also surrounded by

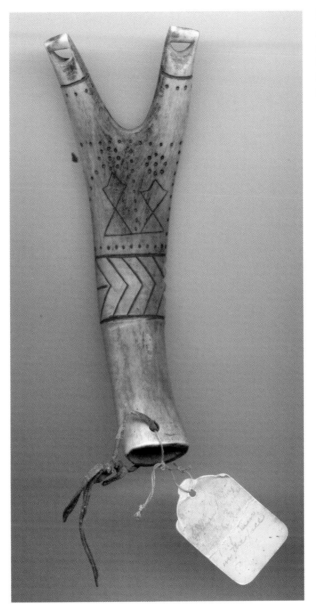

Figure 6.13

A Sioux craftsman fashioned this quirt from an elk antler. It had thongs of hide strung through the holes on the tines.

a thin layer of hard material called cementum. Figure 6.15 shows the structure of a tooth. This is not the tooth of a particular species, but rather an idealized diagram showing the major parts.

Dentine is composed of a mixture of about 70% hydroxlyapatite $(Ca_5(PO_4)_3(OH))$, 20% collagenous proteins and about 10% water. The microscopic structure of dentine consists of microscopic canals called dentinal tubules that radiate out from the pulp cavity to the cementum border. The diameter of these canals varies among different animals, and ranges

Figure 6.14

The handles of these tools are made from antler. The characteristic ridges are clear, and have been smoothed by years of wear on the big knife (top).

from 0.8 to 2.2 μm. At the outer margin of the pulp cavity is a layer of odontoblastic cells that produce the dentin. The primary function of the pulp tissue is to supply nutrients for these cells.

Tooth enamel is the hardest tissue in an animal's body. It is composed almost entirely of inorganic hydroxyapatite, with less than 5% organic components and water. Most tooth enamel is from 1.5 to 2.0 mm thick, and may vary in thickness between teeth and even on a single tooth.

Cementum is a thin layer of hard material that covers the root of a tooth. Its composition is close to that of skeletal bone, with about 65% hydroxyapatite, 23% collagen, and 12% water.

Teeth that are still growing have an open root canal, but in those that have reached maturity, this canal is closed. "Rootless" teeth are those in which the root canal stays open and growth continues indefinitely. These are common in rodents like rabbits and gophers, whose teeth grow continually throughout

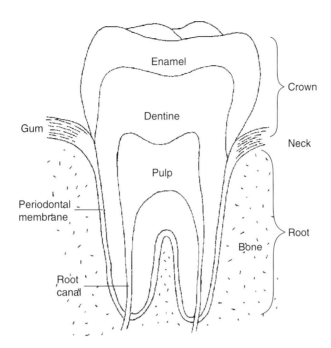

Figure 6.15

Parts of a tooth.

their lives. Most animals have one set of permanent teeth, some of which are preceded by deciduous or milk teeth.

Most vertebrate animals have some kind of teeth. Some reptiles, amphibians, and birds are the exceptions. Teeth are described according to their position in the mouth, their purpose, and their shape. Molars are grinding or masticating teeth, usually along the sides and at the back of the jaw. Molars are multi-rooted, with up to four roots. Incisors are usually in the front of the jaw; single-rooted teeth used for biting and cutting. Canines are intermediary between molars and canines. These single-rooted teeth are smaller than molars, and not as sharp as incisors.

Tooth type and position are often noted with a combination of numbers and letters, depending on the species. Each tooth has a lingual side, adjacent to the tongue, and a labial surface, which is closest to the lips (if there are any). The posterior teeth are at the back of the mouth, and the anterior to the front. The occlusal surface is the area where opposing teeth meet during chewing or biting.

An animal's teeth reflect its eating habits. Omnivores, animals that eat different types of food, including both meat and plants, tend to have all three types of teeth. Their incisors are not large, but may be sharp and pointed. Insectivores, who live on insects, have jagged molars that can be used for crushing hard crunchy bug parts. Meat eaters, or carnivores, have all three types of teeth. Their incisors may be large and sometimes extend well outside

Figure 6.16

The tusks of the walrus (Odobenus rosmarus) *have been used to make decorative items, tools, and weapons.*

the mouth. The canines are long and sharp, and their molars tend to be jagged. Plant eaters, or herbivores, may have incisors, but these teeth are usually chisel-shaped. Molars are large and strong, since they do most of the work for these animals. In some herbivores, there is a gap between molars and incisors, and parts of the anterior jaw may be covered with a horny pad.

Tusk is a general term used to describe large teeth that protrude beyond an animal's lips, such as those produced by elephants and walrus (Figure 6.16). Tusks tend to grow throughout an animal's lifetime, and contain a live, open-pulp cavity. Tusks have two basic layers; an outer homogeneous and fine-grained dentin, and an inner, coarser dentin mass that is created from within, in the pulp cavity.

The narwhal (*Monodon monoceros*) is a toothed Arctic whale that has two tusks, only one of which grows to any size. The unseen tusk is vestigial and may never erupt from the bone, but the other forms a long, straight shaft that may be up to three meters in length. The surface of a narwhal tusk is twisted, but the tooth itself is linear. Like the tusks of elephants and walrus, the narwhal's tusk grows continually during its lifetime.

Muscles and Other Tissues

Tendons are bundles of tough connective tissue fibers that connect muscle to bone. They vary in length and size depending on where they are in the body (and whose body it is). Ligaments are short bundles of fibrous tissue in and around joints. They stabilize the joint by keeping the bones in position both during movement and at rest. Both tendons and ligaments have been used as cordage and to provide stability to structures like baskets. When used in these ways, these materials are often referred to as sinew.

Cartilage consists of specialized cells in a viscous interfibrillar matrix. There are three types, found in different areas of the body, depending on the strength and flexibility needed in each area.

Elastin is the protein in connective tissues that allows them to undergo large shape and size changes without damage or loss of strength.

Muscle and organ tissue make up most of what is referred to as "meat." These materials are composed mostly of proteins and water, and they begin decomposing immediately after the animal's death. These tissues are removed from skin during tanning or taxidermy, although dried remnants may remain. In traditional natural history collections, these materials are usually wet preserved in 70% ethanol as part of whole or partial animals.

Intestines were often used as casings for sausage and other foods. They were also used as condoms and to hold and carry water or other substances. Intestines were sometime slit lengthwise and dried like leather. The stomachs of larger animals were sometimes used as containers for water and other liquids. The stomachs and bladders of animals were used as pouches or bags to store pigments, mixed paints, herbs, medicines, and other powdered materials.

Catgut, which was used for medical suturing and as tough strings on tennis rackets and musical instruments, is not from cats, but comes from the intestines of sheep, horses, and other large mammals.

Eggs

Although some reptiles, fish, amphibians, and a few mammals lay eggs, most egg products come from birds.

Eggshells vary in composition depending on the animal species. Eggs held within the mothers' body are surrounded by organic membranes, but those that are deposited outside the body usually have a protective shell. Eggs that are to be externally fertilized or that will be buried are usually soft or pliable. Those laid by animals that will sit on them or stay with them, like most birds, have hard shells. Bird eggshells are mostly calcite (calcium carbonate), mixed with some keratin.

Birds' eggshells have been used as a base for decorative objects, and to make useful items such as spoons, scoops, and bowls. If an egg is intended for a use that requires it to remain whole, the contents are usually blown out. Two holes are poked into the shell, usually at the small ends, and the contents are then expelled by someone blowing hard into one end. Egg contents can also be sucked out through a single hole. Eggs that do not show evidence the contents have been removed (no holes) may have been simply dried.

Egg white or albumin has been used most often as a medium for paint pigments and as an adhesive. As a glue, it is not strong, but can be applied thinly and it dries quickly. Fresh dry albumin resists water and may have been used in situations where there was a possibility of moisture. It was used by the ancient Egyptians to fasten gold leaf to gesso and wood and as an additive in gesso (gypsum). Later artists also mixed egg albumin with sizing or gesso to prepare canvas or wood for painting. It was used in many cultures as a paint medium. Mixed with ground mineral pigments such as red and yellow ochre (iron oxides) or green malachite (copper carbonate), albumin gives a lustrous paint. Some artists mixed egg albumin with watercolor paints to give their work more permanence and to make it more water-resistant. This technique was often used in hand-colored bookplates.

Keratin Materials

Claws, beaks, horns, hooves, and baleen: these materials may seem like strange companions, but they are all composed of basically the same material, the protein keratin. Hair and feathers are also keratin, but are addressed in detail in previous sections. All of these materials form on the outside of an animal's body, in the skin.

Turtle and tortoise shells are composed of dense keratin plates or skutes that are held together with an underlying network of interlocking bones. The carapace is the dorsal or upper part of the exoskeleton. The plaston is the much flatter ventral or underside portion. In some species, the sex of an individual can be determined by the shape of the plastron; convex for the female and concave for the male. Figure 6.1 shows a pattern of skutes or plates. The actual size and arrangement of the skutes is unique to each species.

Commercial tortoise shell is taken from the carapace (upper shell) and plastron (underside) of several species of large sea turtle. The green sea turtle (*Chelonia mydas*) (Figure 6.17), The loggerhead turtle (*Caretta caretta*), the leatherback turtle (*Dermochelys coriacea)*, and the Hawksbill Turtle (*Eretmochelys imbricata*) are endangered animals today because they have been hunted for their shells and meat. Tortoiseshell is a favored material for some types of personal and decorative objects because it is very light in weight, it is flexible, and its translucent mottled browns and yellows can be very attractive. Although its shape can be changed with pressure and heat, most tortoiseshell is used in its natural form. Most objects made of this material retain some of its original curvature.

The shells of terrestrial tortoises and freshwater turtles have also been used in some of the same ways as the larger marine turtles. Whole turtle bodies, with the soft tissue and most of the skeleton removed, have been made into pouches and specialized containers for personal and ceremonial use.

Figure 6.17

This green sea turtle
(Chelonia mydas) *is one of*
the species that has been
hunted almost to extinction for
its meat and its shell.

Hornbill is a general name given to birds in the family Bucerotidae, in which there are about 50 species named (Figure 6.19). The name comes from the large excrescence or growth on the front of the head, at the base of the bird's bill that sometimes resembles a horn. The hornbill is a large bird native to many parts of the southern hemisphere.

The outside of the horn-like casque is often red, while the inside is a creamy yellow. This material was highly sought-after and, before the invention of firearms, very difficult to obtain. Asian artists produced snuff bottles, buttons, netsukes, and other small objects from this material. Sometimes the entire head of the bird would be retained, parts of it carved and some areas left in their natural state, sometimes even with feathers intact. Hornbill "ivory" is also known as golden jade, crane's crest, crane's bill, and *ho-ting*.

Baleen forms large plates that hang in a row from the upper jaw of baleen whales. These plates are tapered, like a comb, from a wide base at the gum line down to a loose fringe at the end. Whales strain a huge volume of water through these natural sieves every day, capturing their food as the water passes through the comb-like baleen.

Whale hunters were interested in these huge animals for their meat and oil, but also for baleen. In the days before the invention of plastic, baleen was used to make objects that required flexibility and low density. Baleen was also called "whalebone," even though it is not made of bone and does not come

Figure 6.18

These hair ornament are made of plastic, as imitations of tortoiseshell.

from the animal's skeleton. The most common objects made of this material are corset and collar stays, buggy whips, and umbrella ribs.

There are 11 species of baleen whale, which are divided into three groups: gray whales, right whales, and rorqual whales. Right whales were so called because hunters liked them best. They are big, slow swimmers with big baleen plates, and they float when dead. They were the "right ones" to kill.

Claws, nails, and hooves are hard protective coverings that form at the ends of the arms and feet, on the digits (fingers and toes) (Figure 6.20). In vertebrate animals, claws are curved, pointed growths. Talons are the claws of a bird of prey. Some animals have claws that are retractable, like cats, but most are fixed in the "out" position. Some animals use their claws for hunting and defense, while others use them for climbing or digging.

In some cultures, claws have been used as trophies of the hunt, usually to prove that a person has killed a predator or a large, aggressive animal.

Nails are like claws, but they are flatter, with a curved edge instead of a point. Hooves are large toenails. Large hooves have been made into tools or

Figure 6.19

There are about 50 species of hornbill birds, many of which have a thick casque or growth at front of the head. This mass of keratin is used in place of ivory to make small items like buttons.

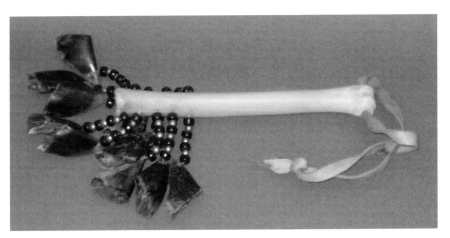

Figure 6.20

This rattle is made from the toes of a deer (keratin), tied to a bone, and decorated with glass and metal beads.

containers, since they are naturally curved, lightweight, slightly flexible, and waterproof. Hooves have also been used in making small decorative or souvenir objects such as hair combs and buttons.

Horns are the hard protuberances that extend from the heads of some animals (Figure 6.22). In most cases, horns have a core of bone that is part of

Figure 6.21

This pin carries the foot, feathers, and talons of a ptarmigan, a relative of quail and pheasants.

Figure 6.22

Structure of horn such as those grown by sheep, buffalo, and cattle.

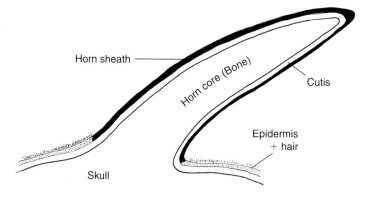

the skull, which is covered by a hollow sheath made of keratin. Pronghorn antelope shed their horn sheaths annually, but most horns are permanent, and grow continually throughout an animal's lifetime (Figure 6.23).

Horns have been used to make containers, like powder horns, by covering or plugging up one end. Horn is curved, lightweight, and flexible, which makes it useful as scoops, spoons, and small bowls. Ornaments made of horn are often

Figure 6.23

The horns of the bighorn sheep (Ovis canadensis) *grow throughout its lifetime.*

similar in appearance to those made of tortoise or turtle shell, having a streaked or mottled brown/yellow/gray color and a naturally smooth surface. Large horn sheaths have also been used as musical instruments, like a simple trumpet.

The horns of a giraffe are solid bone, called ossicorns. They are covered only with skin and hair.

Rhinoceros horns are composed of densely compressed hair-like fibers over a stubby bone core that is part of the skull. They are composed of a dense growth of epidermal cells and dermal papillae, which are similar to thick hair. These are not really true hairs, since they do not grow from a follicle in the skin. Unlike the sheath-like horns of cattle and buffalo, rhino horns are mostly solid.

While rhinoceros horn has been used in powdered form as an aphrodisiac, most of the horns harvested are used for either ornamental or medicinal purposes. Rhino horn is a popular carving material, particularly for handles on daggers and other weapons. In Asia, powdered rhino horn is a remedy against fever.

Products

This section contains a discussion of some of the products produced from vertebrate animals. Some of these materials are not species specific, and are produced from whatever animals are available and suitable for the prescribed purpose.

Tools and Weapons

The hard parts of an animal's body, usually skeletal bone, are hard enough to be useful for making objects that will be subjected to impact and wear. Some teeth and antler may also be used in this way.

For something to be useful as a weapon, it must be either very dense and heavy, or be rigid and pointed. This latter property can be achieved artificially through sharpening or honing. Bones of large animals can be shaped into spear points, knives, and scrapers. Having a general hardness of only about 3 on Mohs' scale, most bone tools may not last long under heavy use. But in many cultures, bone has the advantages of availability and ease of working. In some parts of the world, stone is scarce, but the bones of large animals that are hunted for food are readily available. Bone is not as hard as stone materials that might be used for similar purposes, and so is more easily fashioned. Some large and heavy bones may be useful as clubs or hammers, particularly long bones with the condyle intact.

Brushes for fine or delicate work, such as writing, painting, or applying cosmetics, may be made from animal hair. Bristles, usually from pigs or boar, are stiff hairs that are used for hair brushes and some cleaning tools. Softer hairs for brushes are usually taken from sable, oxen, squirrel, horse, goat, or badger.

Fat, Oil, and Wax

Fat is a general term applied to light-colored animal solids that melt at low temperatures. Oil or grease is liquid fat, and the definitions of these materials vary widely.

Lard is a term used for animal fat, usually from pigs. Before the industrial revolution, it was commonly used in place of butter or vegetable oils, which were more expensive. In some cultures today, it is still an important food additive. Lard is also used to make some kinds of soap.

Tallow is waxy body fat rendered from animal tissue, usually that of beef or sheep. It is isolated by heating, and allowed to solidify. Tallow has been used in leather preparation, as a lubricant, in food preparation, and in making candles and soap. It is used as food for domestic animals, mostly for poultry. Tallow candles burn quickly and have a low melting point. They were generally less expensive than wax candles, and easier to make. Suet is another name for animal fat, usually applied to that from sheep.

Lanolin is an oil or grease made by some wool-bearing animals. It is produced by the sebaceous glands, which are adjacent to hair follicles in the skin. This compound gives an animal's wool a certain amount of water-resistance, and the amount present in a fleece varies by species and variety.

Lanolin is washed or pressed out of wool during the processing of fleece, and is an important by-product of wool production. In concentrated form, lanolin is used in cosmetics and skin ointments, as a water-resistant coating on fabric, metal, and leather, and as a polish. In medicine, lanolin is used to make creams for the treatment of dry skin, burns, chapped lips, and diaper rash.

Squalene is an oil obtained from shark liver and other organs. It is used as a surfactant, and in moisturizing cosmetics.

Turtle or sea turtle oil is taken from the genitalia and muscle tissue of large sea turtles. It is used in cosmetics, soap, and skin cream.

Minks and other animals that live in cold climates may have thick fatty layers under the skin. When a mink's furry pelt is cleaned, this fat is scraped off and rendered into oil. This product is then used in skin treatments, cosmetics, and as an oil for leather. These products usually are referred to as mink oil, or beaver oil, or (insert animal name here) oil.

There are two compounds known as emu oil. One is derived from the fats and tissues of the flightless emu bird. This oil is valued largely for its reported medicinal properties. It is supposed to reduce skin irritation and reduces scarring. It is used on burns and to reduce pain and swelling in joints. The second type of emu oil is derived from plants, but is sold under the same name as the compounds derived from the bird.

Body parts from animals that are either aggressively sexual or just plain aggressive have often been used as aphrodisiacs. These include internal organs, glands, bones, teeth, fat, oil, and soft tissue like skin and muscle. Sometimes these items were carried as charms, but more often they were powdered and taken internally.

Most perfumes and incense are plant products and are discussed in Chapter 4: Plants. Many animals, however, produce body oils that have been used as a base for perfumes. Usually taken from large mammals, these oils tend to have little or no scent themselves when fresh. Whale oil was commonly used in this way.

The musk glands of the male musk deer (*Moschus moschiferus*) have been used in a number of ways because of their strong scent. In Asia, the glands are dried, and sold in powdered form as a sexual aid. Musk is also an important fixative in perfume and incense. Some mosques in the Middle East reportedly were built with musk mixed in with the mortar, which can still be smelled today.

Castoreum or caster is a strongly scented creamy fluid derived from the genitals of male beavers. This name is also applied to similar materials taken from otters and muskrats. These fluids are used by the animals to mark their territories and to attract females. They are reputed to have the same effects on other species, notably humans, when incorporated into perfumes or creams. Castoreum perfume is produced by placing the entire gland into alcohol.

Civet oil is the product of small glands in the anal pouch of the civet cat. It has a strong musky smell, and is used as a perfume fixative.

Ambergris is a waxy substance produced as a concretion in the intestines of sperm whales. It is also known as gray amber, ambre gris, and ambra grisea.

It is a low-density fatty compound produced in the whale's stomach and intestines in response to irritation, possibly from the passing of the hard, sharp beaks of squid, which are a major part of the whale's diet.

Ambergris is excreted into the sea along with the whale's other wastes. Due to its low density, it floats in salt water and is sometimes collected from beaches. It comes in a variety of colors, usually gray or brown, and may have a white powdery surface coating. Ambergris has also been collected from whales killed during hunting, or that died and came to rest on a beach.

The smell of ambergris can vary from mildly sweet and earthy to downright stinky and offensive. It is unsurpassed as a fixative of all kinds of scents and has been sought after for hundreds of years as a necessary component in fine perfume. It is also used in medicines, as an aphrodisiac, and as an flavor-enhancing additive in food and wine. Ambergris has been synthesized with some success.

Sperm whales also carry a quantity of oil in a cavity in their heads. This oil contains a wax compound called spermaceti wax. This wax is white in color, and was used for candles, wax casting, and in medicines.

Adhesives have been made from a wide variety of plant and animal products, sometimes in combination. The most common form of animal glue is largely composed of collagen, which is usually acquired by boiling animal skin, tissue, and bones. The resultant liquid is reduced by further heating until it reaches the desired viscosity.

Gelatin is a light-colored translucent solid that is produced by boiling animal tissue, skin, and bones. It has a very low melting point, and forms a semi-solid colloidal gel when mixed with water. Most gelatin is produced as a by-product of the meat and leather industries. Historically, gelatin has also been produced from the swim bladders of some fish (isinglass), and from antlers (hartshorn jelly).

Gelatin is used in foods, usually as a stabilizer or thickener. It is made into capsules for medicines, in glues and binders, in cosmetics, as sizing in paper, and in photographic emulsions.

Concentrated collagen can also be used as sizing in fabric, or as a coating on leather or fabric. It can increase the strength of materials, as well as enhancing their water resistance.

The process of making soap is called saponification, which most simply involved combining oil or fat with an alkali compound and heating it. Historically, the components were animal fat or vegetable oil combined with sodium hydroxide (lye) made from wood ashes. The properties and usefulness of the resulting product depended on the kind of fat used, how pure the ingredients were, and how long the process lasted. Refinements on the basic process include re-treatment of the initial product by again boiling the crude soap, and the addition of vegetable or animal oils, pigments, or scent. Abrasive or scouring soap may contain sand or ground pumice.

Saponification also takes place in nature, when fatty tissue is buried in a wet alkaline environment. This usually occurs in a bog or other wetland, where the local soils are alkaline and the subsurface conditions are anaerobic. The fats in an animal's body will gradually be converted into insoluble fatty acids, white or light yellow waxy solids that are known as adipocere or grave wax. The soft tissue of human cadavers buried in swamps or bogs may be almost entirely composed of this material after a period of time.

Leather

The tanned or preserved skin of an animal is called leather. This material varies greatly from species to species, and its properties are also affected by the process of tanning. Most of the materials treated in this way come from mammals, but the skins of some fish, birds, reptiles, and amphibians are also occasionally tanned for various purposes.

The processes used to make leather have not changed very much over the years, even though some procedures are now carried out by machines. These methods were developed independently by various cultures around the world.

There are two series of steps involved in making leather, the preparation of the skin, and tanning of the skin. After its removal from the animal, the skin is washed and soaked in water. If the skin will not be tanned immediately, it may be dried or salted to prevent rot. The first treatment step is called fleshing. When done by hand, this involves the careful scraping of tissue from the underside of the skin. This may actually be performed several times during processing, as later soaking may make it easier to get some of it off. This may also be done by machine.

Skin that has been de-fleshed and de-haired, but not otherwise treated is called rawhide. This untanned leather material can be molded and shaped when wet, so that it holds a useful shape when it dries and hardens. Sometimes, rawhide would be improved by smoking. As rawhide has not been tanned, it can absorb moisture and is subject to mold.

The second step in the preparation of the skin is the removal of the epidermis and its load of hair by "bucking," which involves soaking the skin in a solution of water and lime. Early leather workers used wood ash to produce the lye. The hair usually slips off during or after the soaking, and the unwanted upper layer of skin may be then scraped off. In modern tanneries, this process is done by machines, but traditionally it is accomplished by hand. If the desired end-product is a leather that is not flexible or elastic, then the skin can be left in the lye solution for a prolonged period. This is known as "liming." After the hair and upper skin layer have been removed, the skin must be carefully rinsed to get rid of any residual alkalis.

Figure 6.24

*The cape buffalo (*Syncerus caffer*), like other members of the Bovidae, is the source of horn, bone, meat, and skin for leather.*

The final pre-leather step is splitting or shaving, where the treated skin is reduced to the desired even thickness. When done by hand, this is a matter of shaving off small pieces or strips. By machine, a thick skin can be split down the middle, reducing loss and creating a more consistent product. Lastly, the prepared skin is washed again and may, at this time, undergo tempering or softening. If the final leather is to be soft, then at this stage the skin may be subjected to a kind of fermentation to break down some of the linked collagen fibers. This usually involved coating the skin with animal excrement, beer, or fermented grains. This could take days or weeks, and the process had to be monitored carefully lest it proceed too far and destroy the product. After this, the skin is again washed and is ready for tanning.

There are a number of methods used to tan leather. Vegetable tanning involves the immersion of the skin in water with a large amount of tannin-rich plant material, usually tree bark. The bark is chopped fine and soaked in clean water. Minerals or other impurities in the water will result in dark spots or mottling of the finished leather. The skin is put first into a weak tannin solution, and then into a series of progressively stronger baths. If a strong solution is used right from the beginning, the outside of the skin will absorb lots of tannins and shrink, leaving the inside untanned or raw. This is called case hardening or dead tanning. The skins must be moved around in the solution as often as possible. Modern tanners use large rotating tanks for this process, but without mechanical assistance, this process can take months. There are many variations on this basic process, depending upon the kind of skin being made into leather, and the desired end-product.

Figure 6.25

Sports equipment, toys, and other items may include leather, wood, and other natural materials.

The finishing of vegetable leather usually involves oil or grease, since one of the outcomes was to make the product water-resistant. Currying is one process to accomplish this, during which oil or grease, sometimes mixed with tallow or wax, is rubbed into the leather. Dyes are also added at this stage. Historically, currying was done by craftsmen who specialized in these procedures. They were usually not the same people who prepared the skin and tanned the leather.

Another tanning method is "mineral tanning," which involves soaking a skin in a solution of alum and salt. This is called tawing. The products of this process are white and open-pored, and become stiff and hard when dried. Due to its open-pored texture, tawed leather is often treated with additives that fill in some of the irregularities and add to the skin's strength. Historically, these fillers have included flour, grease, egg yolks, and fat.

Chamoising is a less common process that involves rubbing the raw skin with brain tissue. This results in a soft, light brown to yellow leather.

Regardless of which process was used to make the leather, the final step is slow and careful drying. In some cases, this could take months and often required special structures be built to protect the hides while they dried.

Vellum is fine, thin skin, usually from a young lamb (sheep) or goat, has been used as a surface for writing (Figure 6.26). It was most often prepared by chamoising (brain tanning) or chemical tanning, since vegetable tanning usually produces a product that is too dark to be useful as a writing surface. Small paintings, such as portrait miniatures, were often painted on thin vellum that was glued to a paper card. Early playing cards were sometimes used for this purpose.

Leather was sometimes treated with wax to make it harder and more water-resistant. The most effective method was to immerse leather sheets or objects in hot liquid wax for some period of time, long enough for the wax to penetrate all the way through the skin. Leather items too big for this treatment could be coated with wax, but this was not as effective since the wax was then only on the surface. Waxed leather was commonly used for containers liquids, such as buckets, bottles, and cups. It was also used to make protective armor and shields for both people and horses.

In the modern fur trade, fur is defined as a mammal pelt with all or some hair intact, with an intended use for warmth or adornment, and recognized as an item of commerce in the fur industry. This last requirement separates fur items that are taxable when sold from those that are not.

Fur was originally prepared by scraping off the fat and tissue from the inside. The skin was then repeatedly washed, and then oiled with fat or oil from the animal. Oiling required pounding or massaging the fat into the hide. Eskimos do this by chewing the skin. Bark or vegetable tanning is used in some cultures, even though this process results in darkened or stained fur.

Figure 6.26

Leather, vellum, and parchment are important materials in library collections. All three are made from the skin of animals.

Teeth and Ivory

Teeth are sometimes used as trophies or in spiritual or symbolic objects. Hunters sometimes keep the teeth or claws of animals they have killed to prove their skill and experience. These are often made into personal decorations, such as necklaces, or sown to clothing. Teeth have been used as proof of how many animals have been killed, which can be an indication of the hunter's prowess or wealth. For instance, Plains Indian tribes used elk teeth as signs of wealth, and displayed them sewn on clothing.

Ivory is the term used to describe large teeth, usually from mammals. Some large reptile teeth have also been referred to as ivory. Ivory is composed largely of dentine, the compound that makes up the hard substance of a tooth.

While the word ivory usually evokes visions of an elephant's tusks, there are many animals that have contributed to the world's supply. This includes hippopotamus (Figure 6.27), walrus, boar, narwhal, and other toothed whales. Whale ivory was produced as a by-product of the whaling industry, along with baleen, various oils, and bone. The toothed whales are all in the suborder Odontoceti, which is divided into nine families, including dolphins and porpoises. There are three species of sperm whales, three white whales (including the narwhal), twenty-one beaked or bottle-nosed whales, and six pilot or killer whales. All of these animals carry enough teeth to have made them targets for ivory hunters.

Fossilized ivory is a popular material in the few places in the world where it is found in commercial amounts because it does not fall within the restrictions

Figure 6.27

Hippopotamus amphibius *has an impressive array of large teeth, and has been hunted for its ivory for thousands of years.*

Figure 6.28

These are all ivory.
Top: hippopotamus tooth;
center: boar's tusk;
bottom: sperm whale teeth.

of the trade in modern ivory. Most fossil ivory is from Pleistocene-aged walrus and mammoth found in northern Canada, Alaska, and northern Russia.

Ivory has been used for both practical and decorative purposes. In cultures where there were few hard materials available for making tools and weapons, the bones and teeth of large animals were very important for these purposes (Figure 6.28). People living on plains or in arctic areas created a vast array of items from the teeth of large animals. These include hunting tools such as

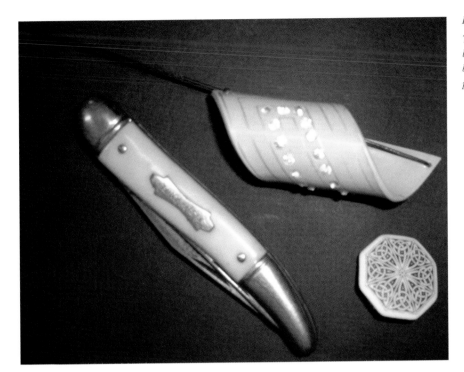

Figure 6.29

These items are made to look like ivory, but they are made of bakelite (knife), celluloid (hat pin), and ceramic (brooch).

spear and arrow points and fish hooks, and household items like scrapers and spoons.

Scrimshaw is an art that involves the incision of a design on the surface of a light-colored material, usually ivory or bone, and the rubbing of ink or other pigment into the grooves. This was a popular pastime among sailors and people living near the sea, and many scrimshaw designs have a nautical theme.

Before plastics were invented, ivory was used to make piano keys, billiard balls, buttons, dice, and many other small items. It was used as an insulator in the handles of metal containers such as teapots and coffee urns. It was, and still is, a popular material for making jewelry and *objects d'art*. Sheets of ivory, which can be made by flattening sections of the outer part of large tusks, has been used as a base for paintings, in bookbinding, boxes, and as veneer or plaques in furniture.

Blood, Milk, and Excrement

Like other body fluids, blood has often been used as a binder in pigments and adhesives. It is a food in some parts of the world, and a food additive. It has been used as a pigment and a paint.

Bois durci is a mixture of blood, usually from cattle, soot, and fine hardwood sawdust. This compound has been molded into a wide variety of shapes, most commonly decorative plaques, picture frames, jewelry, and household objects such as pen trays and inkwells.

Casein is an insoluble protein found in milk. It is used to make adhesives and fillers, water-resistant coatings, and as an additive in some plastics and commercial food products like non-dairy creamers and soy cheese. The milk from cows, sheep, and goats has been used, alone or mixed with fillers, as gesso or as a tempera medium. Casein mixed with fillers such as sawdust or plant materials has been molded into various objects, such as buttons, knitting needles, button hooks, and jewelry. It has been used as an imitation of ivory under the commercial names erinoid and galalith.

The feces or droppings of many animals have been utilized in a variety of ways for thousands of years. While manure rarely appears in museum collections, it should still be considered as a potential element in certain collections. Dried manure may be a normal component of natural history collections. And animal droppings have been occasionally utilized as a medium in modern art. Coprolites, which are fossilized droppings, are trace fossils and may be found in most paleontological collections.

Animal manure is the feces, dung, droppings, or excrement of animals and some birds. The term may also be expanded to include contaminated bedding such as straw or wood shavings.

The excrement most often used is produced by plant-eating animals. The droppings of carnivores or scavengers tends to have a strong, unpleasant smell and contains less of the nutrients that make other animals' excrement useful as fertilizer and soil additives. Dried dung is used as a fuel for fires, particularly in places where other fuels, like wood or coal, are scarce.

Dung has also been used in paper-making. The undigested, masticated plant materials found in the droppings of elephants, horses, llamas, and even kangaroos, can be separated with water and turned into coarse paper.

The term guano refers to the excrement of bats and seabirds. Since these animals tend to live for long periods in a small area, such as caves, vast deposits of guano may build up over time.

Animals in Collections

Animals and animal products appear in museum collections in many forms. Natural history collections contain the widest variety, since their purpose is to document the natural world.

There are different standards of practice for collections of each type of animal. Insects are mostly preserved dry, pinned in specialized trays or boxes. Certain types of insects, like spiders or sometimes the larger beetles, may be fluid preserved in a standard 70% ethanol and water solution. Older collections sometimes include wet-preserved specimens in glycerin, oil, or formalin.

Non-insect invertebrates are kept in both wet-preserved and dry form. Those animals having hard outer shells, like most mollusks, some echinoderms, and corals, may be dried and stored in drawers or trays. Invertebrates having no hard parts, or animals collected whole, are usually preserved in alcohol.

Vertebrate animals may be preserved dry or in fluid. Traditional systematic species collections may include study skins, skeletons, and fluid-preserved animals or body parts. Study skins are, as the name implies, the skin of the animal with hair and feathers intact. In small animals, the bones are often left in place since it would be too difficult and damaging to remove them. In study skins, the eyes and mouth are usually filled with cotton, and the body is stuffed gently with either cotton or acid-free tissue in order to keep the skin extended to its original size and shape. Large animals, such as whales or elephants, require a great deal of preparation and storage space. Some researchers may keep only those parts that are relevant to their collections, like the skull or extremities. Soft tissue or stomach contents may be frozen or preserved in alcohol.

After the skin is removed from the body, all soft tissue is removed by scraping. Tendons and ligaments may be pulled out of joints, through incisions at the joints. The body is washed with water and soap, and then soaked in compounds that will fix or tan the skin, preventing decomposition. Fluids used for this purpose vary according to the type of animal involved, what compounds are available, and the speed at which the preparator wants to work. Mixtures of salt and alum, or salt and mild sulfuric acid were historically popular, particularly for making taxidermy mounts of large animals. These compounds tend to dry, shrink and distort the skin, which make the finished product less useful. A combination of aluminum sulfate and salt in water takes longer to tan a skin, but produces a softer, less shrunken result.

If the skeleton is the only part of an animal to be preserved, the organic components of a body may be removed through a combination of physical and chemical means. The animal is skinned and as much tissue is removed as possible. The body can then be buried in the ground to allow microbes and insects to remove the remainder of the tissue. Depending on the size of the body, this can take weeks to years. Bones cleaned in this way may be stained by pigments occurring in the soil or groundwater. Insects may also be used to clean skeletons. Dermestid beetles are highly efficient protein feeders that can remove the tissue from even the tiniest bones without damaging them. Dermestid colonies must be carefully contained and monitored to insure that the insects do not escape, and to maintain the environmental conditions necessary for their survival. Chemical baths can also be used to decompose tissue.

During skinning, various compounds may be introduced into the specimen for the purposes of dissolving fats (acetone, gasoline, or other solvents), drying fat and tissue (borax, salt, cornmeal, diatomite, or plaster), and to kill insects (arsenic trioxide or borax).

The core of a taxidermy specimen may contain wire, soft wood, and stuffing material, with the skin stretched over it and sewn together. The stuffing can be just about anything. Straw and excelsior were common, but other plant materials or hair have also been used. Taxidermists who need to make mounts of similar animals repeatedly often create body casts in plaster from a mold that can be reused. Modern taxidermists often use pre-cast body molds made of plastic, wood, fiberglass, or compressed paper. The nose, eyes, and other elements of the outer body that were, in life, composed of soft tissue are usually replaced by replicas made of glass, wax, plastic, or resin. Paint and resin or lacquer may have been applied to various areas of the body in an effort to produce a natural color, or to protect the skin. Taxidermy mounts may contain screws, tacks, or bits of wire inside, as part of the frame, and at the surface where they are used to hold various body parts in place, like hooves, antlers, or horn sheaths.

Freeze-drying is another method sometimes used to preserve whole animals, particularly small ones that are too delicate for traditional skinning. Methods have been developed for the impregnation of soft tissues with resin. This is done in a vacuum chamber, and is usually done to preserve specimens of internal organs for teaching purposes.

Fur rugs and wall hangings are created in much the same way as study skins and taxidermy mounts, except that the bones are completely removed and the skin is trimmed into the desired size and shape. An exception to this is the trophy rug, in which the head and sometimes the feet are left intact.

Fish, reptiles, and amphibians are sometimes prepared as whole-body taxidermy mounts, but in collections they are most often preserved in 70% ethanol and water. Dried mounts prepared for display are often painted, since most of the natural pigments change or disappear when the animal dies. Mounted fish, particularly large ones, are often produced as a combination of natural and artificial parts. Large dorsal fins, such as those on sailfish and marlin, are often damaged and are recreated in wax or resin (older mounts) or fiberglass, masonite, or thick cardboard.

If preparation of an animal is done too quickly or without proper care, some natural compounds may remain in the specimen. Even though these compounds were liquid when the animal was alive, they may still be toxic. These include venom in the fangs of insects, snakes, some mollusks, and gila monsters. Mollusk shells in a dry collection may contain toxin if the body of the animal was not removed, but rather left to dessicate inside.

If the scent glands in some animals are not removed properly, the oily residue may remain on the skin around the anus. Moisture may reactivate these compounds, producing a nasty odor.

Environmental and storage conditions that are ideal for a whole animal are generally good for parts of the same animal. Composite objects, however, must be considered for all the different materials they contain, and an environmental compromise reached that will be the best for the thing as a whole.

Table 6.7   Animals in collections.

Animal group	Secondary group	Type of specimens in natural history collections	Derived materials found in museum collections
Invertebrates	With hard parts (mollusks, corals, etc.)	Dry shells, wet-preserved animals	Pearls, shell (M-of-p), coral, sponges
Invertebrates	Insects	Pinned or mounted dry insects, wet	Butterfly wings, beetles (scarabs)
Vertebrates	Mammals	Study skins, pelts, mounted specimens (taxidermy), whole or partial skeletons, teeth, wet-preserved animals, parts, or stomach contents, eggs, nests	Ivory, ruminant horn, rhino horn, antler, bone, claws, skin (leather, vellum), hair (bristles, quills, fur) hooves
Vertebrates	Fish	Whole or partial skeletons, teeth, wet-preserved animals, parts, or stomach contents	Scales
Vertebrates	Reptiles and amphibians	Study skins, mounted specimens (taxidermy), whole or partial skeletons, wet-preserved animals or parts	Tortoise shell, teeth, skin
Vertebrates	Birds	Study skins, mounted specimens (taxidermy), whole or partial skeletons, wet-preserved animals or parts	Feathers, down, beaks, feet

Sometimes it is best for an object to take it apart so that the different parts can be stored separately.

All of the natural history collections described here may also be associated with ancillary collections of data in various forms, and derived specimens such as slide-mounted histological or dissected parts, SEM mounts, photographs, or frozen tissue. Table 6.7 is a basic list of the types of materials associated with each major group of animals.

Appendix A: References and Further Reading

Aldrich, D. (1971). *Creating with Cattails, Cones and Pods*. Hearthside Press Inc., Great Neck, NY.

Barnes-Svarney, P. (1995). *Science Desk Reference*. MacMillan Press & New York Public Library, New York, NY.

Bolton, E.M. (1960). *Lichens for Vegetable Dyeing*. Charles T. Branford Co., Newton Center, MA.

Bonar, A. (1994). *Herbs, A Complete guide to Their Cultivation and Use*. Tiger Books International, London, UK.

Boskey, A.L. and Posner, A.S. (1984). Structure and formation of bone material. In *Natural and Living Biomaterials* (Hastings, G.W. and Ducheyne, P. eds.). CRC Press, Boca Raton, FL.

Brostow, W. (1985). *Science of Materials*. Robert E. Krieger Publishing, Malabar, FL.

Brusca, R.C. and Brusca, G.J. (2002). *Invertebrates*. Second edition. Sinauer Associates Inc., Sunderland, MA.

Campbell, N.A., Reece, J.B. and Mitchell, L.G. (1999). *Biology*. Fifth edition. Addison Wesley Longman Inc., New York, NY.

Cater, D. and Waller, A. (1998). *Care and Conservation of Natural History Collections*. Butterworth-Heinemann, Oxford, UK.

Catling, D. and Grayson, J. (1982). *Identification of Vegetable Fibers*. Chapman & Hall Ltd., London.

Collins, C. (ed.) (1995). *Care and Conservation of Paleontological Material*. Butterworth-Heinemann, Oxford, UK.

Cote, W.S. (ed.) (1980). *Papermaking Fibers: A Photomicrographic Atlas*. Syracuse University Press, Syracuse, NY.

Cronyn, J.M. (1990). *The Elements of Archaeological Conservation*. Routledge, New York, NY.

Curtis, H. (1983). *Biology*. Worth Publishers Inc., New York, NY.

Dana, E.S. and Ford, W.E. (1932). *A Textbook of Mineralogy*. John Wiley & Sons Inc., New York, NY.

Doughty, R.W. (1975). *Feather Fashions and Bird Preservation*. University of California Press, Berkeley, CA.

Douglas, S. (1981). *Feather Arts*. California Academy of Sciences, San Francisco, CA.

Dudley, L.P. (ed.) (1963). *Encyclopedia Americana*. Americana Corporation, New York, NY.

Feirer, J.L. (1975). *Wood: Materials and Processes*. Chas. A. Bennett Co. Inc., Peoria, IL.

Feller, R.L. (1985). Solvents. In *On Picture Varnishes and Their Solvents* (Feller, R.L., Stolow, N. and Jones, E.H. eds.). National Gallery of Art, Washington DC, WA.

Fettner, A.T. (1977). *Potpourri, Incense, and Other Fragrant Concoctions*. Workman Publishing, New York, NY.

Fleischer, M. and Mandarino, J.A. (1991). *Glossary of Mineral Species 1991*. Mineralogical Record Inc., Tucson, AZ.

Forster, I.W. (1984). Structural aspects of tendons and ligaments. In *Natural and Living Biomaterials* (Hastings, G.W. and Ducheyne, P. eds.). CRC Press, Boca Raton, FL.

Freethy, R. (1982). *How Birds Work: A Guide to Bird Biology*. Blandford Press, Dorset, UK.

Gibbons, E. (1962). *Stalking the Wild Asparagus*. Alan C. Hood & Co., Putney, VT.

Gillow, J. and Sentance, B. (1999). *World Textiles*. Thames & Hudson Ltd., London, UK.

Guildbeck, P.E. and MacLeish, A.B. (1985). *The Care of Antiques and Historical Collections*. Second edition. American Association for State & Local History, Nashville.

Harris, B. (1971). *Eat the Weeds*. Barre Publishing, Garre, MA.

Hartley, R.C. and Holliday, J.B. (1980). *Botanical Wreaths: A guide to Collecting, Preserving and Designing with natural Materials*. Flower Press, Warner, NH.

Hastings, G.W. and Ducheyne, P. (1984). *Natural and Living Biomaterials*. CRC Press Inc., Boca Raton, FL.

Heyn, A.N.J. (1954). *Fiber Microscopy*. Interscience Publishers Inc., New York, NY.

Howie, F.M. (1992). *Care and Conservation of Geological Materials: Minerals, Rocks, Meteorites and Lunar Finds*. Butterworth-Heinemann, Oxford, UK.

Kierstead, S.P. (1950). *Natural Dyes*. Bruce Humphries Inc., Boston, MA.

King, R.R. (1985). *Textile Identification, Conservation, and Preservation*. Noyes Publications, Park Ridge, NJ.

Kraus, E.H. and Holden, E.F. (1925). *Gems and Gem Materials*. McGraw-Hill, New York, NY.

Lesch, A. (1970). *Vegetable Dyeing*. Watson-Guptill Publications, New York, NY.

Liddicoat, Jr. R.T. (1977). *Handbook of Gem Identification*. Tenth edition. Gemological Institute of America, Santa Monica, CA.

Linton, G.E. (1966). *Natural and Manmade Textile Fibers*. Duell, Sloan & Pearce, New York, NY.

Long, J. (1998). *Making Bentwood Trelises, Arbors, Gates and Fences*. Storey Books, Pownal, VT.

Lucas, A. and Harris, J.R. (1989). *Ancient Egyptian Materials and Industries*. Fourth edition. Histories & Mysteries of Man Ltd., London, UK.

MacGregor, A. (1985). *Bone, Antler, Ivory and Horn: The Technology of Skeletal Materials Since the Roman Period*. Croom Helm Ltd., Beckenham, Kent, UK.

McFall, W.F. (1975). *Taxidermy Step By Step*. Winchester Press, New York, NY.

Metsger, D.A. and Byers, S.C. (eds.). (1999). *Managing the Modern Herbarium*. Society for the Preservation of Natural History Collections, Washington, DC.

Mills, J.S. and White, R. (1994). *The Organic Chemistry of Museum Objects*. Butterworth Heinemann, Oxford, UK.

Miloradovich, M. (1952). *Growing and Using Herbs and Spices*. General Publishing Co., Toronto, Canada.

Osborne, P.A. (1994). *About Buttons: A Collectors Guide*. Schiffer Publications, Atglen, PA.

Palache, C., Berman, H. and Frondel, C. (1944). *The System of Mineralogy of James Dwight Dana and Edward Salisbury Dana*. Seventh Edition, three volumes. John Wiley Sons Inc., New York, NY.

Pedersen, M.C. (2004). *Gem and Ornamental Materials of Organic Origin*. Elsevier Publishing, Oxford, UK.

Rabineau, P. (1979). *Feather Arts*. Field Museum of Natural History, Chicago, IL.

Raven, P.H. and Curtis, H. (1970). *Biology of Plants*. Worth Publishers Inc., New York, NY.

Sanderson, R.T. (1989). *Simple Inorganic Substances*. Robert E. Krieger Publishing, Malabar, FL.

Shipley, R.M. (1974). *Dictionary of Gems and Gemology*. Sixth edition. Gemological Institute of America, Santa Monica, CA.

Silver, F.H. (1987). *Biological Materials: Structure, Mechanical Properties and Modeling of Soft Tissue*. New York University Press, New York, NY.

Simon, H. (1969). *Feathers Plain and Fancy*. Viking Press, New York, NY.

Stevens, B.C. (1976). *The Collector's Bok of Snuff Bottles*. John Weatherhill Inc., New York, NY.

Storer, T.I., Usinger, R.L., Nybakken, J.W. and Stebbins, R.C. (1977). *Elements of Zoology*. Fourth Edition. McGraw-Hill Book Company, New York, NY.

Strunz, H. (1957). *Mineralogische Tabellen*. Akademische Verlagsgesellschaft, Leipzig, Germany.

Taberner, P.V. (1985). *Aphrodisiacs – The Science and the Myth*. University of Pennsylvania Press, Pittsburgh, PA.

Waterer, J.W. (1968). *Leather Craftsmanship*. G. Bell & Sons Ltd., London, UK.

Weisz, P.B. (1968). *Elements of Zoology*. Fourth Edition. McGraw-Hill Book Company, New York, NY.

Wilbraham, A.C., Staley, D.D. and Matta, M.S. (1997). *Chemistry*. Fourth edition. Addison-Wesley Publishing Co., Menlo Park, CA.

Williams, H., Turner, F.J. and Gilbert, C.M. (1954). *Petrography*. W.H. Freeman & Co., San Francisco, CA.

Wills, G. (1968). *Ivory*. Arco Publications, London, UK.

Wolf, R.F. (1939). *India Rubber Man*. Caxton Printers Ltd., Caldwell, ID.

Woshner, M. (1999). *India-Rubber and Gutta-Percha in the Civil War Era*. O'Donnell Publications, Alexandria, VA.

Appendix B: Glossary

This list includes words used to describe natural materials and some of the objects made from them. Most of these terms are also discussed in more detail in the text.

Acidic   having a pH value of less than 7.

Alkaline   having a pH value greater than 7.

Alloy   a mixture of two or more metals.

Alpha cellulose   the primary compound in plant tissues and fibers.

Amino acid   an organic acid that contains an amino radical (NH_2); the building blocks of all proteins. These simple organic molecules have a similar general formula, containing carbon, hydrogen, oxygen, nitrogen, and occasionally sulfur. There are only 20 common amino acids found in most animal tissue. There are another 100 less common amino acids that are found in plants and some animals.

Amorphous   a substance that has no orderly internal arrangement of atoms (glass).

Aquatic   living in or pertaining to water.

Arboreal   living in or pertaining to trees.

Artery   tube containing oxygen-enriched blood moving away from the heart.

Asterism   a star-like internal reflection of light within a mineral, caused by the crystal structure or aligned inclusions.

Baroque pearl   one that has an irregular shape (not round, oval, etc.).

Bead   a perforated worked object; usually round but may be any shape; may be any material.

Cabochon   a cut stone having a convex, curved upper surface and a flat, convex or concave base; may be of any shape or material.

Cameo   a carving in relief; substance cut away to reveal design; commonly made of layered substances such as onyx, agate, or shell; often cut so that colored layers in the stone accentuate the design.

Capillary   small tube with single-celled walls thin enough to allow diffusion to and from surrounding tissues; connectors between veins and arteries.

Carapace   hard upper shell, part of the exoskeleton, of turtles, tortoises, and crustaceans.

Carbohydrates   sugars and multi-sugar molecules. They are classified according to how many sugar molecules they have: monosaccharide, disaccharide, or polysaccharide, having one, two, and many, respectively. Carbohydrates are the main energy storage molecule in living systems, mostly in the form of cellulose and starch.

Carotinoids   red and yellow pigments in plants and algae, part of the photosynthesis cycle.

Carnivorous   an organism that eats or lives on the tissue of animals (meat).

Cartilage   fibrous collagen in an amorphous gel.

Cellulose   a polysaccharide polymer made of glucose molecules. It is the principal structural molecule in all plants, making up the fibrous part of plant cell walls.

Chitin   polysaccharide, a polymer made of glucose molecules combined with nitrogen-bearing molecules. Tough and chemically resistant, it makes up the exoskeletons of insects and other arthropods, and the cell walls of many fungi.

Chlorophyll   green pigment in plants and algae, part of the photosynthesis cycle.

Clay   a group of complex silicate minerals that have sheet-like molecular structure or any clastic fragment that is less than 1/256 mm in size.

Cleavage   a predictable break along planes that are parallel to crystal faces or structural planes when stress is applied to a substance.

Coccoon   protective covering or envelope surrounding a larva, pupa, or a mass of eggs.

Collagen   a group of common, relatively simple fibrous proteins; over 1400 amino acids long, in three chains that are twisted into a tight helix. Approximately 1/4 to 1/3 of all protein in an organism is usually collagen, and it is the most common protein in vertebrate animals. It is a major structural element in connective tissues: skin, tendons, muscle, and internal organs. It combines with inorganic compounds in bones and teeth.

Conchiolin   a protein that is found in mollusk shells, mixed with calcium carbonate. It is similar in structure to the keratin proteins.

Cornified   hardened or horny keratinous material; like a skin callus, horn, claw, or nail.

Cortex   outermost layer or covering on a structure.

Crystal   a solid mass composed of one or more element in which the internal structure consists of regularly repeating identical unit cells; usually characterized by planar external planes or faces.

Crystalline   a substance having a definite internal structure or pattern, opposite of amorphous.

Cultured pearl   one that is artificially induced by the placement of a foreign body within a mollusk, usually an oyster.

Dentine   central tissue in teeth; composed of collagen, hydroxyapatite (a mineral), and water.

Dermis   living skin beneath the outer epidermal layer.

Enzyme   biological catalysts; proteins that can accelerate chemical reactions without being changed themselves. Most enzymatic reactions occur within a narrow temperature range, from 30 to 40°C. Most enzymes react with only a small number of closely related compounds, and some require the presence of additional small non-protein molecules (coenzymes).

Fluorescence   the light given off by a substance when it is exposed to ultraviolet light.

Fossil   the remains or traces of organisms that have been naturally preserved in the Earth's crust.

Fracture   Fracture describes the way a substance breaks when it neither cleaves nor parts (breaks along plane of weakness). The most common kind of visible fracture is conchoidal, which produces curved, smooth surfaces (glass, quartz).

Freshwater pearl   one that occurs in a freshwater (non-marine) mollusk.

Gem   a general term used to describe precious and semi-precious stones, usually after they have been cut and polished. In archaeology, it refers only to engraved stones (cameo, intaglio, seals, etc.).

Gem-quality   term applied to rough material that is of a quality suitable for cutting or working in some way; varies according to the substance involved.

Hardness   the degree to which the surface of a substance resists scratching.

Hydrocarbon   molecules that contain only carbon and hydrogen. This term is also used sometimes to describe any simple organic molecule, possibly with additional elements such as nitrogen, phosphorus, or oxygen.

Imitation   a substance that looks or behaves like a particular material, but does not have the same chemical composition or internal structure.

Inlay   verb: to set or insert something into the surface of something else; or noun: inlaid work; usually refers to the material that has been set in.

Intaglio   an incised carving; the reverse of a cameo; often intended for use as a seal for wax or clay.

Intarsia   a design made up of fitted pieces having no metal or other binder between them; pieces are cut to fit a specific pattern; usually made of stone or a combination of materials.

Keratin   a group of fibrous proteins, these are the major components of hair, tooth enamel, skin, wool, horns, hooves, fingernails, claws, and feather quills. These proteins contain a lot of the amino acid *cysteine*, one of the few which has sulfur in it.

Lipids   organic compounds that are insoluble in water, including waxes and fats.

Luster   the way the surface of a substance reflects light, independent of color. The two basic types are metallic and non-metallic.

Matrix   the material in which a substance is naturally embedded; also called the groundmass.

Metal   those elements that are good energy conductors, generally opaque, have a metallic luster (usually), are cations (positive ions), fuse easily, and are ductile.

Mineral   a naturally occurring homogeneous solid having a definite chemical composition and an orderly internal structure.

Mineral species   a mineral substance having a specific chemical formula and characteristic physical and optical properties that distinguish it from all others; defined by composition and crystal structure.

Mosaic   a pattern made with small pieces of material, usually stone or glass, of different colors or textures; spaces between the pieces are filled with grout when finished.

Nucleotides   large molecules that combine into the nucleic acids (DNA and RNA), which carry genetic information.

Ore   a natural deposit in which some element or compound occurs in sufficient abundance to make it economically valuable.

Organic   a substance containing carbon compounds (usually hydro-carbons) and derived from organisms.

Oriental pearl   a natural pearl.

Pearl   an abnormal growth within shelled mollusks; consists of concentric layers of nacre (calcium carbonate); can be attached to the shell or loose; various colors and shapes.

Precious stone   the most prized gem species; usually limited to only four: ruby, sapphire, diamond and emerald; all others are "semi-precious"; this is an artificial term used only in marketing and has nothing to do with quality, size, or value.

Proteins   linear chains of amino acids; may contain any combination of the 20 amino acids that are found in natural organic substances. Some proteins may contain thousands of amino acids. Many proteins are specialized, such as enzymes, hormones, antibodies, and those whose job it is to store energy or transport energy or other compounds.

Refractive index   a numerical measure of the degree to which light is bent when it enters a translucent or transparent substance.

Rock   any naturally formed mass of mineral matter; composed of one or more minerals.

Specific gravity   a numerical expression of the ratio between the weight of a substance and the weight of an equal volume of water; a measure of a substance's density.

Synthetic a man-made substance with the same chemical formula as the natural substance it imitates; also has same physical and optical properties as the natural substance.

Tannin large molecule astringent compound found in plants; bonds readily with proteins. Used in tanning leather and medicinally. Found in most plants in some amount, more in some than in others.

Translucency a measure of how much light can penetrate a substance. A substance that transmits light is translucent; one that is clear enough that objects can be seen through it is transparent; and one through which no light can penetrate is opaque.

Vein tube containing oxygen-depleted blood toward from the heart.

Appendix C: Measurements

Measurements of Size

The metric system is the standard for measurements of all branches of science.

To measure	Divisions	Symbol	Numerical expression	Parts of basic unit	English equivalent
Length	Kilometer	km	1000 m	1000 × 1 meter	0.62137 miles
	Meter	m	Basic unit of measure	1 meter	39.4 inches
	Centimeter	cm	0.1 m	1/10 meter	0.3937 inches
	Millimeter	mm	0.001 m	1/100 meter	
	Micron		0.000001 m	1/10,000 meter	
	Nanometer or millimicron	nm or mμ	0.000000001 m	1/100,000,000 meter	
	Angstrom	Å	0.0000000001 m	1/1,000,000,000 meter	
Volume (solid)	Cubic meter	m^3	Basic unit of measure		1.308 cubic yards or cubic feet
	Cubic centimeter	cm^3	0.000001 m^3	1/100,000 cubic meter	0.061 cubic inches
	Cubic millimeter	mm^3	0.00000000 m^3	1/100,000,000 cubic meter	
Volume (fluid)	Liter	l	Basic unit of measure		1.06 quarts or pints
	Milliliter	ml	0.001 liter	1/100 liter	
	Microliter	μl	0.000001 liter	1/100,000 liter	

Measurements of Weight

To measure	Divisions	Symbol	Numerical expression	Parts of basic unit	English equivalent
Weight	Kilogram	kg	1000 g	1000 × 1 gram	2.2 pounds
	Gram	g or gr	Basic unit of measure	1 gram	3.527 ounces
	Carat*	ct	0.2 g	1/5 gram	
	Grain*	gr	0.0648 g	gram	
	Milligram	mg	0.001 g	1/100 gram	
	Point*	pt	0.002 g	1/500 gram	
	Microgram	μg	0.000001 g	1/100,000 gram	

*used for gemstones and/or pearls.

Denier   The denier of filaments or yarn is the gram weight of 9000 meters of it. The higher the number, the coarser the filament.

One pound of 1-denier sized yarn contains 4,464,528 yards

Carat   Measure of weight used for gemstones, part of the metric system.

1 carat = 1/5 gram or 5 carats = 1 gram

Points   Measure of weight used for gemstones, part of the metric system.

1 point = 1/100 carat or 100 points = 1 carat or 500 points = 1 gram

Grains   Measure of weight used for pearls.

1 grain = 0.0648 grams = ¼ carat = 1/20 gram. This unit is sometimes confusing and is best written out "grains," since the accepted abbreviation or symbol for it is "gr," which is also used from grams.

The weight of pearls may be expressed in carats, grains, or momme. The momme is usually used for large pearls or masses of smaller pearls. It is equal to 18.75 carats, or 3.75 grams.

Precious metals are usually weighed in troy ounces.

1 troy ounce (t.oz.) = 31.1035 grams

Measurements of Purity

Karat   24 K = pure gold

18 K = 18 parts gold, 6 parts something else (other metals) or 75% gold

14 K = 14 parts gold, 10 parts other or about 58% gold

10 K = 10 parts gold, 14 parts other or 42% gold

Low-karat gold, usually anything less than 14 K, will tarnish and will not have the malleability or other properties of gold.

Fine silver   99.9% silver

Britannia silver   95.84% silver, up to 4.16% copper

Mexican silver   95% silver, 5% copper

Sterling silver   92.5% silver, alloyed with other metals, usually copper

Coin silver   90% silver, 10% copper

Index

(*Bold page numbers refer to Figures*)

aardvark, 118, 120
abaca, 74, 76
abalone, 101, 111
Abies, 70
abrasives, 122, 150
absorbency, 7
accessory minerals, 42
Acer, 70
acetone, 159
acetylsalicylic acid, 72
achondrites, 50
achroite, 34, 39
acid rain, 8
acids, acidity, 7, 8, 73, 167
Acinonyx jubatus, **127**
Acmaea, 101
acorns, 70, 93
actinolite, 18, 22, 35, 39, 54
adamantine luster, 10
adhesives, 106, 142, 150, 157, 158
adipocere, 151
adularescence, 12, 23
adularia (see also moonstone), 35
afterfeather, 129
aftershaft, 129
agate, 24, **25**, 35, 167
Agave, 76
Agave sisalana, 74
Agnatha, 116
airplane fabric, 74

airplanes, 74
alabaster (see also gypsum), 19, 33, 37
albatross, 119
albite (see also plagioclase, feldspar,
    moonstone), 5, 12, 23, 36, 42
albumin, 142
alcohol (see also ethanol), 94, 112,
    149, 159, 160
alder, 70
alexandrite (see also chrysoberyl), 31,
    32, 37
algae, 59, 60, 66, 91, 118, 168
alkali, alkaline, 7, 150, 151, 167
alkaloid, 72
alligators, 116, 122
allochromatic, 10
allotype, 61
alloys, 7, 26–30, 167, 174
almandine (see also garnet), 17, 33, 37
Alnus, 70
alpaca, 124, 125
alpha cellulose, 167
alpha particles, 8
alpha radiation, 52
alum, 92, 93, 153, 159
aluminum, 15
aluminum sulfate, 159
alveolata, 60
amazonite, 36
amber, 8, 66–67, 132

amber clearing, 67

ambergris, 149–150

amberoid, 67

ambra grisea, 149

ambre gris, 149

ambroid, 67

American ruby, 33

amethyst, 24, 35

ametrine, 24

amino acid, 50, 58, 135, 167, 168, 169, 170

ammonites, 101

amniotes, 116

amoebas, 59, 60

amorphous, 5, 167, 168

amosite, 22

Amphibia, 116

amphibians, 98, 115, 116, 120, 139, 141, 151, 160, 161

amphibole group, 18, 21, 31, 38, 42

amphioxus, 115

amygdaloidal basalt, 43

an isotropic, 11

ancillary collections, 161

andalusite, 17, 33

andesine (see also feldspar), 36, 41

andradite (see also garnet), 17, 33

anemones, 98

angiosperms, 63, 64, 69

anglesite, 53

angora fiber, 124

angora goat, 124, 125

angora rabbit, 124, 126

angstrom, 173

animal dung (see also dung, excrement), 68

animal fat (see also fat), 84

animal hair, 82

animal hair, 122

animal kingdom, 59

animals in collections, 158–161

animals, animalia, 59–60, 97

annelida, 98

anorthite (see also feldspar), 36, 42

anteaters, 118, 120

antelope, 120, 146

antennae, 102

anterior teeth, 139

Antheraea melitta, 104

Antheraea pernyi, 104

anthophyllite, 22, 54

anthophyta, 63

anthracite, 47

antibodies, 58, 170

antigorite, 18, 21, 35, 39

antimonides, 16

antler velvet, 136

antlers, 121, 134–136, **136**, **137**, **138**, 150, 160, 161

ants, 103

Anura, 115

apatite, 17, 33, 42, 135

ape, 120

aphrodisiacs, 103, 147, 149, 150

Apis mellifera, 106

Apoda, 115

aquamarine, 15, 34, 38

aquatic, 167

aragonite (see also calcium carbonate), 5, 15, 17, 19, 33, 37, 46, 107

arboreal, 167

archaea, 60

Archaeognatha, 103

Archaeopteryx, 132

archaezoa, 60

arenite, 43

argillite, 43

arkose, 43

armadillos, 120, 122

armor, 154

arrows, 83

arsenates, 20

arsenic, 16, 51, 52, 53, 159

arsenic trioxide, 51, 159

arsenolite, 51, 53

arsenopyrite, 53

arteries, artery, 167

arthropods, arthropoda, 57, 98, 101–104, 107, 168

Artiodactyla, 120, 128

asbestiform minerals, 22

asbestos, 6, 10, 13, 22

ash, ashes, 70, 81, 150, 151

aspen, 70, 81

asphalt, 47, 91

asphaltum, 91

aspirin, 72

asterism, 13, **13**, 167

astroblemes, 50

atomic mass, 1

atomic number, 1

atoms, 1

auks, 119

autunite, 53

aventurine, 26

Aves, 116, 129

avocets, 119

axinite, 34

azurite, 10, 17, 19, 33, 37

backbone, 97, 115

backscratchers, 122

bacteria, 59, 60, 75

Bactrian camel, 124, 125

baculum, 135

badger, 120, 128, 148

bags (see also containers, pouches), 141

bakelite, 89, **157**

balas ruby, 32

bald cypress, 81

bald eagle, **134**

baleen, 142–144, 155

balloon cloth, 74

bamboo, 71, 75, 81

Bambusa, 71

Banana family, 74

bandicoot, 120

barbiceli, **131**

barbs, 129, 131, **131**

barbules, 129, **131**

barite, 17, 20, 23

bark, 58, 65, 70, 71–72, 73, 77, 79, 87, 90, 91, 94, 152, 154

bark cloth, 71

barley, 78

barnacles, 103, 104

Barong Tagalog, 78

baroque pearl, 167

basalt, 41, 43, 49

bases, 8

baskets (see also woven plant materials), **xii**, 71, 74, 77, 78, 82, 83, 94, 122, 133, 141

bast, 73, 74, 75, 76

bastard cinnamon, 72

batiste, 74

bats, 118, 120, 158

bead, 113, **145**, 167

beaked whales, 120, 155

beaks, 121, 142, 161

beard hairs, 122

bears, 118, 120, 128

beaver oil, 149

beavers, 120, 128, 149

bedding, 78

beech, 70

beef, 148

beer, 152

bees, 103

beeswax, 84, 106

beetles, 103, 158, 159, 161

belts, 72

beluga whales, 120

benitoite, 34

bentwood, 79, 81, 82

Berchemia scandens, 81

berries, 82

beryl, 5, 15, 17, 21, 34, 38, 41

Berzelius, Jons, 15

beta particles, 8

beta radiation, 52

Betula, 70

bighorn sheep, **147**

billiard balls, 88, 157

bills (see also beaks), 143

binomial, 59

biotite, 28, 42

birch, 70, 72, 81

birds, 98, 116–117, 119–120, 129, 131–132, 133, **134**, 139, 141, 143, 144, 149, 151, 158, 161

birds of paradise, 133

birds of prey, **134**, 144

birefringence, 12

bismuth, 16

bitterns, 119, 129

bituminous coal, 46–47

bivalves, 104, 108, **110**, 111

Bivalvia, 101

black coral, 99

black star of India, 13, 35

blackberry, 93

bladders, 141, 150

blankets, 125

blastopore, 97

blastula, 97

blende, 32

blender scent, 90

blisters, 111

blood, 8, 157–158

bloodroot, 93

bloodstone, 24

bluebirds, 119

boar, 148, 155

boar tusk, **156**

boas, 116

boats, 72, 91

body contour feather, **130**

body feathers, 129

Boehmeria nivea, 76

bog oak, 68

bohemian ruby, 24

boiling point, 8

bois durci, 157–158

Bombyx mori, 104

bone, 6, 23, 44, **85**, 108, 116, 119,
    134–136, 138, 140, 142, 143, **145**, 147,
    148, 149, 150, 152, 155, 156, 157, 159,
    160, 161, 168

boobies, 119

book cloth, 74

bookbinding, 74, 88, 157

bookplates, 142

books, **xii**, **154**

boots, 122

borates, 19

borax, 53, 159

Boswellia, 91

botanical specimens, 93–94

bottle-nosed whales, 120, 155

boulders, 42

bouquets, 82

Bovidae, **152**

bowenite, 35

box elder, 81

Brachiopoda, 98

braided straw, 79

brain tissue, 153

branches, 69, 77, 79, 81, 82

brass, 29

brazilianite, 33

breadfruit tree, 71

breccia, 41, 43

bricks, 78

bridges, 81

Brinell hardness test, 7

bristle feathers, **130**, 131

bristles, 126, 148, 161

bristletails, 103

Britannia silver, 28–29, 174

brittleness, 5

brocade, 105

bronze, 29

brooms, 77, 81–82

brown coal, 46

brown ocher, 18

brushes, 76, 77, 81, 82, 148

brushite, 135

bryophyta, bryophytes, 63

bryozoa, 98

Bucerotidae, 143

bucking, 151

buckram, 74

buffalo, 128, 146, 147, **152**

buggy whips, 144

bugs, 103

building materials, 19, 91, 108

burlap, 76

burmite, 67

burn test, 8

Bursa, 109

Burseraceae family, 91

bustards, 119

butter, 89, 148

butter-and-tallow tree, 89

butterflies, 103, 104, **104**, **112**, 161

butterfly maiden, **xiii**

button quail, 119

buttons, 85, 87, 88, 113, 135, 143, 145, 157, 158

byssal threads, 104

byssolite, 22

bytownite (see also feldspar), 36

cables, 77

cabochon, 167

cactus, 106

cadavers, 151

caecilians, 115

cahuchu, 86

cairngorm, 24

calamus, 129, **130**

calcite (see also calcium carbonate), 5, 15, 17, 19, 23, 32, 37, 40, 41, 43, 45, 46, 48, 107, 141

calcium, 15

calcium carbonate see also aragonite, calcite), 5, 15, 17, 19, 23, 32, 37, 41, 43, 45, 46, 48, 107, 108, 141, 168, 170

calcium phosphate, 135

calico, 74

californite, 34

calking, 91

callais, 20

callus, 168

calomel, 53

calves, 121

cambium, 65, **66**

cambric, 74, 76

camel, 120, 125, 135

camel hair, 124, 125

camellids, 124

cameo, 30, 108, **109**, 113, 167, 169

camphor, 88

cancellous tissue, 134

candelilla wax, 89

candles, 89, 90, 91, 106, 148, 150

candy, 88, 89

cane, 71

canine teeth, 139

canines, 140

Cannabis, 74

Cannabis sativa, 76

cannel coal, 47

canoes, 72

cantharidin, 103

canvas, 74, 76, 142

caoutchouc, 86

cape buffalo, **152**

cape ruby, 33

capillary, 167

capybara, 120

carapace, 116, **117**, 142, 168

carat, 174

carats, 111

carbohydrates, 57, 65, 73, 135, 168

carbolic acid, 89

carbonaceous chondrite, 50

carbonate rocks, 45, 46

carbonates, 17, 19, 32

carbuncle, 33

cardboard, 160

cardinals, 119

Caretta caretta, 142

caribou, 120, 135

carnauba wax, 89

carnelian, 24, 35

Carnivora, 120, 128

carnivores, 116, 118, 139, 158

carnivorous, 168

carnotite, 54

carotinoids, 65, 131, 168

carpet (see also rugs), 76

cartilage, 58, 116, 135, 141, 168

carvings, 113, 167

Carya, 70

case hardening, 152

casein, 158

cashmere, 123, 124

cashmere goat, 124, 125

casings, 141

casque, 143, **145**

cassia, 72

cassimere, 123

Cassis, 108, 109
cassiterite, 18
cast iron, 7
Castanea, 70
caster, 149
castoreium, 149
castoreum perfume, 149
cat hair, 124
cat litter, 21
cat's eye, 32, 37
cat's eye effect (see also chatoyancy),
  12, 13
catalysts, 169
catechols, 58
caterpillar, 104, 105
catgut, 141
cations, 170
cats, 118, 120, 124, **127**, 128, 141,
  144, 149
cattails, 82, 83
cattle, 118, 120, 124, 126, 135, 146,
  147, 157
cavalry twill, 123
cave deposits, 42, 45
caves, 158
cedar, 70, 81
celestine, 20
cells, 57, 59
celluloid, 88, 89, **157**
cellulose, 57, 69, 73, 74, 88, 89, 167, 168
cellulose acetate, 74
cement, 43, 69
cementum, 137, 138
centimeter, 173
centipedes, 98
cephalopods, 98, 101
cephalothorax, 102
ceramic glazes, 9, 51
ceramics, 21, 135, **157**
cereal plants, 78
cerote, 89
cerussite, 53
Cervidae, 135, **136**
Cervus elaphus, **136**
ceylonite, 32

chairs, 72
chalcanthite, 20, 53
chalcedony, 24, **25**, 35, 39, 44, 46
chalcedony after bone, 26
chalcedony after crocidolite, 26
chalcedony after riebeckite, 26
chalcedony after wood, 26
chalcopyrite, 5, 28
chalk, 46
challis, 123
Chamaecyparis, 70
chambered nautilus, 101
chameleons, 116
chamois leather, 153
chamoising, 153
charms, 113, 149
Charonia, 109
chatoyancy, 12, 37
cheesecloth, 74
cheetah, **127**, 128
chelicera, 102
Chelicerata, 102
Chelonia mydas, 142, **143**
chemical formulae, 3
chemical groups of minerals, 16–18
chemical sediments, 42, 45
cherry, 70
chert, 23, 42, 46
chestnut, 70
chewing gum, 88, 89
chiastolite, 33
chickadees, 119
chickens, 133
chiffon, 105
china clay, 21
China grass, 73, 76
chinchilla, 120, 128
Chinese "cinnabar", 16, 18
Chinese insect wax, 106
chipmunk, 120
Chiroptera, 120
chitin, 57, 100, 102, 103, 107, 168
chitons, 98
chlamydias, 60
chlorargyrite, 19

chloromelanite, 39

chlorophyll, 65, 168

chocolate, 90

Chondrichthyes, 116

chondrites, 49–50

chondrules, 50

Chordata, 97, 98, 115

chromates, 19

chrome, 93

chrome-diopside, 34

chromista, 60

chromite, 18

chromophore, 10

chrysoberyl, 13, 17, 18, 31, 32, 37

chrysoberyl var. alexandrite, 31, 32, 37

chrysocolla, 18, 35

chrysolite, 33

chrysoprase, 24, 35

chrysotile, 21, 22, 35, 39, 54

cigars, 78

ciliates, 60

Cinchona, 72

cinnabar, 16, 17, 53, 88

cinnabar lacquer, 16, 18

cinnabar ware, 88

cinnamon, 72

Cinnomomum aromaticum, 72

Cinnomomum verum, 72

Cinnomomum zeylandicum, 72

citrine, 24, 35

civet oil, 149

clams (see also bivalves), 98, 108, 111

class, 59

classification of animals, 97–98, 115–119

classification of birds, 119

classification of invertebrates, 97–98

classification of mammals, 120

classification of organisms, 59–60

classification of plants, 63–64

clastics, 168

claudetite, 53

claws, 58, 121, 142, 144, 155, 161,
    168, 169

clay, 16, 18, 42, 43, 74, 78, 168, 169,

claystone, 42, 43

cleavage, 5–6, 168, 169

close plating, 29

Clostridium, 75

cloth, 74

clothing, 71, 73, 74, 78, 83, 86, 125, 127,
    133, 155

club moss, 63

cnidaria, 98, 99

coal, 46, 68, 90, 91, 158

coal tar, 91

coal tar creosote, 91

coal tar pitch, 91

coarse wool, 122

coatings, 88

cob, 78

cobaltite, 53

cobbles, 42, 43

Coccoidea, 105, 106

coccoon, 102, 103, 104, 105, 168

cochineal, 106

cockatoos, 119

cockroaches, 103

coconut, 76

coelenterata, coelenterates, 98, 99

coenzymes, 58, 169

coffee, 93

coin silver, 28, 174

coins, 27

coir, 76, 77

coke, 47, 91

colemanite, 53

collagen, 58, 135, 137, 138, 150, 152,
    168, 169

collar stays, 144

cologne, 90

color, 10, 131

color centers, 11

color fading, 10

coluga, 120

combs, 145

Commiphora, 91

common goat hair, 125

common opal, 26

compact bone, 134

composite objects, **xiii**

conchiolin, 58, 107, 168

conchoidal fracture, 6, 169

concretions, 43

condoms, 87, 141

condors, 119

conductivity, 7

cone shells, 108

cones, 70, 82

conglomerate, 42, 43

coniferophyta, 63

conifers, 63, 69

consolidants, 88

contact metamorphic rocks, 47

containers, 84, 145, 146, 154

contour feathers, 129

Conus, 108

copper, 16, 27, 29, 92, 174

copper salts, 29

copper sulfate, 20

copperas, 92

copperas, 93

coprolites, 158

coral, 19, 45, 46, 98, 99, **99, 100**, 113, 159, 161

Corchorus, 74

Corchorus capsullaris, 76

Corchorus olitorus, 76

cord, cordage, 73–78 106, 125, 141

cordierite, 34

cork, 66, 74, 76

cork floats, 72

cork oak, 72

cormorants, 119

corms, 65

corn, 78

corn broom, 82

corn dollies, 78, **79, 80**

corn husks, 92

corn stalks, 81

cornified, 168

cornmeal, 159

corset stays, 144

cortex, **66**, 122, 168

cortical tissue, 134

corundum (see also ruby, sapphire), 13, 17, 18, 31, 32, 42

cosmetics, 47, 89, 90, 91, 106, 108, 148, 149, 150

cotton, **xii**, 57, 73, 74, 75, 76, 79, 159

cotton cloth, 74

cotton flannel, 74

cotton gabardine, 74

cottonwood, **xii**, **xiii**, 70, 81, 95

cotype, 61

cow hair, 124, 125

cowries, 107

cows, 158

coypu, 128

crabapple, 93

crabs, 102, 103

crane's bill, 143

crane's crest, 143

cranes, 119

craniates, 115

creepers, 119

creosote, 91

creosote bush, 91

crepe, 105

crepe de chine, 105

crickets, 103

crinoids, 98

crocidolite, 22

crocodiles, 116, 122

Crocodylia, 116

crocoite, 19, 53

crosses, 78

crown (tooth), 136, **139**

crown jewels, 31

crows, 119

crust, 15

crustacea, crustaceans, 98, 102, 103, 104

cryolite, 53

cryptocrystalline quartz, 23

crystal, 168

crystal classes, 4

crystal forms, 5

crystal structure, 4–5

crystal symmetry, 4–5

crystal systems, 4

crystalline, 168

cubic zirconia, 11, 36

cuckoos, 119

cucumber family, 84
Cucurbitaceae, 84
cudbear, 93
culms, 81
cultured pearl, 111, 169
cuprosklodowskite, 54
curite, 53
currying, 153
cut steel, 30
cuticle, 65, 122
cutis, **146**
cuttlefish, 101
cyanobacteria, 60
cycadophyta, 63
cycads, 63
cyclosilicate, 17, 21, 34
cymophane, 32
Cyperous papyrus, 72
Cypraea, 107
cypress, 70, 81
cysteine, 58, 169
CZ, 11, 36

daguerreotype-type cases, 88
damask, 76, 105
Dana, James & Edward, 15
Dana's system, 15–18, 54
dead tanning, 152
deciduous trees, 69
deer, 118, 120, 145
deer family, 135, **136**
demantoid, 33
Demospongiae, 98
denier, 174
density, 9, 170
dentin, 58, 135, 136–138, **139**, 140, 155, 169
dentinal tubules, 137
dentistry, 29, 87
dermal cells, 65
dermal papillae, 147
dermestid beetles, 159
dermis, 121, 169
Dermochelys coriacea, 142
Dermoptera, 120
dew retting, 75

diabase, 49
diamond, 5, 6, 11, 15, 16, 17, 31, 32, 38, 39, 170
diamond imitations, 31, **40**
diatomaceous earth, 46, 88
diatomite, 42, 46, 159
diatoms, 46, 60
dice, 157
dichroism, 31
dicots, 64
diffraction of light, 11
dinoflagellates, 60
dinosaurs, 116
diopside, 18, 34
diorite, 41
Diospyros, 69, 70
diplomonads, 60
disaccharide, 57, 168
disinfectant, 91
dispersion, 11
DNA, 170
dodo, 119
dogs, 118, 120, 135
dogwood, 81
doll (see also kachina), **xiii**
dolomite, 42, 45
dolphins, 118, 120, 155
domain, 60
door knobs, 88
dorsal fins, 160
Douglas fir, 69, 70
doum palm, 85
doves, 119, 133
down, down feathers, 129, **130**, 133, 161
dragonflies, 103
dressed pelts, 127
dried plant materials (see also baskets, mats, wreaths), **xii**, 77–85, **112**
dripstone, 42
dromedary camel, 125
droppings (see also excrement, dung), 158
ducks, 119, 131, 132, 133
ductility, 5
dugongs, 120
dull luster, 10

dung (see also excrement), 158

dust, 52, 55

dyes, 31, 51, 66, 91–93, 99, 105–106, 125, 127, 153

eagles, 119, 133, **134**

ear shells, 101

Earth's crust, 15, 20, 22, 40, 44, 169

earwigs, 103

ebonite, 86

ebony, 69, 70

echidna, 120

Echinodermata, 98

echinoderms, 159

Edentata, 120

eels, 116

egg shell, eggshell, 115, 141

egg white, 142

egg yolks, 153

eggs, 102, 103, 115–117, 132, 141–142, 161, 168

egret, 132, **132**, 133

Egretta thula, **132**

Egyptian alabaster (see also calcium carbonate), 32, 46

elasticity, 5

elastin, 141

elbaite (see also tourmaline), 17, 34

elderberry, 93

electrical equipment, 28, 29, 89

electron shells, 3

electrons, 1

electrum, 27

elephants, 120, 140, 155, 158, 159

elk, 120, **136**

elk teeth, 155

elm, 70

embroidery, 74

emerald, 15, 31, 34, 38, 170

emu, 129, 132, 133, 149

emu oil, 149

enamel, 136, 138

enamel (tooth), **139**, 169

Endopterygota, 103

endoskeleton, 113, 116

enstatite, 13, 18, 35

enzymes, 58, 106, 169, 170

epidermal hairs, 73

epidermis, 65–66, **66**, 121, 127, 129, **146**, 147, 151, 169

epidote, 17, 34, 49

Eretmochelys imbricata, 142

erinoid, 158

erionite, 22, 54

Erithzon dorsatum, **126**

ermine, 128

erythrite, 53

esparto grass, 90

esparto wax, 90

essonite, 33

etching, 108

ethanol (see also alcohol), 112, 141, 158, 159, 160

eucalyptus, 69, 70

euglenoids, 60

euglenozoa, 60

eukarya, 60

eukaryotes, 59

Euphorbia, 89

Euporbiaceae, 89

eurypterids, 98, 102

Eutheria, 117

evaporites, 45

excelsior, 160

excrement (see also dung), 44, 152, 157–158

excrescence, 143

Exopteryogota, 103

exoskeleton, 101, 112, 113, 116, 168

external mold, 44

extrusive rocks, 41

fabric, **xii**, **xiii**, 73–77, 82, 86, 87, 89, 91, 94, 95, 104–106, 113, 123, 125, 126, 128, 149, 150

Fagus, 70

faille, 105

falcons, 119

false teeth, 87

family, 59

fangs, 160

fans, 133

fat, 57–58, 84, 148–151, 153, 154, 159, 169

fatty acids, 89

feather color, 131

feather parts, 129, **130**, **131**

feather types, 129, **130**

feathers, **xii**, **xiii**, 11, 58, 77, 82, **84**, 92, 95, 116, 117, **118**, 121, 128–134, **132**, **134**, 142, 143, **146**, 159, 161, 169

feces (see also excrement), 158

feel, 7

feet, 135, 144, **146**, 160, 161

feldspar group, 12, 16, 18, 22, 35, 41, 42, 43

felt, 123, 125

fenders for ships, 77

fermentation, 152

ferns, 63

ferrogedrite, 22, 54

fertility charms, 135

fertilizer, 47, 135, 158

fiber banana plant, 76

fiberglass, 160

fibers, 104

fibroin, 105

fibrous fracture, 6

Ficus, 86

fig tree, 71

filaments, 105, 174

filatex, 87

film, 88

filoplume, 129, **130**

filters, 76

finches, 119

fine silver, 28, 174

fine wool, 122

fingernails, 58, 129, 169

fins, 160

fir, 70

fish (see also sharks, rays), **85**, 98, 104, 116, 120, 141, 150, 151, 160, 161

fishing floats, 84

fishing nets, 78

Fissurella, 101

fixative (scent), 90

fixatives, 149, 150

flamingo, 119, 133

flammability, 8

flannel, 74, 123

flatworms, 98

flavoring, 88

flax, 73, 74, 75, 89

fleas, 103

fleece, 122, 124, 148

fleshing, 151

flexibility, 5

flies, 103

flight feathers, 129, **130**

flightless birds, 117

flint, 23

floor covering (see also linoleum, mats), 74, 77, 78, 81

flotation (see also cork), 84

flour, 153

flowering plants, 63–64

flowers, 64, 66, 82

fluff, 83

fluorapatite, 17, 33

fluorescence, 11, 169

fluorite, 5, 6, 17, 19, 23, 32

fluorospar, 32

flux, 88

follicles, 121, 122, 147, 148

fonts, 109

food, 70, 71, 76, 82, 83, 84, 85, 88, 89, 90, 104, 108, 135, 141, 148, 150, 157, 158

fool's gold, 28

foot (see also feet), 107, **146**

foraminifera, 46, 60

formaldehyde, 89

formalin, 112, 158

formulae, 3

forsterite, 17, 33, 37

fossil ivory, 155, 156

fossil plants (see also coal, amber), 66–68, 90

fossilization, 66

fossils, 23, 44, 113, 131, 169
fossils, radioactive, 8
fox, 120, 128
fracture, 5–6, 169
frames, 88
framework silicates, 22
frankincense, 91
Fraxinus, 70
freeze-drying, 160
French jet, 68
freshwater pearls, 111, 169
frigatebirds, 119
frogs, 115, 116
frozen specimens, 159
fruit, 66
fruit tree wood, 81
fulgarite, 41
Fuller's earth, 46
fungi, fungus, 57, 59, 60, 66, 75, 91, 168
fungicides, 91
fur, 122–128, **127**, 154, 160, 161
furniture, 70, 71, 76, 77, 78, 81, 82, 157

gabardine, 74, 123
gabbro, 41
galalith, 158
galena, 16, 17, 53
gamma particles, 8
gamma radiation, 52
gannets, 119
garnet group, 5, 6, 16, 17, 20, 33, 37, 39, 41, 42
garter snakes, 116
gasoline, 47, 159
gastropods, 101, 111
gastrula, 97
gauze, 105
geese, 119, 131, 132, 133
gelatin, 150
gem, 169
gem-quality, 30, 169
gemstones, 30–40, 174
genitalia, 149
genotype, 61
genus, 59
geological collections, 51–56

georgette, 105
gerbil, 120
German silver, 29
gesso, 19, 142, 158
ghedda, 106
giant clam, 109
giardia, 60
gila monster, 160
gilsonite, 91
gingham, 74
ginkgoes, 63
ginkgophyta, 63
ginseng, 103
giraffe, 120, 147
glands, 149, 160
glass, 5, 6, 10, 11, 13, 36, 39, 40, 41, 46, 51, 54, 82, 88, 160, 167, 169, 170
glass sponges, 98
Glauber's salts, 92
glaucodot, 53
gliders, 74
glossary, 167–171
glucose, 57, 168
glue (see also adhesives), 69, 75, 88, 105, 106, 121, 142, 150
glycerin, 158
glycine, 135
gneiss, 47, 48, 49
gnetophyta, 63
goat hair, 124
goats, 120, 121, 124, 126, 149, 153, 158
goethite (see also iron oxide), 18
gold, 17, 27, 28, 32, 142, 174
golden beryl, 34, 38
golden jade, 143
golf balls, 87
goma de un arbol, 86
Goodyear, Charles, 86
gophers, 120, 138
goshenite, 15, 34, 38
Gossypium, 73, 74
gourds, **84**, 84, 85
grain (plant), 174
grain sizes (sediment), 42
grains (unit of measure), 111, 152
gram, 174

gram-positive bacteria, 60
granite, 9, 41, 42, 49
granitic rocks, 42
grapes, 93
grapevines, 82
graphite, 16
graphite, 15, 17
grass, 64, 71, 77, **79**, **80**, 81, 82, **112**
grass skirts, 78
grasshoppers, 103
grave wax, 151
gravel, 42
gray amber, 149
gray whales, 120, 144
grease, 148, 153
greasy luster, 10
grebes, 119, 133
green sea turtle, 142, **143**
greenockite, 53
greenstone, 48, 49
grossular (see also garnet), 17, 33, 39
ground tissue, 65
groundmass, 170
grouse, 119, 129
grout, 170
grunerite, 22, 54
guanaco, 124
guano, 158
guinea corn, 82
guinea pig, 120
gulls, 119, 133
gum trees, 69, 70
gum turpentine, 87
gum-elastic, 86
Gutenberg bible, 73
gutta percha, 85, 86–88, 94
gymnosperms, 63, 69
gypsum (see also alabaster), 5, 13, 17,
    19, 33, 37, 41, 43, 46, 142

hagfish, 116
hair, **xiii**, 58, 92, 106, 121, 122–128, **123**,
    124, **126**, 129, 142, 151, 154, 159, 160,
    161, 169
hair follicle, 121, 122
halfah grass, 90

Haliaeetus leucocephalus, **134**
halides, 17, 19, 32, 45
Haliotis (see also abalone), 101, 110
Haliotis iris, 110
halite (see also salt), 5, 17, 19
halophiles, 60
hamster, 120
handles (see also tools), 113, 122, 147,
    157
hapantotype, 61
happy camp jade, 34, 39
hard coal, 47
hard fiber, 73
hard rubber, 86, 88
hardness, 6–7, 169
hardwood, 69, 70, 91
hare, 120, 128
hartshorn jelly, 150
harvest-related items, 78, **79**, **80**
hats, 74, 76, 79, 122, 125, 133
hawk's eye, 26
hawks, 119, 133
hawksbill turtle, 142
heads, 160
hedgehog, 120
heishi, 108
heliodor, 15, 34, 38
heliotrope, 24
helmet shells, 108
hematite, 17, 18, 19, 32
hemicellulose, 69, 73
hemlock, 70
hemp, 73, 74, 76
henequin, 76
henna, 92, 93
henna tattoo, 92
herbivores, 118, 140
herbs, 141
heron, 119, 129, 132, 133
hessian, 74
hessonite (see also garnet), 33
Hevea, 86
hexagonal crystal system, 5, 13
Hexapoda, 102
hickory, 70, 81
hiddenite, 35

hide, 135
hippopotamus, 120, 155, **155**
Hippopotamus amphibius, **155**
hippopotamus ivory, **155**, **156**
holly, 70
holotype, 61
honeybee, 106
honeysuckle, 81
hoof (see hooves),
hoofed animals, 118
hookworms, 98
hoopoes, 119
hooves, 58, 109, 121, 129, 142, 144, 145,
    145, **147**, **152**, 160, 161, 169
hormones, 10, 58, 170
horn, 71, 143, 161, 168
horn core, **146**
horn sheath, **146**, 160
horn silver, 28
horn structure, **146**
hornbill, 119, 143, **145**
hornworts, 63
horse hair, 92, **124**, 125
horses, 118, 120, 141, 148, 158
horseshoe crabs, 102
horsetails, 63
hot springs, 45
ho-ting, 143
howlite, 34
huanaco, 124
huarizo, 124
hula skirts, 78
human hair, **123**, **124**
humans, 120
humidors, 72
hummingbirds, 119, 133
hyacinth, 34
hydrocarbons, 3, 57, 67, 91, 169, 170
hydroxyapatite, 58, 135, 137, 138, 169
hydrozoans, 98
hyena, 120
Hyphanae thebaica, 85
hypotype, 61
hyrax, 120
hyroxides, 18

ibis, 119, 133
iceland spar, 32
idiochromatic, 10
idocrase, 20, 34, 39
igneous, 41
Ilex, 70
illustration acknowledgements,
    xvii–xviii
imitations (see also specific materials),
    31, 39, 169
impact craters, 50
incense, 72, 90, 91, 149
inches, 173
incisors, 139, 140
inclusions, 26, 67, 167
index of refraction, 10–12
India rubber, 86
indicolite, 34, 39
indigo, 93
inferior umbilicus, 129
inkstone, 48
inlay, 19, 113, 169
inner bark, 73, 74
inosilicate, 18, 21, 34
insect wax, 106
insecticides, 51, 91
Insectivora, 120, 128
insectivores, 118, 139
insects, 57, 98, 102, 104–107, 113, 118,
    139, 158–161, 168
instar, 103
insulation, 78, 83, 86, 129, 157
intaglio, 30, 169
intarsia, 19, 169
integument, 120
interference of light, 11
internal mold, 44
internal organs (see organs),
intestines, 141, 150
intrusive rocks, 41
invertebrate animal products, 104–112
invertebrate animals, 97–113, 159, 161
invertebrates in collections, 112–113
iolite, 34
iridescence, 12, 131

iridium, 29
Iriquois, 92
iris, 64
iron, 7, 15, 16, 19, 27, 29, 50
iron meteorites, 16, 49
iron oxide (see also hematite, goethite, ochre), 48, 99, 142
isinglass, 21, 150
isometric crystal system, 5, 11
isotropic, 11
ivory (see also fossil ivory), 6, 108, **123**, 135, **155**, **156**, 155–157, 161
ivory imitations, **85**, 88, 135, 143, 145, **157**, 158

jacinth, 34
jackal, 120
jacquard, 105
jade, 21, 34, 35, 39
jadeite (see also jade), 18, 21, 34, 39
Japan wax, 90
Japanese insect wax, 106
jargoon, 34
jasper, 24, 35, 39
jays, 119, 133
jellyfish, 98, 133
jet, 47, 68
Jew's mallow, 76
jewelry, 27, 28, 29, **30**, 39, **40**, 47, 68, 82, **83**, 85, 87, 88, 102, 111, 113, **118**, **123**, **124**, 133, 135, **144**, **146**, 155, **157**, 158
joints, 140, 159
jojoba oil, 89, 90–91
jojoba tree, 89
Juglans, 70
jute, 74, 76, 79

Kachina, **xii**, **xiii**, 70, 95
kangaroos, 120, 158
kaolinite, 21
kapa cloth, 72
karat, 27, 174
kauri gum, 66–67
kenetoplastids, 60
keratin, 142–147

keratin, 58, 116, 122, 128, 141, 142–147, 168, 169
kerosene, 47
khaki, 123
kids, 121
kieselgur, 46
killer whales, 155
kilogram, 174
kilometer, 173
kingdom, 59
kingfishers, 119, 133
kites, 119
knife (see also tools, weapons), **138**, **157**
koala, 120
kunzite, 35
kyanite, 17, 33

labial side (teeth), 139
labradorescence, 12
labradorite (see also feldspar), 23, 36
lac, 106
lac pigment, 106
Laccifer lacca, 106
lace, **75**
lacquer, **80**, 85, 88, 160
lacquer-ware, 88
Lagomorpha, 120, 128
lagomorphs, 118
lamb, 121, 153
lamp shells, 98
lampreys, 116
lamps, 83, 109
lampshade, **112**
lanolin, 122, 148, 149
lapis lazuli, 22, 36, 40
larch, 70
lard, 148
larks, 119
Larrea tridentata, 91
larvae, 102, 103, 113, 115, 168
larvikite (see also labradorite), 23, 36
lastex, 87
lateral root, 64
latex, 85, 87
Latrix, 70

lattan, 29

Laurel family, 72

lavender, 90, 93

lawn, 74

Lawsonia inermis, 92

laxative, 91

lazulite, 40

lazurite (see also lapis lazuli), 18, 22, 36, 40

lead, 27, 53

leather, **xii**, 47, 58, 77, 86, 91, 92, 121, 122, 127, 141, 148, 149 150, 151–154, **153**, **154**, 161, 171

leatherback turtle, 142

leaves, 65, 72, 73, 74, 76, 77, 78, 82, 87, 89, 90

lectotype, 61

leeches, 98

legs, 102

lemons, 85

lemur, 120

length, 173

leopard, 128

lepidochrocite, 26

lepidolite, 21

Libocedrus, 70

library collections, **154**

lice, 103

lichen, 66, 91, 93

licorice root, 103

liddicoatite (see also tourmaline), 34

life jackets, 72

ligaments, 101, 140, 159

light spectrum, 10

lignin, 69, 73

lignite, 46, 47, 68, 90

lilies, 64

lime, 151

limestone, 19, 37, 42, 45, 46, 74

liming, 151

limonite, 18

linarite, 53

linen, **xii**, 73, 74, 75, **75**, 76, 79, 128

linen straw, 79, **80**

lingual side (teeth), 139

Linnaean system, 59, 63

Linnaeus, Carolus, 59

linneaite, 53

linoleum, 74, 76

linseed oil, 74, 76, 89

Linum usitatissimum, 74, 75

lion, 128

Lion Passant hallmark, 28

lipids, 57, 169

lips, 139, 140

liter, 173

liverworts, 63

lizardite, 21, 35, 39

lizards, 116

llamas, 124, 125, 158

lobsters, 103, 112

lodestone, 19

loggerhead turtle, 142

loofahs, 85

loofas, 85

loons, 119

loris, 120

lubricant, 89, 91, 148

Luffa, 85

lumber, 70

luminescence, 11

lunar meteorites, 50

luster, 9, 170

luster wool, 122

lycophyta, 63

lycra, 87

lye, 150, 151

lynx, 128

lynx sapphire, 34

lyre bird, 133

mabe pearls, 111

macaws, 132, 133

Macintosh (clothing), 86

Macintosh, Charles, 86

madder, 93

madeira rio grande, 24

magnesite, 17, 19, 32, 37

magnesium, 15

magnetism, 7

magnetite, 7, 19, 42

magnets, 19, 49

mahogany, 69

mahogany, 70

main scent, 90

malachite, 10, 17, 19, 33, 37, 142

malleability, 5

Mallow family, 74

Mammalia, 116, 118

mammals, 55, 98, 118, 120, 127, 141, 151, 154, 155, 161

mammoth, 156

manatees, 120

Mandibulata, 102

manganese oxide, 48

Manila hemp, 74, 76

mantle, 101

manure, 158

maple, 70, 81

marabou, 133

marble, 19, 37, 48, 49

marcasite, 5, 16, 20, 28, 30, 32, 51

marialite, 18, 36

marlin, 160

marmoset, 120

marmot, 120, 128

mars meteorites, 50

marsh grass, 72

Marsupiala, 120

marsupials, 117

mask, 92

masonite, 160

massicot, 18, 53

mastic, 88

matrix, 170

mats (see also woven plant materials), 71, 74, 77, 78, 81

mattress stuffing (see also upholstery stuffing), 83, 133

meadow goat hair, 125

measurement, 173–174

meat, 107, 108, 117, 118, 121, 132, 139, 141, 143, 150, 152, 168

mechanical sediments, 42, 44

medicine, 58, 70, 72, 82, 86, 87, 89, 91, 106, 108, 141, 147, 149, 150, 171

medium wood, 122

medium-hard wood, 70

medulla, 122, 126

meerschaum, 21, 35

meionite, 18, 36

melanin, 131

melanite, 33

melanterite, 20, 51, 53

Meliaceae, 69, 70

melting point, 8

memorial carvings, 68

memorial jewelry, **123**, **124**

Mercer, John, 74

mercerization, 74

mercury, 16, 51, 53

mesosiderites, 50

metacinnabar, 53

metal, **xii**, **xiii**, 7, 26–30, 149, 169, 170

metallic elements, 27

metallic luster, 9, 170

metamorphic, 41

metamorphic rocks, 47–49

metamorphosis, 103, 104, 115

Metatheria, 117

metazeunerite, 54

metazoa, 97

meteorite fall, 49

meteorite find, 49

meteorites, 7, 16, 30, 42, 49–51

meteoroids, 49

meteors, 49

meter, 173

methanogens, 60

metric system, 173, 174

Mexican onyx, 32, 45, 46

Mexican silver, 28, 174

mica group, 5, 16, 18, 21, 42

microcline (see also feldspar), 5, 18, 23, 36, 42

microgram, 174

microliter, 173

micron, 173

microsporidians, 60

middens, 108

miles, 173

milk, 157–158

milk teeth, 139

milky quartz, 24, 35

millet, 82

milligram, 174

milliliter, 173

millimeter, 173

millimicron, 173

mimetite, 54

mineral, 170

mineral species, 15, 170

mineral tanning, 153

mineral varieties, 15

minerals, 15–26, 40, 135, 152, 167, 168, 170

minerals, radioactive, 8

minium, 18, 53

mink, 128, 149

mink oil, 149

misti, 125

mites, 102

mixed carpet wool, 122

mocha stone, 24

Moh's hardness scale, 6

mohair, 124, 125

moire, 105

molars, 139, 140

mold, 59, 60

moldavite, 36

mole, 120, 128

molecular formula, 3

molecules, 3

Mollusca, mollusks, 46, 58, 98, 100–101, 104, 106, 107, 108, 111, 112, 159, 160, 161, 168, 169, 170

molting, moulting, 133

molybdates, 20

momme, 111, 174

monera, 59

money, 76

money shells, 107

mongoose, 120

monkey, 120

monoclinic crystal system, 5

monocots, 64

Monodon monoceros, 140

monosaccharide, 57, 168

Monotremata, 120

monotremes, 117

montan, 90

montmorillonite, 18, 21

moon meteorites, 50

moonstone, 10, 12, 23, 35, 36

moose, 120

mordant, 93

mordant, 92, 93

morganite, 15, 34, 38

morion, 24

mosaics, 19, 170

Moschus moschiferus, 149

moss, 63

moss agate, 24, **25**

mother-of-pearl (see also nacre), 110, 113, 161

moths, 103, 104

motion picture film, 88

moulting, 131

mouse, 120

mousebirds, 119

mud, 43, 44, 78

mudstone, 42, 43, 48

mulberry tree, 71, 72

murex family, 106

Muricidae, 106

Musa textilis, 74, 76

muscle, 58, 101, 121, 140–141, 149, 168

muscovite, 18, 21, 42

mushrooms, 59, 60

musical instruments, 69–70, 84, 88, 109, 141, 147, 157

musk, 149

musk deer, 149

musk ox, 124, 126

muskrats, 128, 149

musline, 74

mussels, 101, 111

myrrh, 91

Mysticeti, 120

nacre (see also mother-of-pearl), 10, 101, 107, **107**, 109, 110, 111, 113, 170

nacreous layer, 101

naiad, 103

nails, 121, 144, 168

nanometer, 173

naphtha, 86

narwhal, 120, 140, 155

native elements, 2, 16, 17, 27, 29, 32

native iron, 7

natrolite, 18

nautilus, 101

neck (tooth), 136, **139**

needle grass, 90

needle stone, 26

needles, 77, 127

Nematoda, 98

nematodes, 98

Neognathae, 117, 119

neoprene, 87

nephrite (see also jade), 21, 35, 39

nesosilicates, 17, 20, 33, 54

nesosubsilicates, 33

nests, 44, 161

netsuke, **85**, 143

Nettle family, 76

nettles, 74

neutrons, 1

nickel, 27, 29, 50

nightjars, 119

noble metals, 27

noil, 125

non-metallic luster, 9, 170

notochord, 97, 115

nucleic acids, 170

nucleotides, 57, 58, 170

nutria, 120, 128

nuts, 70

nymph, 103

oak, 70, 93

oats, 78

obsidian, 6, 10, 36, 41

occlusal surface, 139

ocelot, 128

ocher, 18, 142

octopus, 101

Odobenus rosmarus, **140**

odontoblastic cells, 138

Odontoceti, 120, 155

oil cloth, 74

oil of turpentine, 87

oil paint, 74, 89

oilbirds, 119

oils (see also petroleum), 57–58, 83, 87–90, 122, 143, 148–151, 153, 154, 155, 158, 160

olibanum, 91

oligoclase, 36

olive oil, 89

olives, 91

olivine group (see also peridot, forsterite), 20, 31, 33, 37, 41, 42, 50

omnivores, 118, 139

onion, 93

onyx, 24, 35, 46, 167

opacity, 9

opal, 12, 18, 22, 26, 35, 42, 46

opalescence, 12

opaque, 171

opercula, operculum, 100, 110, 111

opium cases, 122

opossum, 120

optical properties, 9–13

oranges, 85

orbitals, 3

order, 59

ordinary goat hair, 125

ore, 170

organdy, 74

organic, 170

organic compounds, 57–59

organic molecules, 3

organic sediments, 42, 45

organic tissue, 141

organisms, 57–61

organs, 58, 149, 160, 168

oriental emerald, 32

oriental pearls, 111, 170

oriental sapphire, 24

oriental topaz, 32

orioles, 133

ornamental stones, 31

orpiment, 53

orris root, 90

orthoclase (see also feldspar), 5, 12, 18, 35, 42, 49

orthorhombic crystal system, 5

orthosilicates, 20

os penis, 135

osmium, 29

ospreys, 119

ossicorns, 147

Osteichthyes, 116

ostrich, 129, 132, 133

otters, 120, 128, 149

ounces, 174

ouricuri wax, 89

Ovis canadensis, **147**

owls, 119, 133

oxen, 148

oxides, 2, 17, 18, 32, 54

oxygen, 1, 15

oyster, 101, 111, 108, 169

ozocerite, 90

packing material, 77, 78

paco-llama, 125

Pahlik-mana, **xiii**

paint (see also oil point, watercolor), **xii**, **xiii**, 9, 51, 74, 87, 141, 157, 160

painting, paintings, 74, 142, 148, 153, 157

paktong, 29

Paleognathae, 117, 119

paleontology collections, 102, 158

palladium, 27, 29

pallasites, 50

palm frond ribs, 81

palm leaves, 89

palms, palm trees, 64, 81, 89, 90

pangolin, 120

panther, 128

paper, 70, 71, 72–73, 76, 78, 81, 82, 87, 89, 90, 92, 93, 94, 150, 154, 158, 160

paprika, 103

papyrus, 72

paraffin, 106

paramecium, 59, 60

parasites, 98

paratype, 61

parchment, 73, 121, **154**

parrots, 119, 132, 133

parting, 6, 169

partridge, 119, 133

Passeriformes, 117

Paua shell, 109

peacock, 132

peafowl, 133

pearls, 10, 101, 111–113, 161, 167, 169, 170, 174

pearly luster, 10

peat, 47, 68

pebbles, 42, 43

peccary, 120

pectin, 73, 75

pedicle, 136

pedipalps, 102

pegmatite, 41

pelage, 127

pelecypods, 101

pelicans, 119, 133

pelts, 154, 161

penguins, 119

penile bone, 135

penis bone, 135

Pentadesma butyracea, 89

people (see also humans), 104, 116, 118

pepper, 103

perfume, 90–91, 149

peridot (see also forsterite, olivine), 31, 33, 37

periodic chart or table, 2, 3, 27

periodontal membrane, **139**

periostracum, 100, 101, 107, 112

Perissodactyla, 120

Peruvian bark, 72

pesticide, 47

petiole, 64

petrels, 119

petrified wood, 45

petrolatum, 47

petroleum, 47, 89, 91, 106

petroleum jelly, 47

pewter, 30

pH, 73, 167

pH scale, 7–8

pheasants, 119, 129, 132, 133, 146

phloem, 64, 65, 66, 73

phlogopite, 21

Pholidota, 120

phosgenite, 53

phosphates, 17, 20, 33, 54

phosphorescence, 11

photograph cases, 88

photographic emulsion, 150

photographs, 94

photosynthesis, 65, 66, 168

phyllite, 47, 48, 49

phyllosilicates, 18, 21, 35

Phyllostachys, 71

phylum, 59

physical properties of matter, 4–9, 27

Phytelephas macrocarpa, **85**

piano keys (see also musical
    instruments), 69, 157

Picea, 70

piconite, 32

picture frames, 88

piezoelectricity, 21

pigeons, 119, 133

pigments, **xii**, 10, 65, 88, 89, 92, 99, 110,
    121, 122, 131, 141, 142, 150, 157, 159,
    160, 168

pigs (see also boar), 118, 120, 148

pika, 120

pillows, 83, 133

pilot whales, 155

pina cloth, 78

pina fiber, 78

pinchbeck, 29

pine, 70

pine needles, 70, 77

pine trees, 87

pineapple fiber, 78

pinfeathers, 129

Pinnipedia, 120

pins, 127

pints, 173

pinukpok, 76

Pinus, 70

pipe, **48**

pitch, 72

pith (hair), 122

pith (plant), **66**, 84

placentals, 117

placoid scales, 122

plagioclase feldspar, 18, 36, 42, 50

planaria, 98

plant classification, 63–64

plant fibers, 73, 75, 83

plant fluids, 85–87

plant hairs, 122

plant kingdom, 59

plant latex (see also latex), 84

plant materials, 158

plant materials in collections, 93–94

plant products, 68–85

plant resin, 66, 72, 74, 85, 87, 88, 90

plant sap, 44, 66

plant structure, 64–66, **64**, **66**

plant wax, 89

Plantae, 59, 60

plants, 63–95, 118, 139, 149, 168, 171

plasma, 24

plaster, 159

plastic, **xiii**, 8, 47, **112**, 143, 157,
    158, 160

plastron, 116, **117**, 142

Platanus, 70

plates, 142, 143

platinum, 27, 29, 32

platinum group metals, 29

platyhelminthes, 98

platypus, 120

play of color, 12

pleonaste, 32

plexiglas, 54

plovers, 119

plumes, 133

plutonic rocks, 41
Poaceae, 71, 81
pods, 82
points, 174
poisons, 51, 52, 55
polish, 89, 91, 149
polished cotton, 74
polymers, 57, 168
polymorphs, 15, 19
polypeptide, 135
polysaccharide, 57, 107, 168
polysynthetic twinning, 12
ponies, 116
poodles, 116
poop (see also excrement, dung), 44
poplar, 70
poppy oil, 89
Populus, 70
porcelain, 88, 101, 107, 108, 109, 110
porcupines, 116, 120, **126**, 127
Porifera, 98
porphyrin, 131
porphyry, 41
porpoises, 120, 155
possum (see opossum), 120
posterior teeth, 139
potassium, 15
potpourri, 90
pouches (see also bags, containers), 141, 142
poultice, 83
pounds, 174
powder feathers, 129
powder horns, 146
prase, 24
precious coral, 99
precious metals, 27, 174
precious opal, 26
precious stones, 31, 169, 170
pressed flowers, 82
prickly pear, 106
Primates, 120
privet, 93
Proboscidae, 120

prokaryotes, 59
proline, 135
pronghorn antelope, 146
properties of matter, 4–13
proteins, 57, 58, 135, 137, 141, 158, 167, 168, 169, 170, 171
proteobacteria, 60
Protista, 59, 60
protoconch, 101
Prunus, 70
pseudomorphs, 23, 26, 44, 45
Pseudotsuga, 70
psilophyta, 63
ptarmigan, **146**
pterophyta, 63
Pterygota, 103
puddingstone, 43
puka shells, 108
pulled wool, 124
pulp cavity, 136, 137, 138, **139**, 140
pumice, 150
pupa, 102, 103, 105, 168
pupal case, 103
purity, 174
purses, 122
pyrite, 2, 5, 16, 17, 20, 28, 30, 32, 40, 42, 51
pyromorphite, 54
pyrope (see also garnet), 17, 33, 37
pyroxene group, 18, 21, 34, 39, 41, 42, 50
pyroxylin, 88
pyrrhotite, 7, 19, 28

qiviuq, 126
qiviut, 124, 126
quail, 119, 133, 146
quarts, 173
quartz, 5, 6, 13, 18, 21, 22, 23, 24, 31, 35, 37, 39, 40, 41, 42, 43, 45, 46, 48, 49, 169
quartzite, 48, 49
quatzals, 119
Quercus, 70

Quercus suber, 72
quills, 126, **126**, 127, 161, 169
quinine, 72
quirt, **137**

rabbit, 118, 120, 122, 128, 138
rabbit hair, 126
raccoon, 118, 120, 128
rachis, 129, **130**, **131**, 131
radioactive minerals, 55
radioactivity, 8–9, 52, 54
radiolaria, 46
radon gas, 54–55
radula, 100
raffia, 78
raffia palm, 78
rags, 72, 73, 155
rails, 119
Raphia farinifera, 78
rats, 120, 135
rattan, 81
rattle, **84**, **145**
rawhide, 151
rays, 116, 122
realgar, 52, 53
red cedar, 81
red ochre, 142
red tiger eye, 26
redwood, 70
reed candles, 84
reeds, 77
references, 163–165
refraction, 11, 131
refractive index, 9, 38, 170
refractometer, 12
regional metamorphic rocks, 47
reindeer, 135
reptiles, 98, 116, 117, 120, 122, 131,
    132, 139, 141, 151, 155, 160, 161
Reptilia, 116
resin, 85, 87–90, 106, 160
retting, 75, 76
rhea, 132, 133
rhinestone, 24, 36, 39, **40**

rhino horn, 147, 161
rhinoceros, 120, 147
rhizomes, 64, 65
rhodium, 29
rhodochrosite, 17, 19, 33, 37
rhodolite (see also garnet), 33
rhodonite, 18, 35
rhodophyta, 60
rhombohedral crystal system, 5
Rhus, 90
Rhynchocephalia, 116
rhyolite, 41
rice bran wax, 90
rice wax, 90
rick ornaments, 78
riebeckite, 22, 54
rigging, 77
right whales, 120, 144
ringtail cat, 120
RNA, 170
rock crystal (see also quartz), 24, 35
rocks, 40–49, 170
rocks radioactive, 8
rocks specific gravity of, 9
Rockwell hardness test, 7
Rodentia, 120, 128
rodents, 118, 127, 138
rollers, 119
roofs, 78
root (tooth), 136, **139**
root canal, 136, 138, **139**
root system, 64
rootless teeth, 138
roots (plant), 66, 77, 89, 90, 91, 93, 95
rope, 73, 74, 76, 77, 78, 125
rorqual, 120
rorqual whales, 144
rose quartz, 24, 35
rosemary, 93
rosin, 88
roundworms, 98
rubber, 85, 86, 88, 94
rubellite, 34, 39
rubicelle, 32

ruby (see also corundum), 13, 18, 31, 32, 170
ruby spinel, 32
rugs (see also floor coverings), **xii**, 77, 125, 135, 160
rumanite, 67
rush candle, 83–84
rushes, 77
rushlight, 83–84
ruthenium, 29
rutilated quartz, 23, 26
rutile, 5, 17, 26, 32, 42
rye, 78

sable, 128, 148
sacks, 73
sagenite, 26
sailfish, 160
salamanders, 115, 116
saliva, 8
Salix, 70
salts (see also halite), 5, 19, 43, 45, 153, 159
sand, 42, 43, 44, 150
sand dollars, 98
sandgrouse, 119
sandstone, 9, 42, 43, 48
sap (see also plant sap, plant fluids), 66, 85, 86, 87, 90, 91
Sapium sebiferum, 89
saponification, 150–151
sapphire (see also corundum), 13, 18, 31, 32, 170
saprophytes, 66
sard, 24
sardonyx, 24
sassafras, 70
satin, 105
satin spar, 33
sausage, 141
sausage casing, 76
saussuritized granite, 49
sawdust, 88, 157, 158
scaffolds, 81
scale insects, 103

scales, 121, 122, 131
scallops, 101
scapolite group, 18, 36
scarabs, 161
scavengers, 158
scent glands, 160
scents (see also perfume, incense), 90–91
schappe, 105
scheelite, 20
schist, 47, 48, 49
schleroprotein, 107
scorodite, 54
scorpions, 98, 102
scrimshaw, 135, 157
sculpture, 19
sea anemones, 98
sea cucumbers, 98
sea lion, 120
sea scorpions, 102
sea spiders, 102
sea turtle oil, 149
sea turtles, 117, 142, **143**
seabirds, 158
seagrass, 81
seals (animal), 120, 128
seals (stone), 30, 169
seasoned wood, 69
sebaceous glands, 121, 148
secondary phloem, 65, **66**
secondary scent, 90
secondary xylem, 65, **66**
sectility, 5
sedimentary rocks, 41, 42, 43
sediments, 43
seed leaf, 64
seedlac, 105
seeds, 44, 63, 64, 66, 73, 74, 75, 78, 82, **83**, 89, 90, 91, 93
selenides, 16
semi-plumes, 129
semi-precious stones, 31, 169, 170
semi-transparent, 9
sepiolite (see also meerschaum), 18, 21, 35

Sequoia, 70

serge, 123

sericin, 105

serpentine, serpentinite, 21, 35, 37, 39, 48, 49

shaft (feather), 129

shagreen, 122

shale, 42, 43, 48

shampoo, 89

shark skin, sharkskin, 122, 123

sharks, 116, 122, 149

shaving, 152

shearing, 123

shearwater, 119

shedding, 131

sheep, 73, 120, 121, 122, 124, 125, 141, 146, **147**, 148, 153, 158

Sheffield plate silver, 29

shell (see also nacre, mother-of-pearl, porcelain), 44, 58, 100, 104, 107–111, **107**, **109**, **110**, 112, 113, 159, 160, 161, 168, 169, 170

shell structure, 101

shellac, 88, 105–106

shingles, 91

ship building, 69, 70

shoes, 122

shoot system, 64

shooting stars, 49

shrew, 120

shrimp, 103

siberite, 34, 39

siderite, 23

silicates, 16, 20

silicon, 15

silk, 10, 72, 82, 104–105, 128

silky luster, 10

silt, 42

siltstone, 43

silver, 16, 17, 27, 28, 32, 174

silver bullion, 28

silverfish, 103

simetite, 67

Simmondsia chinensis, 89, 90

sinew, 141

Sirenia, 120

sisal, 74, 76

size, 173

sizing, 74, 121, 142, 150

skeletons, 102, 159, 161

skin, 120–122

skin (see also leather, parchment, vellum), 58, 72, 92, 117, 119, 120–122, 131, 135, 141, 142, 149, 150, 151, 152, 153, 160, 161, 168, 169

skin structure, **121**, 121

skinks, 116

skinning, 159, 160

skins, 135, 159, 161

sklodowskite, 54

skulls, 135, 136, 159

skunks, 118, 120, 128

skutes, **117**, 142

skutterudite, 53

slate, 47, 48, 49

slime eels, 116

slime molds, 60

sloth, 120

slugs, 98, 101

smaragdite, 34

smell, 7

smithsonite, 19

smoky quartz, 24, 35

smoky topaz, 24, 35

snails (see also gastropods), 98, 108

snakes, 116, 160

snipes, 119

snowy egret, **132**

snuff bottles, 85, 122, 143

soap, 148, 149, 150–151

soapstone, 35, **48**

sodalite, 18, 36, 40

sodium, 15

sodium hydroxide, 74, 150

soft fiber, 73

softwood, 69, 70

soldering flux, 88

solubility, 7, 52

solvents, 47, 87, 159

songbirds, 133

soot, 157

sorghum, 82

sorosilicates, 17, 20, 34

sow bugs, 103

Spanish fly, 103

sparrows, 119

species, 59

specific gravity, 9, 170

spectral colors, 12

speleothems, 19, 45

sperm whale, 120, 149, 150, 155

sperm whale tooth, **156**

spermaceti, 91

spermaceti oil, 89

spermaceti wax, 150

spessartine (see also garnet), 17, 33

sphaerocobaltite, 53

sphalerite, 32

sphenophyta, 63

spicules, 98

spider webs, 104

spiders, 98, 102, 104, 158

spinel, 17, 18, 31, 32

spirochetes, 60

splintery fracture, 6

splints, 81

splitting, 152

spodumene, 18, 35

sponges, 85, 97, 98, 161

spongin, 98

spongy bone, 134

sports equipment, **xii**, 70, 141, **153**

spruce, 70

squalene, 149

Squamata, 116

squid, 97, 101, 150

squirrel, 120, 128, 148

stains (see also dyes), 91, 125

stalactites, 45

stalagmites, 45

star effect, 13

starch, 74, 168

starfish, 98, 112

starlings, 119

starlite, 34

steatite, 35, 39, **48**

steel, 7, 29, 30

stem, 75

stems, 65, 69, 70, 72, 73, 74, 75, 78, 82, 83, 84, 89, 94

sterling silver, 28, 29, 174

sticklac, 105, 106

stilts, 119

stingrays (see also rays), 116, 122

Stipa tenacissima, 90

stomach contents, 159, 161

stomachs, 141

stone (see also rocks), 108, 113, 148, 167, 170

stony meteorite, 49–50

stony-iron meteorites, 50

storks, 119, 133

stramenopila, 60

straw, 77, 78, **79**, **80**, 158, 160

strawberry quartz, 26

streak, 11

strings, 141

Strombus, 109

structural color, 10, 11, 131

structural groups of minerals, 16

Strunz classification, 20

Struthioniformes, 119

study skins, 161

sub-bituminous coal, 47, 90

subcutaneous tissue, 121

succulents, 94

suet, 148

sugar, 57, 103, 168

sulfates, 17, 19, 33, 45

sulfides, 16, 17, 29, 32

sulfosalts, 18, 29

sulfur, 5, 17, 53

sulfur turpentine, 87

sulfuric acid, 89, 159

superkingdom, 60

surfactant, 149

susceptibility to toxins, 7

swallows, 119, 133

swans, 119, 133

sweat gland, 121

swifts, 119

swim bladders, 150

sycamore, 70

synthetics, 31, 36, 88, 89, 171

syntypes, 61

taffeta, 105

tagua nut (see also vegetable ivory, ivory imitations), **85**, 85

tailor's chalk, 46

tails, 133

talc, 10, 18, 22, 35, 39, 46, 48

tallow, 148, 153

tallow tree, 89

talons, 144, **146**

tanagers, 133

tangerines, 85

tanned pelts, 127

tannic acid, 92

tanning, 141, 151, 152

tannins, 58, 66, 73, 76, 152, 171

tanzanite, 20, 34

tap root, 64

tapa cloth, 72

tapeworms, 98

tapir, 120

tar, 44, 47, 91

tarnish, 28

Tasmanian devil, 120

taste, 7

tawing, 153

taxidermy, 135, 141, 159–160, 161

Taxodium, 70

tea, 70

teabags, 76

tectosilicates, 18, 22, 35

teeth, 44, 58, 87, 113, 117, 135, 136–140, **139**, 155–157, **155**, 156, 161, 168, 169

tektites, 36, 41–42, 51

tellurides, 16

tellurite, 53

tempera medium, 158

tempering, 152

tenacity, 5

tendons, 58, 135, 140, 159, 168

tents, 74

termites, 69, 103

terns, 119, 133

terrapins, 116

terrycloth, 74

Testudines, 116

tetragonal crystal system, 5

thatched roof, 78

thermophiles, 60

thistles, 82

thorax, 102

thorianite, 53

thread, 73, 74, 75, 76, 87, 104

thrushes, 119

Thuja, 70

thulite, 34

ticks, 98, 102

tiger eye, 26

tigers (see also cats), 128

tin, 27, 29, 92, 93

Tinamiformes, 117, 119

tissue, 111, 140–141, 149, 150, 151, 154, 159, 168, 169

tits, 119

toads, 115, 116

toilet water, 90

tools (see also handles), 29, 70, 87, 108, 109, 113, 122, 135, **137**, **138**, 140, 141, 144, 146, 148, 156, 157, 158

tooth (see also teeth), 136, 137, **139**

tooth enamel, 136, 138, **139**, 169

tooth parts, **139**

tooth types, 139

toothbrushes, 82

topaz, 17, 20, 31, 34, 38, 41

topazolite, 33

topotype, 61

torbernite, 54

torches, 83

tortoise shell, tortoiseshell, 142, 147, 161

tortoises, 116, 142

tortoiseshell imitation, **144**

toucans, 119

tourmalinated quartz, 26

tourmaline group, 5, 16, 17, 21, 26, 34, 39, 41

toxic minerals, 51, 52, 55

toxicity, 7

Toxicodendron, 90

toxins, 7

toys, **xii**, 113, 122, **153**

trace fossils, 44, 158

translucency, 9, 171

translucent, 170, 171

transparent, 9, 170, 171

transvaal jade, 33, 39

travertine, 32, 37, 42, 45, 46

tree bark (see also bark), 58

trellis, 81, 82

tremolite, 22, 35, 54

trichomonads, 60

triclinic crystal system, 5

Tridacna gigas, 109

trilobites, 98, 102

triphane, 35

tripolite, 46

trogons, 119

troy ounces, 174

trumpets (see also musical instruments), 109

Ts'ai Lun, 72

tsavorite (see also garnet), 33

Tsuga, 70

tuataras, 116

tubers, 64, 94

tubules, 137

Tubulidentata, 120

tufa, 42

tulle, 105

tungstates, 20

tunicates, 98, 115

turkeys, 119, 133

turmeric, 93

turpentine, 87, 88

turquoise, 17, 20, 33, 37, **38**

turtle oil, 149

turtle shell (see also tortoise shell), 147

turtles, 116, **117**, 142

tusks, **140**, 140, 155, **156**

Tussah silk, 104

tweed, 123

twigs, 77

twill, 123

twine (see also cordage), 73, 74, 76, 125

type specimens, 60–61

Typha, 83

Ulmus, 70

ultraviolet light, 169

umbrellas, 144

unakite, 34, 49

uneven fracture, 6

uniforms, 74

union cases, 88

Unionidae, 111

untanned leather, 151

upholstery stuffing, 76, 77, 78, 83, 125

uraninite, 53

uranium salts, 9

urchins (see also Echinoderms), 98

urine, 8

Urodela, 115

Urtica dioica, 74

utahlite, 33

uvarovite (see also garnet), 17, 33

vanadates, 20

vanadinite, 54

vanadium oxysalts, 20

vane, 129, **130**

variscite, 17, 20, 33

varnish, 87

vascular cambium, 65, **66**

vascular cells, 65

vascular plants, 63, 69

vascular tissue, 65, 136

vaseline, 47

Vateria indica, 89

vegetable dyes, 92

vegetable ivory, **85**, 85

vegetable leather, 86, 153

vegetable oil (see also oils), 72, 90, 148, 150

vegetable parchment, 73

vegetable sponges, 85

vegetable tanning, 152, 153, 154

vegetable wax, 89

veins, 167, 171

vellum, 73, 121, 153–154, **154**, 161

velour, 123

velvet (antler), 136

velvet (fabric), 105

veneer, 157

venom, 160

Venus hair stone, 26

Venus' flower basket, 98

verdelite, 34, 39

veridine, 24

vertebral column, 97

vertebrata, 115

vertebrate animal products, 147–158

vertebrate animals, 58, 115–158, 161

vertebrate body parts, 119–147

vertebrate classification, 115–116

vesuvian (see also idocrase), 5, 17, 20, 34, 39

Vickers hardness test, 7

Vickers plate, 29

vicunas, 124, 125

vines, 77, 78, 79, 81, 82

violan, 34

vipers, 116

vitreous luster, 10

voile, 74

volcanic ash, 44, 45

volcanic rocks, 41

vole, 120

volume, 173

voucher specimens, 61

vulcanite, 86

vulcanization, 86

vulcanized cotton, 74

vulcanized gutta percha, 87

vulcanized latex, 94

vulcanized rubber, 86

vultures, 119

wacke, 43

walking sticks, **71**

wallaby, 120

walnut, 69, 70, 93

walnut oil, 89

walrus, 120, 135, **140**, 140, 155, 156

wampum, 107

warblers, 119

wasps, 103

water, 3–4, 57, 58

water buffalo, 135

water containers, 141

water molds, 60

water pipes, 87

water resistance, 142, 148, 150, 153, 154

water resistant coating, 76, 89, 91, 149, 158

water sapphire, 34

watercolor paint, 142

waterproof, waterproofing, 74, 85, 86, 87, 91, 122, 129

water-repellent, 106

wavelengths of light, 10

wax, 10, 57, 73, 83, 84, 87–90, 105, 106, 148–151, 153, 154, 160, 169

waxed leather, 154

waxy luster, 10

weapons, **xii**, 86, 87, 122, 135, 140, 147, 148, 154, 156, 157

weasel, 120, 122

webs, 104

weight, 174

wet-preserved specimens, 94, 112, 141, 158, 159

whale ivory, 155, **156**

whale oil, 149

whale tooth, **156**

whalebone (see also baleen), 143

whales, 97, 104, 118, 120, 140, 143, 144, 150, 155, 159

wheat, 78

whisk ferns, 63

whiskers, 131

Whitby jet, 47

white mica, 21

white whales, 155

Whittaker, Robert, 59

wicker, 77, 81

Widmanstatten figures, 50

williamsite, 35

willow, 70, 72, 77

wine, 150

wings, 102, 103, **104**, 117, 133

wisteria, 81

witherite, 53

wolf, 120

wombat, 120

wood, **xii**, 23, 57, 65, 68, 69–71, **71**, 77, 78, **80**, 81, **83**, **84**, 90, 91, 92, 94, 95, 104, 113, 142, 153, 158, 160

wood creosote, 91

wood dust, 74

wood of steel, 81

wood pulp, 73

wood seasoning, 69

wood shavings, 158

wood splints, 71, 81

wood turpentine, 87

woodpeckers, 119

wool, **xii**, **xiii**, 58, 73, 95, 122–125, 128, 129, 148, 169

wool flannel, 123

wool grease, 122

wool harvesting, 123

woolens, 123

worms, 98

worsted, 123

woven plant materials, **xii**, 71, 74, 77–85, 94, 122, 133, 141

wreaths, 82

wrens, 119

wulfenite, 20, 54

x-rays, 111

xylem, 64, 65

YAG, 36

yarn, 76, 123, 125, 128, 174,

yellow ocher (see also goethite, iron oxide), 18, 142

yttrium aluminum garnet, 36

zebra, 120

zeolites, 18, 22, 23

zeunerite, 54

zinc, 16, 27, 29

zinc blende (see also sphalerite), 32

zincite, 18

zircon, 11, 17, 20, 31, 34, 38, 42

zoisite, 17, 20, 34

Zygentomas, 103

zygote, 97